Data Modeling Essentials
2nd Edition

Graeme C. Simsion

Revised & Updated
by Graham C. Witt, Graeme C. Simsion

The Coriolis Group, LLC

Data Modeling Essentials 2nd Edition

The Coriolis Group, LLC
14455 N. Hayden Road, Suite 220
Scottsdale, Arizona 85260

(480) 483-0192
FAX (480) 483-0193
www.coriolis.com

Library of Congress Cataloging-in-Publication Data
Simsion, Graeme C.
Data modeling essentials / by Graeme Simsion.--end ed.
   p. cm.
ISBN 1-57610-872-4
     1. Databases design. 2. Data structures (Computer
     science) I. Title.
QA76.9.D26 S54 2000
005.74--dc21   00-050859

Printed in the United States of America
10 9 8 7 6 5 4 3 2 1

President and CEO
Keith Weiskamp

Publisher
Steve Sayre

Acquisitions Editor
Charlotte Carpentier

Marketing Specialist
Tracy Rooney

Project Editor
Charlotte Carpentier

Technical Reviewer
Kevin D. Weeks

Production Coordinator
Kim Eoff

Cover Designer
Jody Winkler

Layout Designer
April Nielsen

This second edition of *Data Modeling Essentials* is dedicated to the memory of our friend and colleague, Robin Wade, who put the first words on paper for the original edition, and whose cartoons illustrated many of our presentations.

About the Authors

Graeme C. Simsion is Principal of Simsion Bowles & Associates, a division of Tier Technologies Inc., in Melbourne, Australia, and a regular speaker and publisher on the subject of data modeling and data management.

Graham C. Witt is a Senior Consultant with Simsion Bowles, specializing in data modeling, database design, and data management. He is also an experienced teacher of data modeling and publishes regularly.

Preface to the First Edition

Some years ago, I was interviewing a bank manager about the information he needed to assess customer profitability. I began to explain the information system changes that would be required. A look of exasperation crossed his face as he realized that this was going to be an expensive and time-consuming exercise. Finally, he interrupted. "I know that all the information I need is going into those blue boxes. How can it be so difficult to get it out?"

On another occasion, I watched a large insurance company struggling to introduce a new product. The hold-up was the time required to develop a supporting information system. Meanwhile, one of the company's competitors was able to introduce a similar product, making use of an existing information system, and win a major share of the market.

Three banks of approximately the same size, using similar technology, spent several years developing information systems to address their core business. Their budgets varied by more than a factor of five. Yet an independent study found that only one had gained a competitive advantage – the bank that had spent the *smallest* amount[1].

These are familiar themes for information systems developers and users: access to information, the ability to cope with change, and systems development productivity. What may not be so obvious is the central importance of data organization. The bank manager's requirements could not be met economically because the data held in the central databases was not organized to meet his needs. The insurance company's existing database was not adaptable enough to support the new product. The successful bank attributed the lower cost of its system to innovative data organization.

The task of specifying what data is to be stored, and how it is to be organized, is called *data modeling*. As both business requirements and database technology become more sophisticated, the need for good data modeling is increasingly apparent. Modern methodologies and computer-aided software engineering (CASE) tools now include data modeling as a key phase in the development life cycle, and the data model has taken its place alongside the functional specification as one of the major deliverables of systems analysis. Data modeling, once a specialist discipline is now a required skill for virtually anyone involved in information systems design.

---

[1] Broadbent, M., and Weill, P., "Improving Business and Information Strategy Alignment: Learning from the Banking Industry," *IBM Systems Journal*, Vol. 32, No 1 (1993), pp 162 – 179.

This book is intended both as an introduction to data modeling and a guide to handling the more common problems that arise in practice. It differs from other books on the subject in several important ways.

First, it is written *by* a practitioner *for* practitioners. I believe that academics and students will also find it useful, but my prime aim has been to convey the knowledge, techniques, and guidelines my colleagues and I use in designing data models for commercial information systems. The language and diagramming conventions reflect industry practice, as supported by the leading documentation products and database management systems.

Second, it recognizes the element of *choice* in data modeling. For a given problem there will usually be many possible models that satisfy the basic rules of sound design. To select the best model, we need to consider a variety of criteria, which will vary in importance from case to case. Throughout the book, the emphasis is on understanding the merits of different solutions, rather than prescribing a single "correct" answer.

Third, it examines the *process* by which data models are developed. Too often, authors assume that once we know the language and basic rules of data modeling, producing a data model will be straightforward. This is like suggesting that if we understand architectural drawing conventions, we can design buildings. In practice, data modelers draw on past experience, adapting models from other applications. They also use rules of thumb, standard patterns, and creative techniques to propose candidate models. These are the skills that distinguish the expert from the novice.

Finally, I have been strictly honest in describing how I do data modeling in practice. In writing or teaching, there is always a temptation to tell the reader how it should be done – "do as I say, not as I do." But there are usually reasons for short cuts, simplifications, and deviations from the theoretical ideal. So the examples in the book include the awkward situations that crop up in real life, and the answers reflect solutions I would actually propose.

The book is in two parts. Part 1 covers the basics of data modeling. I suggest that you read these chapters in sequence before tackling Part 2. Part 2 builds on the techniques covered in Part 1 to examine more advanced topics. The sequence is designed to minimize the need for "forward references." If you decide to read it out of sequence, you may need to refer to earlier chapters from time to time.

Preface to the Second Edition

Much has changed since the first edition of *Data Modeling Essentials* was published. The Internet, object oriented techniques, data warehouses, business process re-engineering, knowledge management, extended relational database management systems, business rules, data quality – all of these were unknown or of little interest to most practitioners in 1992. We have also seen a strong shift towards buying rather than building large applications, and devolution of much of the systems development that remains.

Despite these changes, the essentials of data modeling have remained sufficiently constant that the first edition of this book has continued to be used by practitioners and teachers. Some of the ideas that were controversial when it was originally published are now widely accepted, in particular the importance of patterns in data modeling. Others have continued to be contentious: an article in *Database Programming and Design*[2] in which I restated the central premise of this book – that data modeling is a design discipline - attracted record correspondence.

I have felt the need to revise the book for some time, to cover some contemporary issues in data modeling and to rectify a number of omissions and deficiencies of which I was all too aware. However, in the last few years, much of my time has been devoted to the business of growing Simsion Bowles, and while I retain an interest in data modeling and data management issues, I can no longer claim to be a full-time practitioner.

I therefore asked my colleague Graham Witt, an expert data-modeling practitioner who teaches our master classes and has published on the subject, to work with me on the second edition. Together we reviewed the book, made numerous changes, and developed a substantial amount of new material. While no chapter escaped revision, the major updates are to the chapters on attribute definition and business rules (based largely on material introduced by Graham). New chapters have been included to cover modeling for the data warehouse and data marts, and to expand on the organization of the modeling task.

---

[2] Simsion, G.C: "Data Modeling - Testing the Foundations," *Database Programming and Design*, (February, 1996).

We considered including exercises to make the book more useful in teaching. In the end, we decided instead to work with some of the users of the book to develop a teaching pack, including presentation material, course outlines and exercises. We expect to post this on the Simsion Bowles website www.sba.com.au.

While Graham and I divided the work, the final product represents our joint view – after surprisingly little conflict. Throughout the book, "I" should be read as "Graeme Simsion and Graham Witt" – "we" generally means you (the reader) and "I" as we make the journey together.

Acknowledgments

I had no idea when I started writing a book about a subject that I both practice and teach that it would take so long, raise so many questions, and generally be as demanding as it turned out to be. The fact that it was completed at all is due in a very large part to the support I received from others, particularly my colleagues at Simsion Bowles and my wife, Anne.

A number of people contributed directly to the content. Chief among these was my colleague Hu Schroor, who reviewed each chapter as it was produced, frequently covering the reverse side of every page with notes and suggestions. Graham Witt, Geoff Bowles, John Giles, Hugh Williams, Bill Haebich, Geoff Rasmussen, David Lawson, Chris Waddell, Mike Barrett, and Sue Huckstepp provided valuable input to individual chapters. Daryl Joyce of Ericssons and Steve Naughton of National Australia Bank reviewed the book as potential users, and made numerous suggestions to improve its clarity.

Graeme Shanks of Monash University and Edward Stow of Charles Sturt University provided an academic perspective – and the benefit of extensive teaching experience in the field. Their comments did much to improve the book's rigor, but they are most certainly not responsible for any failings in this area. In many instances, particularly in Part 1, I have deliberately deviated from a strict progressive development of concepts in order to give the reader a "flavor" of the topic. Undefined terms, informality, and any errors are entirely my responsibility.

Valuable and constructive as all this input was, I occasionally felt like offering the standard response to the critic: "Where were you when the paper was blank?" The person who *was* there at the beginning was Robin Wade, who worked from my dictation and briefings to produce an initial set of notes for the main chapters.

Others have contributed in an indirect but equally important way. Peter Fancke introduced me to formal data modeling in the late 1970s, when I was employed as a database administrator at Colonial Mutual Insurance, and provided an environment in which formal methods and innovation were valued. In 1984, I was fortunate enough to work in London with Richard Barker of Oracle Corporation. His extensive practical knowledge highlighted to me the missing element in most books on data modeling, and encouraged me to write my own. Richard beat me to it by writing *CASE Method Entity-Relationship Modelling* (Addison Wesley) in 1990, and it is this book I have recommended to practitioners since then. Hu Schroor, whose direct contribution I have already acknowledged, has been a constant source of ideas, insights, and encouragement. I have also learnt much from working with expert practitioners like Keith Finkelde, Brin Thiedeman, Hugh Drummond, and John Alexander, and from clients and students who ask the hard questions.

In putting the book together, I relied on Fiona Tomlinson, who produced the diagrams and camera-ready copy, and Sue Coburn who organized the text, changing innumerable "modelling"s to "modeling" and "normalisation"s to "normalization." Our other office staff provided valuable support. Ted Gannan and Rochelle Ratnayake of Thomas Nelson Australia, and Dianne Littwin, Chris Grisonich, and Risa Cohen of Van Nostrand Reinhold all provided encouragement and advice.

Finally, the most important contribution came from my wife Anne, who put up with weekends and evenings devoted to "the book," while managing two children, a career, an interstate move, and her own book.

In producing a second edition, Graham and I had the benefit of input from several lecturers who use the book in teaching, in particular Associate Professor Graeme Shanks (now at the University of Melbourne), Professor Jon Patrick (Sydney University), Clare Atkins (Massey University, NZ), and Daniel Moody (who shares his time between the University of Melbourne and working with us at Simsion Bowles). Clare also contributed material on how to approach data modeling, and Daniel developed the approach to presenting large data models described in Appendix B.

We owe particular thanks to some former colleagues who provided help at short notice. Fiona Beckley (formerly Tomlinson) "reverse engineered" the old files into MS Word format, and John Giles and Mark Kortink made important contributions to the chapter on data warehousing, John in particular providing insightful reviews at short notice. Our current colleagues, Paul Taylor and Glenn Cogar provided advice on object oriented approaches and data warehousing respectively. Cathie Lange took on the unenviable responsibility not only of recreating all of the diagrams and reformatting the material to camera-ready standard, but also of keeping Graham and me on schedule.

The Data Management Associations (DAMA) in the USA and Australia, and the Information Resource Managers Association of Canada (IRMAC) in Canada, deserve special thanks for supporting conference presentations and chapter visits which have enabled us to hear feedback from a wide range of data modeling practitioners.

Final thanks go to our partners, Janine and Anne, for whom the Second Edition of *Data Modeling Essentials* was a mere bagatelle compared with everything else they put up with.

Table of Contents

Part I

Overview of Data Modeling

Chapter 1

What Is Data Modeling?

"Ask not what you do, but what you do it to!"

– Bertrand Meyer

Introduction

This book is about one of the most critical stages in the development of a computerized information system – the design of the *data model*. We begin by addressing some fundamental questions:

What is a data model?

Why is data modeling so important?

What makes a good data model?

Where does data modeling fit in systems development?

Who is involved in data modeling?

A Data-Centered Perspective

We can usefully think of an information system as consisting of a database, containing stored data, together with programs that capture, store, manipulate, and retrieve the data (Figure 1-1). The programs are designed to meet a **function specification**, describing the business functions that the system is to perform. In the same way, the database is specified by a **data model**, describing what sort of data will be held, and how it will be organized.

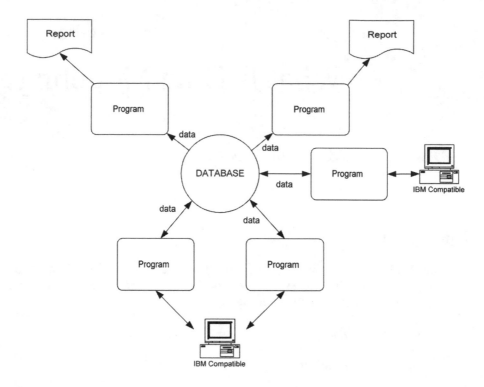

Figure 1-1. An Information System

A Simple Example

Before going any further, let's look at a simple data model. Figure 1-2 shows some of the data needed to support an insurance system.

POLICY TABLE

Policy No.	Date Issued	Type	Customer No.	Commission	Maturity Date
V213748	02/29/1989	E20	HAZED01	12%	02/29/2009
N065987	04/04/1984	E20	WALSH01	12%	04/04/2004
W345798	12/18/1987	WOL	ODEAJ13	8%	06/12/2047
W678649	09/12/1967	WOL	RICHB76	8%	09/12/2006
V986377	11/07/1977	SUI	RICHB76	14%	09/12/2006

CUSTOMER TABLE

Customer No.	Name	Address	Postcode	Gender	Age	Date of Birth
HAZED01	D Haze	3/1 Collins St	3000	F	25	06/23/1975
WALSH01	H Walsh	2 Allen Crt	3065	M	53	04/16/1947
ODEAJ13	J O'Dea	69 Black St	3145	M	33	06/12/1967
RICHB76	B Rich	181 Kemp Rd	3507	M	59	09/12/1941

Figure 1-2. A Simple Data Model

We can see a few things straight away:

- The data is organized into simple tables. This is exactly how a modern relational database stores data, and we could give the model to a technical database designer to build, just as an architect gives a house plan to a builder. Our job as data modelers is essentially to decide what tables and column headings are required. I've shown a few rows of data for illustration; in practice the database might contain thousands or millions of rows in the same format.

- The data is divided into two tables - one for policy data and a separate one for customer data. Typical data models may specify anything from one to several hundred tables.

- There is nothing technical about the model. You don't need to be a database expert or programmer to understand or contribute to the design.

A closer look at the data suggests some questions:

What exactly is a customer – the beneficiary or the person insured? Or perhaps the person who pays the premiums? Could a customer be more than one person – for example, a married couple? If so, how would we interpret Age, Gender, and Date of Birth?

Do we really need to record customers' ages? Wouldn't it be easier to calculate them from Date of Birth whenever we needed them?

Is the Commission Rate always the same for a given Policy Type? For example, do policies of type E20 always earn 12 percent commission? If so, we will end up recording the same rates many times. How do we record the commission rate for a new type of policy if we haven't yet sold any of that type?

Customer Number consists of an abbreviated surname, initial, and a two-digit "tie-breaker" to distinguish customers who would otherwise have the same numbers. Is this a good choice?

Would it be better to hold customers' initials in a separate column from their family names?

Answering questions of this kind is what data modeling is about. In some cases, there is a single, correct approach. Far more often, there will be several options that represent different trade-offs amongst a set of objectives. Answering the questions and choosing the best options requires a detailed understanding of the relevant business area, as well as knowledge of general data modeling principles. Professional data modelers therefore work closely with business specialists, usually the prospective users of the information system, in much the same way that architects work with the owners and prospective inhabitants of the buildings they are designing.

Design, Choice, and Creativity

The architect analogy is particularly appropriate, because architects are *designers*, and data modeling is also a design activity. In design, we do not expect to find a single correct answer, although we will certainly be able to identify many that are patently *incorrect*! Two data modelers (or architects) given the same set of requirements may produce quite different but nevertheless acceptable solutions.

We should not be too surprised that data modeling is not a deterministic process. At least three factors contribute to there being more than one workable answer in most practical situations:

First, our objective is to organize or classify data into tables and columns, and there is usually more than one way of doing this. In our insurance model, we might, for example, have specified separate tables for personal customers and corporate customers, or for accident insurance policies and life insurance policies.

Second, the requirements from which we work in practice are flexible enough to accommodate a variety of different solutions. Again, we have the architect analogy: rather than the client specifying the exact size of each room (which would give the architect little choice), he or she provides some broad objectives, and then evaluates the architect's suggestions in terms of how well they meet these, and what else they offer.

Third, in designing an information system, we have some choice as to which part of the system will handle each business requirement. For example, we might decide to write the rule that policies of type E20 had a commission rate of 12 percent into the relevant programs, rather than including it in the database. Working in the other direction, we might decide that the formulae for calculating benefits at maturity could be held in the database rather than in program logic. Either of these decisions would affect the data model simply by altering what was to be included.

Finally, and perhaps most importantly, new information systems seldom deliver value simply by automating the current way of doing things. For most organizations, the days of such "easy wins" have long passed. To fully exploit information technology, we generally need to change our business processes – and the data required to support them. The data modeler becomes a player in helping to design the new business model, rather than merely reflecting the old.

Unfortunately, data modeling is not always recognized as being a design activity. The widespread use of the term "data analysis" as a synonym for data modeling has no doubt contributed to the confusion. The difference between analysis and design is sometimes characterized as one of *description versus prescription*[3]. We tend to think of analysts as being engaged in a search for truth rather than the generation and evaluation of alternatives. No matter how inventive or creative they may need to be in carrying out the search, the ultimate aim is to arrive at the single correct answer. A classic example is the chemical analyst using a variety of techniques to determine the make-up of a compound.

In simple textbook examples of data modeling, it may well seem that there is only one workable answer (although the experienced modeler will find it an interesting exercise to look for alternatives). In practice, data modelers have a

---

[3] Olle, Hagelstein, MacDonald, Rolland, Sol, Van Assche, and Verrjin-Stuart, *Information Systems Methodologies - A Framework for Understanding*, Addison Wesley (1991).

wealth of options available to them and, like architects, cannot rely on simple recipes to produce the best design. Unfortunately, the terminology that is used in the information systems field tends to confuse the issue. The "analysis" phase within a systems development method often includes design activities, and data modeling is very likely to be the responsibility of a person with the job title of "systems analyst" or "business analyst."

The distinction between analysis and design is nevertheless important, particularly when we discuss creativity. In analysis, creativity suggests interference with the facts. No honest accountant wants to be called "creative." On the other hand, creativity in design is valued highly. In this book, I try to emphasize the choices available at each stage of the data modeling process. I want you to learn not only to produce sound, workable models (buildings that won't fall down), but to be able to explore and compare a range of options, and occasionally experience the "aha!" feeling as a flash of insight produces an innovative solution to a problem. I use the term "creative modeling" when I want to emphasize the importance of actively searching for alternatives rather than merely selecting the most obvious option.

We will look more closely at the creative process throughout this book, but let's clarify one thing now. In recognizing the importance of choice and creativity in data modeling, we are not "throwing away the rule book" or suggesting that "anything goes," any more than we would allow architects or engineers to work without rules or to ignore their clients' requirements. On the contrary, creativity in data modeling requires familiarity with a full range of techniques, and rigorous evaluation of candidate models against a variety of criteria.

Why Is the Data Model so Important?

At this point, you may be wondering about the wisdom of devoting a lot of effort to developing the best possible data model, rather than just accepting the first adequate design. Should we not put similar effort into exploring alternative designs for programs, report layouts, and other system components?

Leverage

The key reason for focusing on data organization is *leverage*: a small change to the data model may have a major impact on the system as a whole. For most commercial information systems, the programs are far more complex and take much longer to specify and construct than the database. But their content and structure are heavily influenced by the database design. Look at Figure 1-1 again. Most of the programs will be dealing with data in the database – storing, updating, deleting, manipulating, printing, and displaying it. Their structure will therefore be strongly influenced by the way the data is organized – in other words, by the data model.

The dependency of program design on data organization has important practical consequences.

A well-designed data model can make programming simpler and cheaper. Even a small change to the model may lead to significant savings in total programming cost.

Another consequence is that poor data organization is often expensive to fix. In the insurance example, imagine that we need to change the rule that each customer can have only one address. The change to the data model may well be reasonably straightforward – perhaps we will need to add a further two or three address columns to the Policy table. With modern database management software, the database can probably be reorganized to reflect the new model without much difficulty.

But the real impact is on the rest of the system. Report formats will need to be redesigned to allow for the extra addresses; screens will need to allow input and display of more than one address per customer; programs will need loops to handle a variable number of addresses, and so on. Changing the shape of the database may in itself be straightforward, but the costs come from altering all of the programs that use the affected part. In contrast, fixing a single incorrect program, even to the point of a complete rewrite, is a (relatively!) simple, contained exercise.

Problems with data organization arise not only from failing to meet the initial business requirements, but from changes to the business after the database has been built. A telephone billing database that allows only one customer to be recorded against each call may be correct initially, but be rendered unworkable by changes in billing policy, product range, or telecommunications technology. The cost of making changes of this kind has often resulted in an entire system being scrapped, or the business being unable to adopt a planned product or strategy.

Conciseness

A data model is also a very powerful tool for expressing and communicating business requirements. Its value lies partly in its *conciseness*. It implicitly defines a whole set of screens, reports, and functions needed to capture, update, retrieve, and delete the specified data. A thorough verification of a data model can therefore be far more valuable than a cursory evaluation of a function specification amounting to many hundreds of pages. The data modeling process can similarly take us more directly to the heart of the business requirements. In their book *Object Oriented Analysis*[4], Coad and Yourdon describe the analysis phase of a typical project:

> *"Over time, the DFD [data flow diagramming or function modeling] team continued to struggle with basic problem domain understanding. In contrast, the Data Base Team gained a strong, in-depth understanding."*

Data Quality

The data held in a database is usually a valuable business asset, built up over a long period. Inaccurate data (poor *data quality*) reduces the value of the asset and can be expensive or impossible to correct.

Frequently, problems with data quality can be traced to a lack of consistency in defining and interpreting data. In our insurance example, is Date of Birth in U.S. or European date format (mm/dd/yyyy or dd/mm/yyyy?) Inconsistent assumptions here by people involved in data capture and retrieval could render a large proportion of the data unreliable.

The data model plays a key role in achieving good data quality by establishing a common understanding of what is to be held in each table and column, and how it is to be interpreted. To summarize: the data model is a relatively small part of the total systems specification but has a high impact on the quality and useful life of the system. Time spent producing the best possible design is very likely to be repaid many times over in the future.

---

[4] Coad, P., and Yourdon, E., *Object Oriented Analysis*, Second Edition, Prentice Hall (1991).

Evaluation Criteria

What constitutes a "good" data model? If we are to evaluate alternative data models for the same business problem, we need some measures of quality. In the broadest sense, we are asking the question: "how well does the model support a sound overall system design that meets the users' requirements?" But we can be a bit more specific than this, and list some general criteria. We will come back to these again and again as we evaluate data models and data modeling techniques, and their suitability in a variety of situations.

Completeness

Does the model support all the necessary data? Our insurance model lacks, for example, a column to record a customer's occupation, and a table to record premium payments. If this data is required by the system, then these are serious omissions. More subtly, we have noted that we might be unable to register a commission rate if no policies had been sold at that rate. We also need to consider completeness in terms of reusability, discussed below. Perhaps the model omits some data about persons or policies that is not required for the current application, but will be difficult to add later as new uses for the data are found.

Nonredundancy

Does the model specify a database in which the same fact could be recorded more than once? In the example we saw that the same commission rate could be held in many rows of the Policy table. The Age column would seem to record essentially the same fact as Date of Birth, albeit in a different form. If we added another table to record insurance agents, we could end up holding data about people who happened to be both customers and agents in two places. Recording the same data more than once increases storage requirements, requires extra processes (and processing) to keep the various copies in step, and leads to consistency problems if the copies get out of step.

Enforcement of Business Rules

How accurately does the model reflect and enforce the rules of the business? It may not be obvious at first glance, but our insurance model enforces the rule that each policy can be owned by only one customer, as there is provision for only one Customer Number in each row of the Policy table. No user or even programmer of the system will be able to break this rule: there is simply nowhere to record more than one customer against a policy (short of such extreme measures as holding a separate row of data in the *Policy* table for each customer associated with a policy). If this rule correctly reflects the business requirement, the resulting database will be a powerful tool in enforcing correct practice. On the other hand, any misrepresentation of business rules in the model may be very difficult to correct later – or to code around!

Data Reusability

Will the data stored in the database be reusable for purposes beyond those anticipated in the function specification? Once an organization has captured data to serve a particular requirement, other potential uses and users almost invariably emerge. An insurance company might initially record data about policies to support the billing function. The sales department then wants to use the data to calculate commissions; the marketing department wants demographic information; regulators require statistical summaries. Seldom can all of these needs be predicted in advance.

If data has been organized with one particular application in mind, it is often difficult to use for other purposes. There are few greater frustrations for system users than to have paid for the capture and storage of data, only to be told that it cannot be made available to suit a new information requirement without extensive, and costly, reorganization.

Since the 1970s, many information systems strategists and researchers have argued that data is a valuable (and expensive) corporate resource, which should be properly managed for the benefit of all current and potential users. This has given rise to the discipline of *data management*, and many organizations now have data management teams responsible for ensuring that their computerized data is well organized, centrally documented, secure, and available to all those who require it. These teams place great emphasis on promoting sound data modeling practices as a means of improving data shareability. Data management is discussed in more detail in Chapter 14.

Stability and Flexibility

How well will the model cope with possible changes to the business requirements? Can any new data required to support them be accommodated in existing tables? Alternatively, will simple extensions to the model suffice? Or will we be forced to make major structural changes, with corresponding impact on the rest of the system?

The answers to these questions largely determine how quickly the system can respond to business change. In many cases, that in turn determines how quickly the business as a whole can respond to change. The critical factor in getting a new product on the market or responding to a new regulation may well be how quickly the computer systems can be adapted. Frequently the reason for redeveloping a system is that the underlying database either no longer accurately represents the business rules or requires costly ongoing maintenance to keep pace with change.

A data model is **stable** in the face of a change to requirements if we do not need to modify it at all. We can sensibly talk of models being more or less stable, depending on the level of change required. A data model is **flexible** if it can be readily extended to accommodate likely new requirements with only minimal impact on the existing structure.

Our insurance model is likely to be more stable in the event of changes to the product range if it uses a generic Policy table rather than separate tables (and associated processing, screens, reports, etc). for each type of policy. New types of policies may be able to be accommodated in the existing Policy table, and take advantage of existing programming logic common to all types of policies.

Flexibility depends on the type of change proposed. The insurance model would appear relatively easy to extend if we needed to include details of the agent who sold each policy. We could add an Agent Number column to the Policy table, and set up a new table containing details of all agents, including their Agent Numbers. However, if we wanted to change the database to be able to support up to, say, three customers for each policy, the extension would be less straightforward. We could add columns called Customer Number 2 and Customer Number 3 to the Policy table, but, as we shall see in Chapter 2, this is a less than satisfactory solution. Even intuitively, most information systems professionals would find it untidy, and likely to disrupt existing program logic. A proper solution would involve moving the original Customer Number from the Policy table, and setting up an entirely new table of Policy Numbers and associated Customer Numbers. Doing this would significantly disrupt our existing programming logic, screens, and report formats for handling the customers associated with a policy. So, simplistically for the moment, our model is flexible in terms of adding agents, but less flexible in handling multiple customers for a policy.

Simplicity and Elegance

Does the data model provide a reasonably natural and elegant classification of the data? If our Customer table were to include only insured persons, and not beneficiaries, we might need a separate Beneficiary table. To avoid recording the same fact more than once, we would need to exclude beneficiaries who were already recorded as Customers. Our Beneficiary table would then contain "beneficiaries who are not otherwise customers," an inelegant classification that would very likely lead to a clumsy system.

"Elegance" can be a difficult concept to pin down. But elegant models are typically simple, consistent, and easily described and summarized. ("This model recognizes that our basic business is purchasing raw materials and transforming them into beer through a number of brewing stages – the major tables hold data about the various raw, intermediate, and final products.") Functions and queries that are central to the business can be met in a simple, reasonably obvious way by accessing relatively few tables.

The difference in development cost between systems based on simple, elegant data models, and those based on highly complex ones can be considerable indeed. The latter models are often the result of incremental business changes over a long period without any rethinking of processes and supporting data. Instead, each change is accompanied by requirements for new data and a corresponding increase in the complexity of the model. In our insurance model, we could imagine a proliferation of tables to accommodate new products and associated persons as the business expanded. Some rethinking might suggest that all of our products fall into a few broad categories, each of which could be supported by a single table, and that a simple "Person" table could accommodate all of the beneficiaries, policyholders, guarantors, assignees, etc.

The huge variation in the development costs for systems to support common applications, such as retail banking or asset management, can often be traced to the presence or absence of this sort of thinking during the data modeling phase of systems design.

Communication Effectiveness

How effective is the model as a communication tool? Do the tables and columns represent business concepts that the users and business specialists are familiar with, and can easily verify? The quality of the final model will depend very much on feedback from these people, who need to be comfortable with the model presented to them.

The most common communication problems arise from high levels of complexity, new concepts, and unfamiliar terminology. A model of even twenty or thirty tables will be overwhelmingly complex for most non-specialists, unless presented in a summary form, ideally using graphics. Larger models need to be presented at different levels of complexity to allow the reader to take a "divide and conquer" approach to understanding (see Appendix B).

Unfamiliar terminology is frequently the result of the data modeler striving to be rigorous and consistent in constructing table and column names, sometimes at the expense of familiar terms and concepts.

Conflicting Objectives

In many cases, the above aims will conflict with one another. In striving for completeness, we may err towards redundancy. An elegant but radical solution may be difficult to communicate to conservative users. A model that accurately enforces a large number of business rules will be unstable if some of those rules change.

Our overall objective is to develop a model that provides at least a good (ideally, the best) trade-off amongst these comparative objectives. As in other design disciplines, this is a process of proposal and evaluation, rather than a step-by-step progression to the ideal solution. We may not realize that a better solution or trade-off is possible until we see it!

Performance and Implementation Issues

You may have noticed an important omission from our list of criteria – performance. Certainly, the system user will not be satisfied if our complete, nonredundant, flexible, and elegant database cannot meet throughput and response-time requirements. However, performance differs from our other criteria, in that it is *primarily* a problem for the physical (technical) database designer rather than the data modeler. This warrants some explanation, as the respective roles are frequently poorly defined or misunderstood.

Logical and Physical Database Designs

Figure 1-3 shows an important feature of the organization of a modern database. The three-layer (or **three schema**) approach allows us to separate those aspects of the database of relevance to programmers and users from those related to the physical storage of data in the computer. In effect, we are able to keep the technical part of the design out of sight, and, more importantly, make changes to it without affecting programs. In more formal texts, the terms **internal schema**, **database schema**, and **external schema** are used for physical database design, logical database design, and views, respectively[5].

---

[5] Even these terms are not used consistently. The usage here reflects Jardine, D.A., "Concepts and Terminology for the Conceptual Schema and the Information Base," *Computers and Standards 3* (1984) pp. 3-17. If using a relational database management system, it would be appropriate to use the term *relational schema* as an alternative to database schema. Some use the term *conceptual schema* in this role; others argue that the term should be used only for an implementation-independent design (i.e., our *data model*).

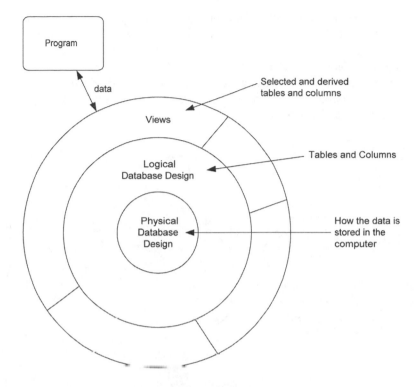

Figure 1-3. Separation of Logical and Physical Components of Database Design.

The **logical database design** describes the organization of the data into tables and columns, as in our insurance example. Programs may work with these tables and columns either directly or via views, which restrict access to certain data or present data in a different way. A view can only select or rearrange data that is already specified in the logical database design.

The **physical database design** is invisible to programmers and users. We can think of it as the inside of a black box, or the engine under the hood. (To pursue the architecture analogy, it represents the foundations, electrical wiring, and hidden plumbing: the owner will want only to know that the house will be sound and that the lights and faucets will work).

The physical database design specifies how the data will be physically stored and accessed, using the facilities provided by a particular database management system (DBMS). For example, the data might be organized so that all the policies for a given customer were stored close together, allowing them all to be retrieved into the computer's memory in a single operation. An index might be provided to enable rapid location of customers by name. All this is the responsibility of the physical database designer, whose approach will be strongly influenced by the capabilities and features of the DBMS.

Figure 1-4 is an overview of the inputs and outputs of the database design task. The job of the database designer is essentially to implement the data model so as to provide adequate performance for predicted transactions, using available hardware and DBMS software.

Figure 1-4. Database Design Inputs and Outputs

So why differentiate between the data model and the logical database design? Ideally, they would be identical. There are three main reasons why they may not be.

Earlier I stated that in modern *relational* databases, data is organized into tables. The logical database design can therefore be an exact copy of the tables specified by the data model. But not all database management systems (DBMSs) are based around or restricted to simple tables. Some older products require that data be organized into hierarchies and/or networks, and, more recently, we have seen relational DBMSs extended to support different data types as well as subtypes (discussed in Chapter 4) and repeating groups (Chapter 2).

For the older DBMSs, the translation from a relational model is largely mechanical, and is discussed in most texts on database design[6]. We will not pursue it further in this book. The extensions to relational DBMSs pose a more difficult problem. Although a standard has been defined (SQL3[7]), DBMSs still differ significantly in what they support beyond basic relational structures (i.e., tables and columns holding a fairly simple set of data types). If you cannot be sure what DBMS will be used to implement the model, or need to be able to change in the future, the safest course is to produce a pure relational model, steering well clear of assumptions about what implementation facilities will be available. On the other hand, if you know you will be implementing the model using a DBMS with particular extensions, it is reasonable to develop an extended model that takes advantage of those features.

The second reason is the opposite of the first. There are advantages in extending the *data model* to include more than just tables, even if the target DBMS doesn't support the extensions. For example, we might want to show that customers could be subclassified into personal customers and corporate customers. If we are using a traditional relational DBMS (without extensions to represent subtypes directly), then ultimately we will still have to specify tables, but the richer model can help us make better decisions as to what those tables should be. For example, we could choose between having separate tables for the different types of customers, or a single table for both. In effect, we can represent different options side by side in the same model.

The third reason is that sometimes the physical designer is unable to meet the performance requirements for all the specified functions with the available hardware and DBMS facilities. If this happens, one option is to implement a logical database design that is not a direct equivalent of the data model, but incorporates some compromises. Naturally, this needs to be done in consultation with the data modeler, and ultimately the person(s) paying for the system, just as a builder unable to implement an architect's design would need to consult with the architect and client. The client may well prefer to sacrifice some performance, or to buy more powerful hardware, rather than compromise flexibility or economy of programming.

---

[6] For example, Hawryskziewycz, I.T., *Database Analysis and Design*, Second Edition, Maxwell MacMillan International Editions (1991).

[7] ANSI/ISO/IEC 9075.

In this book, we work towards a standard relational model, but in the process gather and document most of the information needed to utilize an extended relational DBMS, and to make informed decisions about the impact of changes to improve performance.

Modifying the Data Model to Improve Performance

The alternative to implementing a logical database design that is not a direct translation of the data model is to modify the model itself. Perhaps the model can be changed to improve performance without prejudicing other objectives. More than once, an idea that has been prompted by the need to improve performance has led to improvements in other areas. The important thing is to keep in mind the fundamental premise of creative modeling: that there will be more than one workable solution. The aim should be to arrive at a model that still meets the original business objectives, as well as providing good performance. This is clearly a job for the data modeler, and is the reason I stated earlier that performance was *primarily* the responsibility of the physical database designer. Once the logical design is affected, the data modeler needs to be involved.

Roles of Data Modeler and Physical Database Designer

Unfortunately, the distinct roles and skills of the data modeler and physical database designer are not always recognized in practice. Data modelers frequently try to anticipate performance issues and compromise the data model even before the physical designer sees it. This is a mistake because the physical designer is generally far better placed to estimate performance, and to employ the full range of facilities available to optimize it. (Many data modelers have served apprenticeships as database designers, but are often not up to date with current database technology). Even more importantly, the separation of stages in the process enables us to distinguish clearly "the design the business wants" from "what is possible using current technology."

Data modelers are not the only offenders in failing to separate the roles. Physical database designers (like some builders) do not always feel bound by the specification. Many a data model change has been introduced by a database designer under the guise of performance, often without adequate consultation with data modelers or the users whom they represent.

For data modelers, the best practical approach is to ignore performance issues in the initial modeling stage, and to present the database designer with an ideal logical database design. The data modelers also need to insist that any request for a change to the logical database design be fully justified with a *quantitative* assessment of impact (e.g., estimated transaction response times), and that data modelers and system owners are involved in proposing solutions and choosing the best trade-off. *On no account should physical database designers make any change to the logical database design without such consultation.* In my experience, organizations that have adopted this discipline find that the number of compromises actually required is relatively small.

In our favor is the fact that vendors of database management systems (the software component of the equation) are continually striving to improve what can be achieved at the physical level, without compromising the data model.

When Performance Is Paramount

Occasionally, it is clear even before systems specification begins in earnest that achieving adequate performance will be a major challenge. The systems that fall into this category are usually core transaction processing systems that need to support high throughput and rapid response times. There is often a push to omit the data modeling phase and move directly to database design, on the basis that the ideal data model is likely to be unimplementable, and that the design will be largely determined by performance issues.

This is a *serious* mistake. Performance is of no value if the system does not provide the functionality required by the business. If anything, the need for good data modeling is even greater when we are going to be forced to consider difficult compromises among objectives. The data modeler's role in these circumstances, as always, is to help propose alternatives, and ensure that business needs and impact are properly taken into account.

Where Does the Data Model Fit In?

It should be fairly clear by now that we should not undertake database design without a complete and properly documented data model. Any sound methodology for systems development will therefore include a data modeling phase to be completed prior to database design. The main difference in methodologies is whether the data model is produced before, after, or in parallel with the function specification.

Function-Driven Approaches

Traditional "function-driven" or "data-flow-driven" approaches focus on the function specification[8]. This is hardly surprising: we naturally tend to think of systems in terms of what they *do*. We first identify all of the functions and the data that each requires. The data modeler then designs a data model to support this fairly precise set of data requirements, typically using "mechanical" techniques such as normalization (the subject of Chapter 2). Some methodologies say no more about data modeling. If you are using a function-driven approach, I strongly suggest treating the initial data model as a "first cut" only, and reviewing it in the light of the evaluation criteria outlined earlier. This may result in alterations to the model, and subsequent amendments to the function specification to bring it into line.

---

[8] See, for example, De Marco, T., *Structured Analysis and Systems Specification*, Yourdon Inc. (1978).

Data-Driven Approaches

"Data-driven" approaches[9] are more recent, but have been widely adopted, particularly by the vendors of CASE (Computer-Aided Software Engineering) tools, which provide automated support for systems developers.

The emphasis is on developing the data model *before* the detailed function specification, in order to:

- Promote reusability of data. We aim to organize the data independently of the function specification; on the basis that the functions that it describes are merely the *initial* set that will access the data. The function specification then becomes a test of the data model's ability to support a variety of unanticipated functions.

- Establish a consistent set of names and definitions for data. If we develop the function specification prior to the data model, we will end up *implicitly* defining the data concepts. A function called "Assign salesperson to customer" implies that we will hold data about salespersons and customers. But a second function "Record details of new client" raises the question (if we are alert): What is the difference between a client and a customer? Designing the data model prior to the detailed function specification largely eliminates the need to sort out problems of this kind.

- "Mechanically" generate a significant part of the function specification. Just by looking at the insurance model, we can anticipate that we will need programs to:

    Store details of a new policy;

    Update policy details;

    Delete policy details;

    Report on selected policy details;

    List all policies belonging to a nominated customer;

    Store details of a new customer; etc.

---

[9] Sometimes called "Information Engineering" approaches.

We don't need to know anything about insurance to propose these functions. In defining the data we intend to store, we have implicitly (and very concisely) identified a whole set of functions to capture, display, update, and delete that data. Some CASE tools make heavy use of the data model to generate programs, screens, and reports.

• Provide a very concise overview of the system's scope. As discussed above, we can infer a substantial set of functions just by looking at the data. Not all of these will necessarily be implemented, but we can at least envision specifying them and having them built without too much fuss. Conversely, we can readily see that certain functions will *not* be supportable, simply because the necessary data has not been specified. More subtly, we can see what business rules are supported by the model, and assess whether these will unduly constrain the system. The data model is thus an excellent vehicle for setting the boundaries of the system – far more so than the often overwhelmingly large function specification.

Data-Driven versus Function-Driven

Having grasped this theoretical distinction between function-driven and data-driven approaches, don't expect to encounter a pure version of either in practice. It is virtually impossible to do data modeling without some investigation of functions, or to develop a function specification without considering data. At the very least, this means that function modelers and data modelers need to communicate regularly (they may well be the same person). An increasing number of methodologies now specify that the function specification and data model be developed in parallel[10].

Object-Oriented Approaches

In the last few years, we have seen increased use of object-oriented approaches to system specification and development, and for a while it seemed (at least to some) that these would largely displace conventional "data-centric" development.

---

[10] For example *SSADM - Structured Systems Analysis & Design Methodologies*, NCC Blackwell.

It is beyond the scope of this book to discuss the object-oriented approach in detail[11], or to compare it with conventional approaches. From the perspective of the data modeler, the key points are:

- Many information systems remain intrinsically "data-centric" – containing large volumes of consistently structured data. Experience has shown that the basic principles of good data modeling are relevant, regardless of whether an object-oriented or conventional approach is taken to their development. In short, if you're an object modeler working on "conventional" business applications, you should still read this book!

- True Object-Oriented DBMSs are not widely used. In most cases, data associated with object-oriented applications is stored in a conventional or extended relational DBMS – which of course will be ultimately be specified by a conventional data model.

- Unified Modeling Language (UML) has gained acceptance as a diagramming standard for both conventional models and object models. The UML option is shown as an alternative to the more popular standards in Chapters 3 and 4.

Prototyping Approaches

Finally, a few words on prototyping or Rapid Applications Development (RAD) approaches, which have in many quarters displaced the traditional "waterfall"[12] approaches to systems development. Rather than spend a long time developing a detailed paper specification, the prototyper adopts a "cut and try" approach – build something, show it to the client, modify it in the light of comments, show it to the client again, and so forth. My experiences with prototyping have generally been positive, but they bear out what other experienced prototypers have observed: *you need to design a good data model early in the process*. It comes back to the very high impact of a change to the data model in comparison with the relatively low cost of changing a program. Once prototyping is under way, nobody wants to change the model. So prototypers need to adopt what is effectively a data-driven approach.

---

[11] Booch, G., *Object-Oriented Analysis and Design with Applications*, Benjamin Cummings (1994).

[12] So called because there is no going back. Once a step is completed, we move on to the next, with no intention of doing that step again. In contrast, an *iterative* approach allows for several passes through the cycle, refining the deliverables each time.

Who Should Be Involved in Data Modeling?

In Chapter 6, we look more closely at the *process* of developing a data model. At this stage, let's just note that at least the following people have a stake in the model, and should expect to be involved in its development or review.

The system users, owners, and/or sponsors will need to verify that the model meets their requirements. Our ultimate aim is to produce a model that provides the most cost-effective solution for the business, and the users' *informed* agreement is an important part of ensuring that this is achieved.

Business specialists (sometimes called "subject matter experts") may be called upon to verify the accuracy and stability of business rules incorporated in the model, even though they themselves may not have any direct interest in the system. For example, we might involve strategic planners to assess the likelihood of various changes to product range.

The data modeler has overall responsibility for developing the model, and ensuring that other stakeholders are fully aware of its implications for them: "Do you realize that any change to your rule that each policy is associated with only one customer will be very expensive to implement later?"

Function modelers (analysts responsible for the function specification) and program designers will need to specify programs to run against the database. They will want to verify that the data model supports all the required functions, and assess whether it will necessitate complex or sophisticated design and programming.

The database designer will need to assess whether the model can be implemented to provide adequate performance, or whether compromises will need to be negotiated.

The data administrator will be interested in how the new database will fit into the bigger picture: are there overlaps with other databases; does the coding of data follow organizational or external standards; have other users of the data been considered; are names and documentation in line with standards? In encouraging consistency, sharing, and reuse of data, the data administrator represents business needs beyond the immediate project.

Organizing the modeling task to ensure that all of these views are properly taken into account is one of the major challenges of data modeling.

Costs and Benefits of Data Modeling

Whatever approach to systems development you use, it must include a formal data modeling phase. Project leaders and managers frequently ask me: "How much does data modeling add to the cost of a system?" or, conversely, "What are the benefits of data modeling?" The simple answer is that *data modeling is not optional*; no database was ever built without at least an implicit model, just as no house was ever built without a plan. In some cases the plan or model is not documented; but just as an architect can draw the plan of a building already constructed, a data modeler can examine an existing database and derive the underlying data model. The choice is not whether or not to model, but whether to do it *formally*, whom to involve, and how much effort to devote to producing a good design. If these issues are not explicitly addressed, the decisions are likely to be, respectively, "no," "a technical database specialist," and "not enough."

A formal data modeling phase, staffed with appropriate people, should reduce the costs of both database development (through the greater efficiency of properly qualified people), and the overall system (through the leverage effect of a good quality model). Unfortunately the question of cost is sometimes prompted by past problems with data modeling. In my experience, the two most common complaints are excessive, unproductive time spent in modeling, and clashes between data modelers and physical database designers. Overly long exercises are sometimes due to lack of familiarity with data modeling principles and standard approaches to problems. Surprisingly often, modeling is brought to a standstill by arguments as to which of two or more candidate models is correct – the "one-right-answer" syndrome. Arguments between data modelers and physical database designers often reflect misunderstandings about roles and a lack of hard data to support opinions. Finally, some data modeling problems are just plain difficult, and may take some time to sort out. But we won't solve them any more easily by leaving them to the physical database designers.

It is certainly possible for data modeling to cost too much, just as any activity that is performed incorrectly or not properly managed can cost too much. The solution, however, is to address the causes of the problem, rather than abdicating the job to people whose expertise is in other fields.

Is Data Modeling Still Relevant?

A broader question is: is data modeling still relevant to today's information systems practitioners?

Data modeling, as we now know it, emerged in the late 1960s, in line with the commercial use of database management systems, and the basic concepts have changed remarkably little since then. In those days, information systems – even such common applications as payroll and accounting systems – were generally developed in-house, and most large organizations employed teams of systems developers, often including specialist data modelers. Good data modeling was essential, even if its importance wasn't always recognized.

That picture has changed substantially, with many organizations adopting a policy of "buy not build," as packaged software is now available for a wide range of applications. Such applications arrive with the data structures largely predefined, and the role of the information systems practitioner focuses largely on tailoring of functionality and helping the organization adopt the new ways of working.

What is the role of data modeling in a world dominated by packages?

Obviously enough, the original development of packaged software requires data modeling – and of a very high standard. Such software needs to be comprehensive and adaptable to suit the differing needs of the vendors' clients. As we have discussed, flexibility starts with the data model.

In organizations using packaged software, rather than producing their own, there is still important work for data modelers, beginning at the selection phase.

The selection of a suitable package needs to be based on an understanding of the organization's requirements. These may need to be formally documented to support a tendering process whereby a number of vendors are invited to propose solutions. A data model should be a basic part of such a statement of requirements, and the data modeler faces the challenge of being comprehensive without restricting creativity or innovation on the part of the vendors. This is an important example of the importance of recognizing choice in data modeling. Far too often, I have seen data modelers develop the "one right model" for an application, and look for the product which most closely matches it, overlooking the fact that a vendor may have come up with a different but equally or more effective solution.

Once we are in a position to look at candidate packages, one of the most useful ways of getting a quick and relatively deep understanding of their designs and capabilities is to examine the underlying data models. An experienced data modeler should be able to ascertain fairly rapidly the key business rules enforced by each model – and whether the business can work effectively within them. This does presuppose that the vendors are able and willing to provide models. In my experience the situation has improved considerably in recent years – perhaps because vendors now more frequently have a properly documented model to show!

With the package purchased, we may still have considerable say as to how individual tables and attributes are defined and used. There is plenty of room for expensive errors here – and thus plenty of room for data modelers to ensure that good practices are followed. If modifications and extensions are to be made, the data modeler will be concerned to ensure that the database is used as intended.

Integration remains a major issue, even in these days of Enterprise Resource Planning (ERP) packages that aim to cover a large proportion of the client's business. Data will need to be communicated between applications, and uncontrolled duplication will incur storage and update costs. To address these issues, data models for each application may need to be maintained, and a large-scale corporate model or "town plan" may be necessary to provide an overall picture or plan.

It may also be necessary to develop a *Data Warehouse* – a specialized database that draws together data from a variety of applications to support management information needs. The data model for the warehouse will usually need to support high volumes of data subject to complex ad hoc queries, and accommodate data formats and definitions inherited from independently-designed packages and legacy systems. This is challenging work for any data modeler, and the subject of a full chapter of this book (Chapter 13).

Finally, it is worth noting the impact of personal computers. Today's professionals or knowledge workers use personal computers as essential "tools of trade" and frequently have direct access to a DBMS such as Microsoft Access. Owning a sophisticated tool is not the same thing as being able to use it effectively, and much time and effort is wasted by amateurs attempting to build applications without an understanding of basic design principles.

The discussion about the importance of data models earlier in this chapter should have convinced you that the single most important thing for an application designer to get right is the data model. A basic understanding of data modeling makes an enormous difference to the quality of the results that an inexperienced designer can achieve. Alternatively, the most critical place to get help from a professional is in the data modeling phase of the project. Organizations that encourage (or allow) end-user development of applications would do well to provide specialist data modeling training or consultancy as a relatively inexpensive and nonintrusive way of improving the quality of those applications.

With all of this, the role of the data modeler in most organizations has changed. But as long as we need to deal with substantial volumes of structured data, we need to know how to organize it – and the implications of the choices that we make in doing so. And that's essentially what data modeling is about.

Terminology – "Data Model"

In data modeling, as in all too many other fields, academics and practitioners have developed their own terminologies, and do not always employ them consistently. We have already seen an example in the descriptions of different levels of database design: conceptual schema, database schema, internal schema, and external schema versus data model, logical database design, physical database design, and view. The professional data modeler will need to be familiar with both sets, if only to be able to read the literature. In this book, I stick as closely as possible with the terminology used by practitioners in industry, with passing references to the more formal academic terms.

The most important difference at this stage is the term "data model" itself. Practitioners use it as I have in this chapter, to refer to a representation of the data required to support a particular function or set of functions. Data models may be presented in different ways (e.g., with or without sample data; as tables or diagrammatically; in full or in summary form).

Academics use "data model" to describe a particular way of representing data: for example, in tables, hierarchically, or as a network. Hence they talk of the "relational model" (tables), the "entity relationship model," or the "network model." Be aware of this as you read texts aimed for the academic community or in discussing the subject with them. And encourage some awareness and tolerance of practitioner terminology in return!

Alternative Approaches to Data Modeling

Practitioners differ from academics in another important way: their approach is heavily constrained by available tools. From a practical perspective, there is not much value in adopting a data modeling language that is not compatible with current database management systems or documentation products. In contrast, much of the academic literature on data modeling is devoted to exploring different languages, conventions, and database management system architectures.

As a practicing data modeler, I am often frustrated by the limitations of current tools. But in this book, I have stuck to the most widely used conventions, for documenting data models, and assumed that the models will be implemented using a traditional database management system.

Where to from Here?

Let's now take a brief look at how the rest of this book is organized.

In the next five chapters, which complete Part 1 of the book, we look at the basic principles of data modeling.

In Chapter 2 we cover *normalization*, a formal technique for organizing data into tables. Normalization enables us to deal with certain common problems of redundancy and incompleteness according to straightforward and quite rigorous rules. In some texts, particularly those advocating a function-driven approach, this is all that is taught about data modeling. If you are new to the subject, Chapter 2 should give you a feeling for what a sound data model looks like.

In Chapter 3, we introduce a more convenient way of presenting complex models. In working with the insurance model, you may have found that some of the more important business rules (such as only one customer being allowed for each policy) were far from obvious. As we move to more complex models, it becomes increasingly difficult to see the key concepts and rules among all the detail. A typical model of 100 tables with five to ten columns each will appear overwhelmingly complicated. We need the equivalent of an architect's sketch plan to present the main points.

In Chapter 4, we look at subtyping and supertyping, and their use in exploring alternative designs and handling complex models. We have already touched on these when we discussed the possible breakdown of the Person table into separate tables for personal and corporate customers. Subtypes and supertypes are often treated as an advanced topic, and not all CASE tools provide support for them (though this is rapidly changing). On the contrary, I believe they are an important basic technique of modeling, and we will use them extensively in the remainder of the book.

Chapter 5 covers the problem of actually designing a model in practice. It is possible to be very familiar with modeling conventions and principles of good design, but not be capable of applying them to model actual business requirements. I have confronted this often with graduate students who have studied modeling extensively, but actually developed few, if any, models for themselves.

Chapter 6 looks at the organization of the data modeling task within a real project: who should be involved, how interviews and workshops should be conducted, and what deliverables should be produced.

Part 2 of the book expands on some of the topics covered in Part 1, and looks at problems and structures that the practicing data modeler will encounter regularly. While you may want to "dip in" to Part 2 as required, the sequence has been designed to introduce new concepts progressively. If you dip in, you may have to refer to earlier chapters from time to time.

In particular, Chapter 13 looks at the particular challenges of developing data models for data warehouses and data marts, and the special techniques and structures required to address them, and in Chapter 14 we look at large scale (corporate) data modeling as a technique for information systems planning and coordination.

Finally, Appendix A is a checklist for data model review, summarizing material from throughout the book, and Appendix B describes an approach to presenting large data models.

Summary

Data and databases are central to information systems. Every database is specified by a data model, even if only an implicit one. The data model is an important determinant of the design of the associated information systems. Changes in the structure of a database can have a radical and expensive impact on the programs that access it. It is therefore essential that the data model for an information system be an accurate, stable reflection of the business it supports.

Data modeling is a *design* process. The data model cannot be produced by a mechanical transformation from hard business facts to a unique solution. Rather, the modeler generates one or more candidate models, using analysis, abstraction, past experience, heuristics, and creativity. Quality is assessed according to a number of factors including completeness, nonredundancy, faithfulness to business rules, reusability, stability, elegance, and communication effectiveness. There are often trade-offs involved in satisfying these criteria.

Performance of the resulting database is an important issue, but is primarily the responsibility of the physical database designer. The data modeler will need to be involved if changes to the data model or logical database design are contemplated.

In developing a system, data modeling and function modeling usually proceed in parallel. Data modeling principles remain important for object oriented development, particularly where large volumes of structured data are involved. Prototyping approaches rely on a stable data model being developed at an early stage.

Despite the wider use of packaged software and end-user development, data modeling remains a key technique for information systems professionals.

Chapter 2

Basic Normalization

"A place for everything and everything in its place."

– Homespun advice on kitchen organization.

In this chapter, we introduce *normalization*, a set of techniques for organizing data into tables, in such a way as to eliminate certain types of redundancy and incompleteness. Normalization is one of the most thoroughly researched areas of data modeling, and you will have little trouble finding other texts and papers on the subject. However, most take a fairly formal, mathematical approach. Here, I've tried to focus more on the steps in the process, what they achieve, and the practical problems you are likely to encounter. I have also highlighted areas of ambiguity and opportunities for choice and creativity.

The majority of the chapter is devoted to a rather long example. I encourage you to work through it. By the time you have finished, you will have covered virtually all of the issues involved in basic normalization.

An Informal Example of Normalization

Normalization is essentially a two-step task:

1. Put the data into tabular form (by removing repeating groups).

2. Remove duplicated data to separate tables.

A simple example will give you some feeling for what we are trying to achieve. Figure 2-1 shows a paper form (it could equally be a computer input screen) used for recording data about employees and their qualifications.

Employee Number: 01267		Employee Name: Clark		
Department Number: 05		Department Name: Auditing		Department Location: HO
Qualification		**Year**		
Bachelor of Arts		1970		
Master of Arts		1973		
Doctor of Philosophy		1976		

Figure 2-1. Employee Qualifications Form

If we want to store this data in a database, our first task is to put it into tabular form. But we immediately strike a problem: because an employee can have more than one qualification, it's awkward to fit the qualification data into one row of a table (Figure 2-2). How many qualifications do we allow for? Murphy's law tells us that there will always be an employee who has one more qualification than the table will handle!

Employee Number	Employee Name	Department Number	Department Name	Department Location	Qualification 1	
					Description	**Year**
01267	Clark	05	Auditing	HO	Bachelor of Arts	1970
70964	Smith	12	Legal	MS	Bachelor of Arts	1969
22617	Walsh	05	Auditing	HO	Bachelor of Arts	1972
50607	Black	05	Auditing	HO		

Qualification 2		Qualification 3		Qualification 4	
Description	**Year**	**Description**	**Year**	**Description**	**Year**
Master of Arts	1973	Doctor of Philosophy	1976		
Master of Arts	1977				

Figure 2-2. Employee Qualifications Table

We can solve this by dividing the data between two tables: one for the basic employee data, and the other for qualification data – one row per qualification (Figure 2-3). In effect, we have removed the "repeating group" of qualification data to its own table. We hold employee numbers in the second table to serve as a cross-reference back to the first, because we need to know to whom each qualification belongs. Now the only limit on the number of qualifications we can record for each employee is the maximum number of rows in the table – in practical terms, as many as we will ever need.

Employee Table

Employee Number	Employee Name	Department Number	Department Name	Department Location
01267	Clark	05	Auditing	HO
70964	Smith	12	Legal	MS
22617	Walsh	05	Auditing	HO
50607	Black	05	Auditing	HO

Qualification Table

Employee Number	Qualification Description	Qualification Year
01267	Bachelor of Arts	1970
01267	Master of Arts	1973
01267	Doctor of Philosophy	1976
70964	Bachelor of Arts	1969
22617	Bachelor of Arts	1972
22617	Master of Arts	1977

Figure 2-3. Separation of Qualification Data

Our second task is to remove duplicated data. For example, the fact that department number "05" is "Auditing" and is located at "HO" is repeated for every employee in that department. This means that updating data is complicated: if we wanted to record that the Auditing department had moved to another location, we would need to update several rows in the employee table. This is a nice example of the "elegance" requirement being violated. We also waste space.

The basic problem is that department names and addresses are really data about *departments* rather than employees, and belong in a separate Department table. We therefore establish a third table for department data, resulting in the three-table model of Figure 2-4. Again we leave Department Number in the Employee table to serve as a cross-reference.

Employee Table

Employee Number	Employee Name	Department Number
01267	Clark	05
22617	Walsh	05
70964	Smith	12
50607	Black	05

Department Table

Department Number	Department Name	Department Location
05	Auditing	HO
12	Legal	MS

Qualification Table

Employee Number	Qualification Description	Qualification Year
01267	Bachelor of Arts	1970
01267	Master of Arts	1973
01267	Doctor of Philosophy	1976
70964	Bachelor of Arts	1969
22617	Bachelor of Arts	1972
22617	Master of Arts	1977

Figure 2-4. Separation of Department Data

This is a very informal example of what normalization is about. The rules of normalization have their foundation in mathematics, and have been very closely studied by researchers. On the one hand, this means that we can have confidence in normalization as a technique; on the other, it is very easy to become lost in mathematical terminology and proofs, and miss the essential simplicity of the technique. The apparent rigor can also give us a false sense of security, by hiding some of the assumptions that have to be made before the rules are applied. Remember that data modeling is *design* – we should be wary of any process that seems to lead us to a single "right" answer.

You should also be aware that many data modelers profess not to use normalization, in a formal sense, at all. They would argue that they reach the same answer by other means, including common sense and intuition. Certainly, most practitioners would have had little difficulty solving the employee qualification example in this way.

However, common sense and intuition come from experience, and these experienced modelers have a good idea of what sound, normalized data models look like. Think of this chapter, therefore, as a way of gaining familiarity with some sound models, and, conversely, with some important and easily classified design faults. As you gain experience, you will find that you arrive at properly normalized structures as a matter of habit.

Nevertheless, even the most experienced professionals make mistakes, or encounter difficulties with sophisticated models. At these times, it is helpful to get back onto firm ground by returning to first principles such as normalization. And when you encounter someone else's model which has not been properly normalized (a common experience for data modeling consultants!), it is useful to be able to demonstrate that some generally accepted rules have been violated.

Relational Notation

Before tackling a more complex example, we need to get used to a more concise notation. The sample data in the tables takes up a lot of space, and is not strictly necessary to document the design (although it can be a great help in communicating it). If we eliminate the sample rows, we are left with the table names and columns.

Figure 2-5 shows the normalized model of employees and qualifications using the *relational* notation of table name followed by column names in brackets. (The full notation requires that the key of the table be underlined   discussed in this chapter). This convention is widely used in textbooks, and is convenient for presenting the minimum amount of information needed for most worked examples. In practice, however, we usually want to record more information about each column: format, optionality, and perhaps a brief note or description. Practitioners therefore usually use lists as in Figure 2-6.

EMPLOYEE (Employee Number, Employee Name, Department Number)

DEPARTMENT (Department Number, Department Name, Department Location)

QUALIFICATION (Employee Number, Qualification Description, Qualification Year)

Figure 2-5. Employee Model Using Relational Notation

EMPLOYEE
>   **Employee Number: 5 Numeric – Allocated by HR Dept**
>   **Employee Name: 60 Characters – Surname plus initial**
>   **Department Number: Department which pays employee's salary**

DEPARTMENT
>   **Department Number: 2 Numeric – To be reallocated**
>   **Department Name: 30 Characters**
>   **Department Location: 30 Characters – city where located**

QUALIFICATION
>   **Employee Number**
>   **Qualification Description: 30 Characters**
>   **Qualification Year Date: Optional**

Figure 2-6. Employee Model Using List Notation

A More Complex Example

Armed with the more concise relational notation, let's now look at a slightly more complex example, and introduce the rules of normalization as we proceed. The rules themselves are not too daunting, but we'll spend some time looking at exactly what problems they solve.

The form in Figure 2-7 is based on one used in an actual survey of antibiotic drug usage in Australian hospitals. The survey team wanted to determine which drugs and dosages were being used for various operations, to ensure that patients were properly prescribed for, and that the public was not paying for unnecessary drugs.

One form was completed for each operation. A little explanation is necessary to understand exactly how the form was used.

Each hospital in the survey was given a unique hospital number to distinguish it from other hospitals (in some cases two hospitals had the same name). All hospital numbers were prefixed "H" (for "hospital.")

Operation numbers were assigned sequentially by each hospital.

Hospitals fell into three categories: "T" for teaching, "P" for public, and "V" for private. All teaching hospitals were public ("T" implied "P.")

Hospital Number: H17		Hospital Name: St Vincent's		Operation Number: 48		
Hospital Category: P			Contact at Hospital: Fred Fleming			
Operation Name: Heart Transplant			Operation Code: 7A		Procedure Group: Transplant	
Surgeon Number: S15		Surgeon Speciality: Cardiology		Total Drug Cost: $75.50		
Drug Code	Full Name of Drug	Manufacturer		Method of Admin.	Cost of Dose ($)	Number of Doses
MAX 150mg	Maxicillin	ABC Pharmaceuticals		ORAL	$3.50	15
MIN 500mg	Minicillin	Silver Bullet Drug Co.		IV	$1.00	20
MIN 250mg	Minicillin	Silver Bullet Drug Co.		ORAL	$0.30	10

Figure 2-7. Drug Expenditure Survey

The operation code was a standard international code for the named operation. Procedure group was a broader classification.

The surgeon number was allocated by individual hospitals to allow surgeons to retain a degree of anonymity – the prefix "S" stood for "surgeon" (of course!).

Total drug cost was the total cost of all drug doses for the operation. The bottom of the form recorded the individual antibiotic drugs used in the operation. A drug code was made up of a short name for the drug plus the size of the dose.

As the study was extended to more hospitals, it was decided to replace the heaps of forms with a computerized database. Figure 2-8 shows the initial database design, using the relational notation. It consists of a single table, named Operation because each row represents a single operation. Don't be put off by the table's size: after the first 10 columns, there is a lot of repetition (which we are going to clean up once we start normalizing). But it's certainly not elegant.

OPERATION (Hospital Number, Operation Number, Hospital Name, Hospital
   Category, Contact Person, Operation Name, Operation Code, Procedure
   Group, Surgeon Number, Surgeon Specialty, Total Drug Cost,
   Drug Code 1, Drug Name 1, Manufacturer 1, Method of Administration 1,
   Cost of Dose 1, Number of Doses 1,
   Drug Code 2, Drug Name 2, Manufacturer 2, Method of Administration 2,
   Cost of Dose 2, Number of Doses 2,
   Drug Code 3, Drug Name 3, Manufacturer 3, Method of Administration 3,
   Cost of Dose 3, Number of Doses 3,
   Drug Code 4, Drug Name 4, Manufacturer 4, Method of Administration 4,
   Cost of Dose 4, Number of Doses 4)

Figure 2-8. Initial Drug Expenditure Model

The data modeler (who was also the physical database designer and the
programmer) took the simplest approach, exactly mirroring the form. Indeed, it
is interesting to consider who really did the data modeling. Most of the critical
decisions were taken by the designer of the form.

When I present this example in training workshops, I give participants a few
minutes to see if they can improve on the design. I strongly suggest you do the
same before proceeding. It's easy to argue *after* seeing a worked solution that
the same result could be achieved intuitively – try it first!

Determining Columns

Before we get started on normalization proper, we need to do a little
preparation and tidying up. Normalization relies on certain assumptions about
the way data is represented, and we need to make sure that these are valid.
There are also some problems that normalization does not solve, and it is better
to address these at the outset, rather than carrying excess baggage through the
whole normalization process. The following steps are necessary to ensure that
our initial model provides a sound starting point.

One Fact per Column

First we make sure that *each column in the table represents one fact only*. The
Drug Code column holds both a short name for the drug and a dosage size, two
distinct facts. The dosage size in turn consists of a numeric size and a unit of
measure. The three facts should be broken up into separate columns. We'll see
that this decision makes an important difference to the structure of our final
model.

A subtler example of a multifact column is the Hospital Category. We are identifying whether the hospital is public or private (first fact) as well as whether the hospital provides teaching (second fact). We should establish two columns, Hospital Type and Teaching Status, to capture these distinct ideas. (It's interesting to note that in the last few years, some Australian private hospitals have been accredited at teaching hospitals. The original design would not have been able to accommodate this change as readily as the "one fact per column" design).

The identification and handling of multifact columns is covered in more detail in Chapter 10.

Hidden Data

The second piece of tidying up involves making sure that we have not lost any data in the translation to tabular form. The most common problem here is that *we cannot rely on the rows of the table being stored in any particular order*. Suppose the original survey forms had been filed in order of return. If we wanted to preserve this data, we would need to add a Return Date or Return Sequence column. If the hospitals used red forms for emergency operations and blue forms for elective surgery, we would need to add a column to record the category if it was of interest to the database users.

Derivable Data

We need to remove any data that can be derived from other data in the table, and amend the columns accordingly. Remember our basic objective of nonredundancy. The Total Drug Cost is derivable by adding together the Drug Costs multiplied by the Numbers of Doses. We therefore remove it, noting in our supporting documentation how it can be derived (someone is bound to notice it missing, and we need to be able to prove to them that it can be reconstructed).

We might well ask why the total was held in the first place. In some cases, derived data is included unknowingly; more often it is added with the intention of improving performance. Even from that perspective, we should realize that there will be a trade-off between data retrieval (faster if we don't have to assemble the base data and calculate the total each time) and data update (the total will need to be recalculated if we change the base data). Far more importantly, though, performance is none of our business at this stage. If the physical designers cannot achieve the required performance, then carrying redundant data is *one* option we might consider and properly evaluate.

We can also drop the practice of prefixing Hospital Numbers with "H" and Surgeon Numbers with "S." The prefixes add no information, as we will always look at the hospital numbers and surgeon numbers in the context of their column headings.

Determining the Key

Finally, we determine a key for the table. The subject of keys warrants a full chapter (Chapter 9); for the moment we'll simply note that the key *is a minimal set of columns that contain a different combination of values for each row of the table*. Another way of looking at it is that each value of the key uniquely identifies one row of the table. In this case, a combination of Hospital Number and Operation Number will do the job. To clarify: if we nominate a particular hospital number and operation number, there will be at most one row with that particular combination of values. The purpose of the key is exactly this: to enable us to refer unambiguously to a specific row of a table ("Give me the row for hospital number 33, operation 109.") We can check this with the user by asking: "Could there ever be more than one form with the same combination of Hospital Number and Operation Number?" Incidentally, any combination that includes these two columns (e.g., Hospital Number, Operation Number and Surgeon Number) will also identify only one row, but will violate our requirement that the key be minimal (i.e., just big enough to do the job).

Figure 2-9 shows the result of tidying up the initial model of Figure 2-8. Note that Hospital Number and Operation Number are underlined. *This is the standard convention for identifying the columns that form the key*.

> **OPERATION (<u>Hospital Number</u>, <u>Operation Number</u>, Hospital Name, Hospital Type, Teaching Status, Contact Person, Operation Name, Operation Code, Procedure Group, Surgeon Number, Surgeon Specialty, Drug Short Name 1, Drug Name 1, Manufacturer 1, Size of Dose 1, Unit of Measure 1, Method of Administration 1, Cost of Dose 1, Number of Doses 1, Drug Short Name 2, Drug Name 2, Manufacturer 2, Size of Dose 2, Unit of Measure 2, Method of Administration 2, Cost of Dose 2, Number of Doses 2, Drug Short Name 3, Drug Name 3, Manufacturer 3, Size of Dose 3, Unit of Measure 3, Method of Administration 3, Cost of Dose 3, Number of Doses 3, Drug Short Name 4, Drug Name 4, Manufacturer 4, Size of Dose 4, Unit of Measure 4, Method of Administration 4, Cost of Dose 4, Number of Doses 4)**

Figure 2-9. Drug Expenditure Model after Tidying Up

Repeating Groups and First Normal Form

Let's start cleaning up this mess! Earlier we saw that our first task in normalization was to put the data in tabular form. It might seem that we've done this already, but in fact we've only managed to hide a problem with the data about the drugs administered.

Limit on Maximum Number of Occurrences

The drug administration data is the major cause of the table's complexity and inelegance, with its Drug Short Name 2, Drug Name 4, Number of Doses 3, and so forth. The columns needed to accommodate up to four drugs account for most of the complexity. And why only four – why not five or six or more? Four drugs represented a maximum arrived at by asking one of the survey team, "What would be the maximum number of different drugs ever used in an operation?" In fact, this number was frequently exceeded, with some operations using up to ten different drugs. Part of the problem was that the question was poorly put: a line on the form was required for each *drug-dosage* combination, rather than just for each different drug. And even if this had been allowed for, drugs and procedures could later have changed in such a way as to increase the maximum likely number of drugs. The model rates poorly against the completeness and stability criteria.

With the original clerical system, there wasn't much of a problem. Many of the forms were returned with a piece of paper taped to the bottom, or with additional forms attached with only the bottom section completed to record the additional drug administrations. In a computerized system, the change to the database structure to add the extra columns could be easily made, but the associated changes to programs would be much more painful. Indeed, the system developer decided that the easiest solution was to leave the database structure unchanged, and to hold multiple rows for these operations, suffixing the Operation Number with "a," "b," or "c" to indicate a continuation. This also involved changes to program logic and compromised the original simplicity of the system.

So one problem with our "repeating group" of drug administration data is that we have to set an arbitrary maximum number of repetitions. Ten repetitions is at least untidy and possibly inefficient, considering that 75 percent of operations used no antibiotic drugs at all. But this is not the major problem.

Data Reusability and Program Complexity

The main difficulties are with data reusability and complexity of program logic. It is relatively easy to write a program to answer questions like "How many operations were performed by neurosurgeons?" or "Which hospital is spending the most money on drugs?" A simple scan through the relevant columns will do the job. But it gets more complicated when we ask a question like "How much money was spent on the drug Ampicillin?" Similarly, "Sort into Operation Code sequence" is simple to handle, but "Sort into Drug Name sequence" can't be done at all without first copying the data to another table in which each drug appears only once in each row.

You might argue that some enquiries are always going to be intrinsically more complicated than others. But consider what would have happened if we had designed the table on the basis of "one row per drug." This might have been prompted by a different data collection method – perhaps the hospital drug dispensary filling out one survey form per drug. We would have needed to allow a repeating group (probably with many repeats!) to accommodate all the operations that used each drug, but we would find that the queries that were previously difficult to program had become straightforward, and vice versa. Here is a case of data being organized to suit a specific set of processes, rather than as a resource available to all potential users.

Consider too the problem of updating data within the repeating group. Suppose we wanted to delete the second drug administration for a particular operation (perhaps it was a nonantibiotic drug, entered in error). Would we shuffle the third and fourth drugs back into slots two and three, or would our programming now have to cater to intermediate gaps? Either way, the programming is messy because our data model is inelegant.

Recognizing Repeating Groups

To summarize: we have a set of columns repeated a number of times – a "repeating group" – resulting in inflexibility, complexity, and poor data reusability. The table design hides the problem by using numerical suffixes to give each column a different name.

We are better off to face the problem squarely, and document our initial structure as in Figure 2-10. The curly brackets indicate a repeating group with an indefinite number of occurrences: it's a useful convention, but it describes something we can't implement with a simple table. In technical terms, our data is *unnormalized*.

OPERATION (<u>Hospital Number</u>, <u>Operation Number</u>, Hospital Name, Hospital Category, Teaching Status, Contact Person, Operation Name, Operation Code, Procedure Group, Surgeon Number, Surgeon Specialty, {Drug Short Name, Drug Name, Manufacturer, Size of Dose, Unit of Measure, Method of Administration, Cost of Dose, Number of Doses})

Figure 2-10. Drug Expenditure Model Showing Repeating Group

At this point we should also check whether there are any repeating groups that have not been marked as such. To do this, we need to ask whether there are any data items that could have multiple values for a given value of the key. For example, we should ask whether more than one surgeon can be involved in an operation and, if so, whether we need to be able to record more than one. If so, the data items describing Surgeons (Surgeon Number and Surgeon Speciality) become another repeating group.

Removing Repeating Groups

A general and flexible solution should not set any limits on the maximum number of occurrences of repeating groups, and should also neatly handle the situation of few or no occurrences (the drug-free operation).

This brings us to the first step in normalization:

STEP 1: Put the data in tabular form by identifying and eliminating repeating groups.

The procedure is to split the table into multiple tables: one for the basic operation data and one for each repeating group, as follows:

1. Remove each separate set of repeating group columns to a new table, so that each occurrence of the group becomes a row in the new table.

2. Include the key of the original table in each new table, to serve as a cross reference (we call this a foreign key).

3. If the sequence of any original repeating group had business significance, introduce a "Sequence" column to the corresponding new table.

4. Name each new table.

5. Identify and underline the key of each new table, as discussed in the next subsection.

Figure 2-11 shows the two tables that result from applying these rules to the Operation table.

> OPERATION (<u>Hospital Number</u>, <u>Operation Number</u>, **Hospital Name, Hospital Type, Teaching Status, Contact Person, Operation Name, Operation Code, Procedure Group, Surgeon Number, Surgeon Specialty**)
>
> DRUG ADMINISTRATION (<u>Hospital Number</u>, <u>Operation Number</u>, <u>Drug Short Name</u>, <u>Size of Dose</u>, <u>Unit of Measure</u>, <u>Method of Administration</u>, **Cost of Dose, Number of Doses, Drug Name, Manufacturer**)

Figure 2-11. Repeating Group Removed to Separate Table

We have named the new table Drug Administration, since each row in the table records the administration of a particular drug dose, just as each row in the original table records an operation.

Determining the Key of the New Table

Finding the key of the new table wasn't easy (in fact this is usually the trickiest step in the whole normalization process). We had to ask, "What is the minimum combination of columns needed to uniquely identify one row (i.e., one specific administration of a drug?)" Certainly we needed Hospital Number and Operation Number to pin it down to one operation, but to identify the individual administration we had to specify not only the Drug Short Name, but also the Size of Dose, Unit of Measure, and Method of Administration – a six-column key.

In verifying the need for this long key, we would need to ask: "Can the same drug be administered in different dosages for the one operation?" (yes), and: "Can the same drug and dose be administered using different methods for the one operation?" (yes again).

The reason for including the key of the Operation table in the Drug Administration table should be fairly obvious – we need to know which operation each drug administration applies to. It does, however, highlight the importance of keys in providing the links between tables. It's worth considering the problems that would arise if we could have two or more operations with the same combination of Hospital Number and Operation Number. There would be no way of knowing which of these operations a given drug administration applied to.

To recap: keys are an essential part of normalization.

In determining the key for the new table, you will *usually* need to include the key of the original table, as in this case (Hospital Number and Operation Number form part of the key). This is not always so, despite what some widely read texts, including Codd's[13] original paper on normalization, suggest (see the example of insurance agents and policies in Chapter 8).

The sequence issue is often overlooked. In this case, the sequence of the drugs was not, in fact, significant, but the original data structure did allow us to distinguish between first, second, third, and fourth administrations. A sequence column in the Drug Administration table would have enabled us to retain that data if needed. Incidentally, the key of the Drug Administration table could then have been Hospital Number, Operation Number, and the sequence column.

First Normal Form

Our tables are now technically in *First Normal Form* (often abbreviated to 1NF). What have we achieved?

- All data of the same kind is now held in the same place: for example, all drug names are now in a common column. This translates into elegance and simplicity in both data structure and programming (we could now sort the data by Drug Name, for example).

- The number of different drug dosages that can be recorded for an operation is limited only by the maximum possible number of rows in the Drug Administration table – effectively unlimited. Conversely, an operation that does not use any drugs will not require any rows in the Drug Administration table.

---

[13] Codd, E., "A Relational Model of Data for Large Shared Data Banks," *Communications of the ACM* (1970). This was the first paper to advocate normalization as a data modeling technique.

Second and Third Normal Forms

Problems with Tables in First Normal Form

Look at the Operation table in Figure 2-11.

Every row that represents an operation at, say, hospital number 17 will contain the facts that the hospital's name is St. Vincent's, that Fred Fleming is the contact person, that its teaching status is T, and its type is P. At the very least, our criterion of nonredundancy is not being met. There are other associated problems. Changing any fact about a hospital (e.g., the contact person) will involve updating every operation for that hospital. And if we were to delete the last operation for a hospital, we would also be deleting the basic details of that hospital. Think about this for a moment. If we have a transaction "Delete Operation," its usual effect will be to delete the record of an operation only. But if the operation is the last for a particular hospital, the transaction has the additional effect of deleting data about the hospital as well. If we want to prevent this, we will need to explicitly handle "last operations" differently, a fairly clear violation of our elegance criterion.

Eliminating Redundancy

We can solve all of these problems by removing the hospital information to a separate table, in which each hospital number appears once only (and therefore is the obvious choice for the table's key). Figure 2-12 shows the result. We keep Hospital Number in the original Operation table to tell us which row to refer to in the Hospital table if we want relevant hospital details. Once again, it's vital that Hospital Number identifies one row only, to prevent any ambiguity.

> **OPERATION (<u>Hospital Number</u>, <u>Operation Number</u>, Operation Name, Operation Code, Procedure Group, Surgeon Number, Surgeon Specialty)**
>
> **HOSPITAL (<u>Hospital Number</u>, Hospital Name, Hospital Type, Teaching Status, Contact Person)**
>
> **DRUG ADMINISTRATION (<u>Hospital Number</u>, <u>Operation Number</u>, <u>Drug Short Name</u>, <u>Size of Dose</u>, <u>Unit of Measure</u>, <u>Method of Administration</u>, Cost of Dose, Number of Doses, Drug Name, Manufacturer)**

Figure 2-12. Hospital Data Removed to Separate Table

We've gained quite a lot here. Not only do we now hold hospital information once only; we are also able to record details of a hospital even if we don't yet have an operation recorded for that hospital.

Determinants

It's important to understand that this whole procedure of separating hospital data relied on the fact that for a given hospital number there could be only one hospital name, contact person, hospital type, and teaching status. In fact we could look at the dependency of hospital data on hospital number as the cause of the problem: every time a particular hospital number appeared in the operation table, the hospital name, contact person, hospital type, and teaching status were the same. Why hold them more than once?

Formally, we say that Hospital Number is a *determinant* of the other four columns. We can show this as:

Hospital Number =>> Hospital Name, Contact Person, Hospital Type, Teaching Status

where we read "=>>" as "determines" or "is a determinant of."

Determinants need not consist of only one column; they can be a combination of two or more columns, in which case we use the + sign to indicate such a combination. For example: Hospital Number + Operation Number =>> Surgeon Number.

This leads us to a more formal description of the procedure:

1. Identify any determinants, other than the key, and the columns they determine (we qualify this rule slightly in the section on candidate keys).

2. Establish a separate table for each determinant and the columns it determines. The determinant becomes the key of the new table.

3. Name the new tables.

4. Remove the determined columns from the original table. Leave the determinants to provide links between tables.

Of course, it's easy to say "Identify any determinants." A useful technique for doing this is to:

1. Look for columns that appear by their names to be identifiers ('code', 'number', 'ID,' and – sometimes – 'Name' being obvious candidates). These are potential determinants – or components of determinants.

2. Look for columns that appear to describe something other than what the table is about – in our example, hospitals rather than operations. Then look for other columns that identify this "something" – Hospital Number in this case.

Our "other than the key" exception in step 1 of the procedure is interesting. The problems with determinants arise when the same value appears in more than one row of the table. Because hospital number 17 could appear in more than one row of the Operation table, the corresponding values of Contact Person and other columns that it determined were also held in more than one row – hence the redundancy. But each value of the key itself can appear only once, by definition.

We've already dealt with "Hospital Number =>> Hospital Name, Contact Person, Hospital Type, Teaching Status."

Let's check the tables for other determinants. We find:

Operation Table

   Hospital Number + Surgeon Number =>> Surgeon Specialty

   Operation Code =>> Operation Name, Procedure Group

Drug Administration Table

   Drug Short Name =>> Drug Name, Manufacturer

   Drug Short Name + Method of Administration + Size of Dosage + Unit of Measure=>> Cost of Dose

How did we know that, for example, each combination of Drug Short Name, Method of Administration, and Size of Dose would always have the same cost? Without knowledge of every row that might ever be stored in the table, we had to look for a general rule. In practice, this means *asking the business specialist*. Our conversation might have gone along the following lines:

Modeler: What determines Drug Cost?

User: It depends on the drug itself and the size of the dose.

Modeler: So any two doses of the same drug and same size would always cost the same?

User: Assuming, of course, they were administered by the same method – injections cost more than pills.

Modeler: Ah, and wouldn't cost vary from hospital to hospital (and operation to operation?)

User: Strictly speaking, that's true, but it's not what we're interested in. We want to be able to compare prescribing practices, not how good each hospital is at negotiating discounts. So we use a standardized cost.

Modeler: So maybe we could call this column "Standard Cost" rather than "Cost." By the way, where does the Standard Cost come from?

Note that if the business rules were different, some determinants might well be different. For example, the "we use a standardized cost" rule: if this did not apply, the determinant of Drug Cost would include Hospital Number as well as the other data items identified.

And so on. Finding determinants may look like a technical task, but in practice most of the work is in understanding the business requirements.

The determinant of Surgeon Specialty is interesting. Surgeon Number alone will not do the job, because the same surgeon number could be allocated by more than one hospital. We need to add Hospital Number to form a true determinant. Think about the implications of this means of identifying surgeons. The same surgeon could work at more than one hospital, and would be allocated different surgeon numbers. Because we have no way of keeping track of a surgeon across hospitals, our system will not fully support queries of the type "List all the operations performed by a particular surgeon." As data modelers, we need to ensure the user understands this limitation of the data, a result of the strategy used to ensure surgeon anonymity.

By the way, are we sure that a surgeon can have only one specialty? If not, we would need to show Surgeon Specialty as a repeating group. For the moment, we'll assume that the model correctly represents reality, but the close examination of the data that we do at this stage of normalization often brings to light issues that may take us back to the earlier stages of preparation for normalization and removal of repeating groups.

Third Normal Form

Figure 2-13 shows the final model. Every time we removed data to a separate table, we eliminated some redundancy, and allowed the data in the table to be stored independently of other data (for example, we can now hold data about a drug, even if we haven't used it yet).

> OPERATION (<u>Hospital Number</u>, <u>Operation Number</u>, Operation Code, Surgeon Number)
>
> SURGEON (<u>Hospital Number</u>, <u>Surgeon Number</u>, Surgeon Specialty)
>
> OPERATION TYPE (<u>Operation Code</u>, Operation Name, Procedure Group)
>
> DRUG DOSAGE (<u>Drug Short Name</u>, <u>Method of Administration</u>, <u>Size of Dose</u>, <u>Unit of Measure</u>, Standard Cost)
>
> DRUG (<u>Drug Short Name</u>, Drug Name, Manufacturer)
>
> HOSPITAL (<u>Hospital Number</u>, Hospital Name, Hospital Category, Contact Person)
>
> DRUG ADMINISTRATION (<u>Drug Short Name</u>, <u>Size of Dose</u>, <u>Unit of Measure</u>, <u>Method of Administration</u>, <u>Hospital Number</u>, <u>Operation Number</u>, Number of Doses)

Figure 2-13. Fully Normalized Drug Expenditure Model

Intuitive designers call this "creating look-up tables." Using normalization terminology we say that the model is now in *third normal form* (3NF). I'll anticipate a few questions right away.

What happened to Second Normal Form?

Our approach took us directly from first normal form (data in tabular form) to third normal form. Most texts treat this as a two-stage process, dealing first with determinants that are part of the table's key, and later with nonkey determinants. For example, Hospital Code is part of the key of Operation, so we would establish the Hospital table in the first stage. Similarly, we would establish the Drug and Dose tables as their keys form part of the key of the Drug Administration table. At this point we would be in Second Normal Form (2NF), with the Operation Type and Surgeon information still to be separated out. The next stage would handle these, taking us to 3NF.

But be warned: most explanations that take this line suggest that you handle determinants which are part of the key first, then determinants which are made up entirely from nonkey columns. What about the determinant of Surgeon Specialty? This is made up of one key column (Hospital Number) plus one nonkey column (Surgeon Number), and is in danger of being overlooked. *Use the two stage process to break up the task if you like, but run a final check on determinants at the end.*

Most importantly, we only see 2NF as a stage in the process of getting our data fully normalized, never as an end in itself.

Is "Third Normal Form" the same as "Fully Normalized?"

Unfortunately, no. There are three further important normal forms: Boyce-Codd Normal Form (BCNF), Fourth Normal Form (4NF), and Fifth Normal Form (5NF). We'll discuss these in Chapter 8. The good news is that in most cases, including this one, data in 3NF is already in these other normal forms. In particular, 4NF and 5NF problems usually arise only when dealing with tables in which every column is part of the key. By the way, "all key" tables are legitimate and occur quite frequently, usually without causing any 4NF and 5NF problems.

What about performance?
Surely all those tables will slow things down?

There are certainly a lot of tables for what might seem to be relatively little data. This is partly because I deliberately left out quite a few columns, such as Hospital Address, which did not do much to illustrate the normalization process. This is done in virtually all illustrative examples, so they have a "stripped down" appearance compared with those you'll encounter in practice.

Thanks to advances in the optimizers within database management systems, the number of tables is less likely to be an important determinant of performance than it might have been in the past.

But the important point, made in Chapter 1, is that *performance is not an issue at this stage*. We don't know anything about performance requirements, data and transaction volumes, or the hardware and software to be used. Yet time after time modelers given this problem will do (or not do) things "for the sake of efficiency." For the record, the actual system was implemented completely without compromise, and performed as required.

Finally, recall that in preparing for normalization, we split the original Drug Code into Drug Short Name, Size of Dose, and Unit of Measure. At the time, I mentioned that this would affect the final result. We can see now that had we kept them together, the key of the Drug table would have been the original compound Drug Code. A look at some sample data from such a table will illustrate the problem this would have caused (Figure 2-14).

Drug Code	Drug Name
Max 50mg	Maxicillin
Max 100mg	Maxicillin
Max 200mg	Maxicillin

Figure 2-14. Drug Table Resulting from Complex Drug Code

We are carrying the fact that "Max" is the short name for Maxicillin redundantly, and would be unable to neatly record a short name and its meaning unless we had established the available doses – typical symptoms of unnormalized data.

Definitions and a Few Refinements

We've taken a rather long walk through what was, on the surface, a fairly simple example. In the process, though, we've encountered most of the problems that arise in getting data models into 3NF. Because we'll be discussing normalization issues throughout the book, and because you'll encounter them in the literature, it's worth clarifying the terminology, and picking up a few additional important concepts.

Determinants and Functional Dependency

We've already covered determinants in some detail. Remember that a determinant can consist of one or more columns, and must fit the following formula:

"For each value of the determinant, there can only be one value of some other nominated column(s) in the table at any point in time." Equivalently we can say that the other nominated columns are *functionally dependent* on the determinant.

The determinant concept is what 3NF (and BCNF) is all about – we are simply grouping data items around their determinants.

Primary Keys

We've introduced the underline convention to document the key of each table, and emphasized the importance of keys in normalization. More precisely we are talking about the **primary keys**. A primary key is a nominated column or combination of columns that has a different value for every row in the table. Each table has only one primary key. When checking this with a businessperson, I say, "If I nominated, say, a particular Account Number, would you be able to *guarantee* that there was *never* more than one Account with that number?" We look at primary keys in more detail in Chapter 9.

Candidate Keys

Sometimes more than one column or combination of columns could serve as a primary key. For example, we could have chosen Drug Name rather than Drug Short Name as the primary key of the Drug table (assuming, of course, that no two drugs could have the same name). We refer to such possible primary keys, whether chosen or not, as **candidate keys**. From the point of view of normalization, the important thing is that candidate keys that have not been chosen as the primary key, such as Drug Name, will be determinants of every column in the table, just as the primary key is. Under our normalization rules, as they stand, we would need to create a separate table for the candidate key and every other column (Figure 2-15).

> **DRUG 1 (<u>Drug Short Name</u>, Drug Name, Manufacturer)**

> **DRUG 2 (<u>Drug Name</u>, Drug Short Name, Manufacturer)**

Figure 2-15. Separate Tables for Each Candidate Key

All we've done here is to create a second table that will hold exactly the same data as the first – albeit with a different primary key.

To cover this situation formally, we need to be more specific in our rule for which determinants to use as the basis for new tables. We previously excluded the primary key; we need to extend this to all candidate keys. Our first step then should strictly begin:

> "Identify any determinants, *other than candidate keys* …"

A Formal Definition of Third Normal Form

The concepts of determinants and candidate keys provide a nice lead-in to a more formal definition of 3NF:

> A table is in 3NF if the only determinants of nonkey columns are candidate keys.

This makes sense: our procedure took all determinants other than candidate keys, and removed the columns they determined. The only determinants left should therefore be candidate keys. Once you've come to grips with the concepts of determinants and candidate keys, this definition of 3NF is a succinct and practical test to apply to data structures. The oft-quoted maxim "Each nonkey column must be determined by the key, the whole key, and nothing but the key" is a good way of remembering first, second, and third normal forms, but not quite as tidy and rigorous.

Incidentally, the definition of BCNF is even simpler: a table is in BCNF if the only determinants of *any* columns (i.e., including key columns) are candidate keys. The reason that we defer discussion of BCNF to Chapter 8 is that identifying a BCNF problem is one thing – fixing it may be another!

Foreign Keys

Recall that when we removed repeating groups to a new table, we carried the primary key of the original table with us, to cross-reference or "point back" to the source. Similarly, in moving from first to third normal form, we left determinants behind as cross-references to the relevant rows in the new tables.

These cross-referencing columns are called **foreign keys**, and are our means of linking data from different tables. For example, Hospital Number (the primary key of Hospital) appears as a foreign key in the Surgeon and Operation tables, in each case pointing back to the relevant hospital information. Another way of looking at it is that we are using the foreign keys as surrogates or abbreviations for hospital data – we can always get the full data about a hospital by looking up the relevant row in the Hospital table.

Note that "elsewhere in the data model" may include "elsewhere in the same table." For example, an Employee table might have a primary key of Employee Number. We might also hold the employee number of each employee's manager (Figure 2-16). The Manager's Employee Number would be a foreign key. This structure appears quite often in models as a means of representing hierarchies. The traditional convention for highlighting the foreign keys in a model is an asterisk, as shown.

EMPLOYEE (<u>Employee Number</u>, Name, Manager's Employee Number*, …)

Figure 2-16. Foreign Key Convention

For the sake of brevity, I use the asterisk convention in this book. But when dealing with more complex models, and recording the columns in a list as in Figure 2-6, I suggest you distinguish each foreign key by labeling the columns FK-Hospital, FK-Drug, etc., identifying the tables to which they point. Some columns will be part of more than one primary key, and hence potentially of more than one foreign key: for example, Hospital Number is the primary key of Hospital, but part of the primary keys of Operation, Surgeon, and Drug Administration.

It is a good check on normalization to mark all the foreign keys, and then to check whether any column names appear more than once in the overall model. If they are marked as foreign keys, they are serving the required purpose of cross-referencing the various tables. If not, there are three likely possibilities:

1. We have made an error in normalization – perhaps we have moved a column to a new table, but forgotten to remove it from the original table.

2. We have used the same name to describe two different things – perhaps we have used the word "Unit" to mean both "unit of measure" and "(organizational) unit in which the surgeon works" (as in fact actually happened in the early stages of designing this model).

3. We have failed to correctly mark the foreign keys.

In Chapter 3, foreign keys will play an important role in translating our models into diagrammatic form.

Referential Integrity

Imagine we are looking at the values in a foreign key column – perhaps all of the hospital numbers in the Operation Table, which point to the relevant Hospital records.. We would expect every hospital number in the Operation table to have a matching hospital number in the Hospital table. If not, our database would be internally inconsistent; critical information about the hospital at which an operation was performed would be missing.

Modern database management systems provide *referential integrity* features that ensure automatically that each foreign key value has a matching primary key value. Referential integrity is discussed in more detail in Chapter 12.

Denormalization and Unnormalization

As we know, from time to time it is necessary to compromise one data modeling objective in favor of another. Occasionally, we will be obliged to implement database designs that are not fully normalized in order to achieve some other objective – almost invariably performance. When doing this, it is important to look beyond "normalization" as a goal in itself, to the underlying benefits it provides: completeness, nonredundancy, flexibility of extending repeating groups, ease of data reuse, and programming simplicity. These are what we are sacrificing when we implement unnormalized or only partly normalized structures.

In many cases, these sacrifices will be prohibitively costly, but in others they may be acceptable. Figure 2-17 shows two options for representing data about a fleet of aircraft. The first model consists of a single, unnormalized table; the second is a normalized version of the first, comprising four tables.

(a) Unnormalized Model

> **AIRCRAFT (<u>Aircraft Tail Number</u>, Date Purchased, Model Name, Variant Code, Variant Name, Manufacturer Name, Manufacturer Supplier Code)**

(b) Normalized Model

> **AIRCRAFT (<u>Aircraft Tail Number</u>, Date Purchased, Variant Code*)**
>
> **VARIANT (<u>Variant Code</u>, Variant Name, Model Name*)**
>
> **MODEL (<u>Model Name</u>, Manufacturer Name*)**
>
> **MANUFACTURER (<u>Manufacturer Name</u>, Manufacturer Supplier Code)**

Figure 2-17. Normalization of Aircraft Data

If we were to find (through calculations or measurement, not just intuition!) that the performance cost of accessing the four tables to build up a picture of a given aircraft was unacceptable, we might consider a less-than-fully-normalized structure, although not necessarily the single table model of Figure 2-17(a). In this case, it may be that the Variant, Model, and Manufacturer tables are very stable, and that we are not interested in holding the data unless we have an aircraft of that type. Nevertheless, we would expect that there would be some update of this data, and would still have to provide the less-elegant update programs no matter how rarely they were used.

Considered decisions of this kind are a far cry from the database design folklore which regards denormalization as the first tactic in achieving acceptable performance, and sometimes even as a standard implementation practice regardless of performance considerations! Indeed, the words "denormalization" and "unnormalization" are frequently used to justify all sorts of design modifications that have nothing to do with normalization at all. I once saw a data model grow from 25 to 80 tables under the guise of "denormalization for performance."

To summarize:

- Normalization is aimed at achieving many of the basic objectives of data modeling, and any compromise should be evaluated in the light of the impact on those objectives.

- There are other techniques for achieving better database performance, many of them affecting only the physical design. These should always be thoroughly explored before compromising the logical database design.

- Database management system optimizers are reducing the importance of denormalization as a technique for improving performance.

- No change should ever be made to a logical database design without consultation with the data modeler.

Choice, Creativity, and Normalization

Choice and creativity have not featured much in our discussion of normalization. Indeed, normalization itself is a deterministic process, which makes it particularly attractive to teachers – it's always nice to be able to set a problem with a single right answer. The rigor of normalization, and the emphasis placed on it in teaching and research, has sometimes encouraged a view that normalization is the only technique required in modeling.

On the contrary, normalization is only one part of the modeling process. Let's look at our example again with this in mind.

We started the problem with a set of columns. Where did they come from? Some represented well-established classifications – Operation Code was defined according to an international standard. Some classified other data sought by the study – Hospital Name, Contact Person, Surgeon Specialty. And some were "invented" by the form designer (the *defacto* modeler) – the study group had not asked for Hospital Number, Drug Short Name, or Surgeon Number.

We'll look at column definition in some detail in Chapter 10; for the moment, let's note that there are real choices possible here. For example, we could have allocated nonoverlapping ranges of surgeon numbers to each Hospital so that Surgeon Number alone was the determinant of Specialty. And what if we hadn't invented a Hospital Number at all? Hospital Name and Contact Person would have remained in the Operation table, with all the apparent redundancy that would imply. We couldn't remove them, because we would not have a reliable foreign key to leave behind.

All of these decisions, quite outside the normalization process, and almost certainly "sellable" to the business users (after all, they accepted the *unnormalized* design embodied in the original form), would have affected our final solution. The last point is particularly pertinent. We invented a Hospital Number and, at the end of the normalization process, we had a Hospital table. Had we not recognized the concept of "hospital" (and hence the need for a hospital number to identify it) before we started normalization, we wouldn't have produced a model with a Hospital table. There's a danger of circular reasoning here: we implicitly recognize the need for a hospital table, so we specify a Hospital Number to serve as a key, which in turn leads us to specify a hospital table.

A particularly good example of concepts being embodied in keys is the old account-based style of banking system. Figure 2-18 shows part of a typical savings account file (a savings account *table*, in modern terms). Similar files would have recorded personal loan accounts, checking accounts, etc. This file may not be normalized (for example, Account Class might determine Interest Rate), but no amount of normalizing will provide two of the key features of many modern banking data models: recognition of the concept of "customer," and integration of different types of accounts. Yet we can achieve this very simply by adding a Customer Number (uniquely identifying each customer) and replacing the various specific account numbers with a generic Account Number.

SAVINGS ACCOUNT (Savings Account Number, Name, Address, Account Class, Interest Rate, ...)

Figure 2-18. Traditional Savings Account Model

Let's be very clear about what's happening here. At some stage in the past, an organization may have designed computer files or manual records and invented various "numbers" and "identifiers" to identify individual records, forms, or whatever. If these identifiers are still around when we get to normalization, our new data model will contain tables that mirror these old classifications of data, which may or may not suit today's requirements.

In short, uncritical normalization perpetuates the data organization of the past.

In our prenormalization tidying-up phase, we divided complex facts into more primitive facts. There is a degree of subjectivity in this. By eliminating a multifact column, we add apparent complexity to the model (the extra columns); on the other hand, if we use a single column, we may hide important relationships amongst data, and will need to define a code for each allowable combination.

We will need to consider:

- The value of the primitive data to the business:

A retailer might keep stock in a number of colors, but would be unlikely to need to break the color codes into separate primary color columns (Percentage Red, Percentage Yellow, Percentage Blue); but a paint manufacturer who was interested in the composition of colors might find this a workable approach.

- Customary and external usage:

If a way of representing data is well established, particularly outside the business, we may choose to live with it rather than become involved in "reinventing the wheel" and translating between internal and external coding schemes. Codes that have been standardized for electronic data interchange are frequently overloaded, or suffer from other deficiencies, which we'll discuss in Chapters 9 and 10. Nevertheless, the best trade-off often means accepting these codes with their limitations.

Finally, identification of repeating groups requires a decision about *generalization*: in the example we decide that (for example) Drug Name 1, Drug Name 2, Drug Name 3, and Drug Name 4 are in some sense the "same sort of thing," and represent them with a generic "Drug Name." It's hard to dispute this case, but what about the example in Figure 2-19?

> **CURRENCY (Currency ID, Date, Spot Rate, Exchange Rate 3 Days, Exchange
> Rate 4 Days, Exchange Rate 5 Days, …)**

Figure 2-19. Currency Exchange Rates

Here we have different currency exchange rates, depending on the number of days until the transaction will be settled (i.e., money actually changing hands). There seems to be a good argument for generalizing most of the rates to a generic Rate, giving us a repeating group, but should we include Spot Rate, which covers settlement in two days? On the one hand, renaming it "Exchange Rate 2 Days" would probably push us towards including it; on the other, the business has traditionally adopted a different naming convention, perhaps because they see it as somehow different from the others. In fact, spot deals are often handled differently, and I've seen experienced data modelers in similar banks choose different options, without violating any rules of normalization.

Common examples of less-than-obvious repeating groups include sequences of actions and roles played by people (Figure 2-20).

> **APPLICATION (<u>Application ID</u>, Submission Date, Submitted By, Registration
> Date, Registered By, Examination Date, Examined By, Approval Date,
> Approved By, …)**
>
> **SCHOOL (<u>School ID</u>, Principal, Principal's Contact Number, Deputy Principal,
> Deputy Principal's Contact Number, Secretary, Secretary's Contact
> Number, …)**

Figure 2-20. Generalization Produces Repeating Groups

In this section, we've focused on the choices that are not usually explicitly recognized in the teaching and application of normalization theory, in particular the degree to which key selection preempts the outcome. It is tempting to argue that we might as well just define a table for each concept, and allocate columns to tables according to common sense. This approach would also help to overcome another problem with the normalization process: the need to start with all data organized into a single table. In a complex "real world" model, such a table would be close to unmanageably large.

Indeed, this is the flavor of Chapter 3. In practice, however, normalization provides a complementary technique to ensure that columns are indeed where they belong, and that we haven't missed any of the less obvious tables. We will see how normalization can be complemented with a top-down approach, which gives us a first-cut set of tables, and then uses normalization as a final test to ensure that these tables are free of the avoidable problems we have discussed in this chapter.

Terminology

In this chapter we've used terminology based around *tables*: more specifically *tables*, *columns*, and *rows*. These correspond fairly closely with the familiar (to older computer professionals!) concepts of *files*, *data items* (or *fields*), and *records*, respectively.

Most theoretical work uses the relational terminology: *relations*, *attributes*, and *tuples*, respectively. This is because much of the theory of tabular data organization, including normalization, comes from the mathematical areas of relational calculus and relational algebra.

All that this means to most practitioners is a proliferation of different words for essentially the same concepts. We'll stick with tables, columns, and rows, but will call models in this form relational models. If you are working with a relational database management system, you'll almost certainly find the same convention used, but be prepared to encounter the full relational terminology in books and papers, and to hear practitioners talking about files, records, and items. Old habits die hard!

Summary

Normalization is a set of techniques for organizing data into tables in such a way as to eliminate certain types of redundancy and incompleteness. The modeler starts with a single file and divides it into tables based on dependencies among the data items. The process is mechanical, but the initial data will always contain assumptions about the business that will affect the outcome.

Normalization relies on correct identification of determinants and keys. In this chapter, we covered normalization to third normal form (3NF). A table is in 3NF if every determinant of a nonkey item is a candidate key. A table can be in 3NF but still not fully normalized. Higher normal forms are covered in Chapter 8.

In practice, normalization is used primarily as a check on the correctness of a model developed using a top-down approach.

Chapter 3

The Entity-Relationship Approach

"'What is the use of a book,' thought Alice, 'without pictures or conversations.'"

– Lewis Carroll, Alice's Adventures in Wonderland

Introduction

This chapter presents a top-down approach to data modeling, supported by a widely used diagramming convention. In Chapter 2, the emphasis was on confirming that the data organization was technically sound. The focus of this chapter is on ensuring that the data reflects business requirements.

We start by defining a procedure for representing existing models in diagrammatic form. We then look at developing the diagrams directly from business requirements, and introduce a more business-oriented terminology, based around entities (things of interest to the business) and the relationships among them. Much of the chapter is devoted to the correct use of terminology and diagramming conventions, which provide a bridge between technical and business views of data requirements[14].

---

[14] It is tempting to say "a common language" rather than merely a "bridge between views" - but in reality most nonspecialists do not have the ability, experience or inclination to develop or interpret data model diagrams directly. The data modeler usually needs to provide the various participants in the modeling process with material derived from the model, such as:
1. the business sentences that can be generated from relationships and from the use of subtypes
2. specimen forms that can be generated from prototyping tools.

A Diagrammatic Representation

Figure 3-1 is the model we produced in Chapter 2 for the drug expenditure example. Imagine for a moment that you are encountering it for the first time. Whatever its merits as a rigorous specification for a database designer, its format does not encourage a quick appreciation of the main concepts and rules. For example, the fact that each operation can be performed by only one surgeon (because each row of the Operation table allows only one surgeon number) is an important constraint imposed by the data model, but it may not be immediately apparent. This is as simple a model as we're likely to encounter in practice. As we progress to models with more tables and more columns per table, the problem of presentation becomes more serious.

> **OPERATION (<u>Hospital Number*</u>, <u>Operation Number</u>, Operation Code*, Surgeon Number*)**
>
> **SURGEON (<u>Hospital Number*</u>, <u>Surgeon Number</u>, Surgeon Specialty)**
>
> **OPERATION TYPE (<u>Operation Code</u>, Operation Name, Procedure Group)**
>
> **STANDARD DRUG DOSAGE (<u>Drug Short Name*</u>, <u>Method of Administration</u>, <u>Size of Dose</u>, <u>Unit of Measure</u>, Standard Cost of Dose)**
>
> **DRUG (<u>Drug Short Name</u>, Drug Name, Manufacturer)**
>
> **HOSPITAL (<u>Hospital Number</u>, Hospital Name, Hospital Category, Contact Person)**
>
> **DRUG ADMINISTRATION (<u>Drug Short Name*</u>, <u>Method of Administration*</u>, <u>Size of Dose*</u>, <u>Unit of Measure*</u>, <u>Hospital Number*</u>, <u>Operation Number*</u>, Number of Doses)**

Figure 3-1. Drug Expenditure Model in Relational Format

Function (or process) modelers solve this sort of problem by using diagrams, such as Data Flow Diagrams, showing the most important features of their models. Complex function models can be handled by leveled diagrams, with diagrams at each level showing different amounts of detail.

We can approach data models the same way. This chapter introduces a widely used convention for diagrammatic representation of data models. Chapter 4 and Appendix B look at some practical approaches to presenting complex models.

The Basic Symbols

Our data model diagrams (sometimes called *data structure diagrams*) are based on two symbols:

1. A "box" (strictly speaking, a rectangle with rounded corners) represents a table.

2. A line drawn between two boxes represents a foreign key pointing back to the table where it appears as a primary key.

The first part is easy. Simply draw a box for every table in the model (Figure 3-2), with the name of the table inside it.

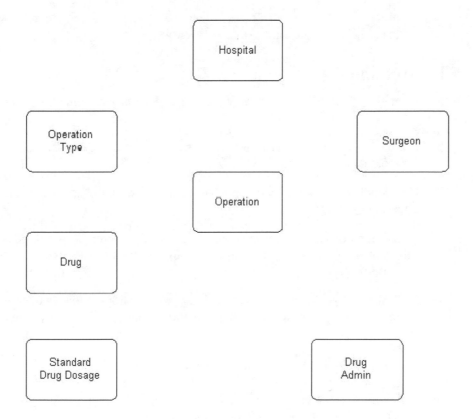

Figure 3-2. Boxes Representing Tables

Diagrammatic Representation of Foreign Keys

To understand how to draw the lines, look at the operation and Surgeon tables. The primary key of Surgeon (Hospital Number + Surgeon Number) appears in the operation table as a foreign key. Therefore draw a line between the two boxes, and indicate the direction of the link by putting a "crow's foot" at the foreign key end (Figure 3-3). If you like, you can think of the crow's foot as an arrow pointing back to the relevant surgeon for each operation.

Figure 3-3. Foreign Key Represented by Line and Crow's Foot

Interpreting the Diagram

If presented only with this diagram, we could deduce at least four important things:

1. The model specifies a Surgeon table (hence we want to keep data about Surgeons).

2. The model specifies an Operation table (hence we want to keep data about Operations).

3. Each Operation can be associated with only one Surgeon (because there is only provision for the key of Surgeon to appear once in each row of the Operation table).

4. Each Surgeon could be associated with many Operations (because there is nothing to stop many rows of the Operation table pointing to the same Surgeon).

The first two rules would have been obvious from the relational representation, the other two much less so. With the diagram, we have succeeded in summarizing the relationships between tables implied by our primary and foreign keys, without having to actually list any column names at all.

We could now ask a business specialist, referring to the diagram: "Is it true that each operation is performed by one surgeon only?" It is possible that this is not so, or cannot be relied upon to be so in future. Fortunately, we will have identified the problem while the cost of change is still only a little time reworking the model (we would need to represent the Surgeon information as a repeating group in the Operation table, then remove it using the normalization rules).

Another possible answer to our question could be that while more than one surgeon could participate in an operation, the client is only interested in recording details of one – perhaps the surgeon who *managed* the operation. Having made this decision, it is worth recording it on the diagram (Figure 3-4), first to avoid the question being revisited, and second to specify more precisely what data will be held. It is now clear that the database will not be able to answer the question: "In how many operations did surgeon number 12 at hospital number 18 *participate*?" It *will* support "How many operations did surgeon number 12 at hospital number 18 *manage*?"

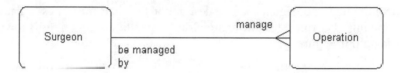

Figure 3-4. Annotated Relationship

As well as annotating the diagram, we should change the name of the Surgeon Number column in the Operation table to Managing Surgeon Number.

Optionality

The diagram may also raise the possibility of operations that don't involve any surgeons at all: "We don't involve a surgeon when we are attending to a patient who presents with a small cut, but we still need to record whether any drugs were used." In this case, some rows in the Operation table may have a null value for Surgeon Number. We can show whether the involvement of a surgeon in an operation is *optional* or *mandatory* by using the conventions of Figure 3-5. You can think of the circle as a zero and the perpendicular bar as a one, indicating the minimum number of surgeons per operation or (at the other end of the line) operations per surgeon.

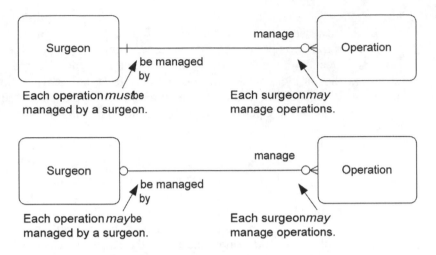

Figure 3-5. Optional and Mandatory Relationships

Our diagram now contains just about as much information about the Surgeon and Operation tables and their inter relationships as can be recorded without actually listing columns and text descriptions of their meanings[15]. The result of applying the rules to the entire drug expenditure model is shown in the diagram in Figure 3-6.

Verifying the Model

The diagram provides an excellent starting point for verifying the model with users and business specialists. Intelligent, thorough checking of each line on the diagram will often reveal unsound assumptions and misunderstandings or, equally useful, increase confidence in the model on the part of both user and modeler.

---

[15] This is not quite all we can usefully record, but few documentation tools support more than this. See Chapter 7 for a diagramming convention for nontransferability. Some tools support the *weak entity* concept discussed in Chapter 9.

We have already looked at the relationship between Operation and Surgeon. Now, consider the relationship between Operation and Operation Type. It prompts the question: "Are we sure that each operation can be of only one type?" This is the rule held in the model, but how would we represent a combined gall bladder removal and appendectomy? There are at least two possibilities:

1. Allow only "simple" operation types such as "Gall Bladder Removal" and "Appendectomy." If this course was selected, the model would need to be redesigned, based on the operation type information being a repeating group within the operation; or

2. Allow complex operation types such as "Combined Gall Bladder Removal and Appendectomy."

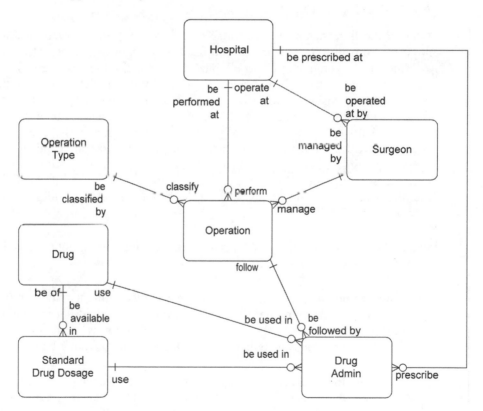

Figure 3-6. Diagram of Drug Expenditure Model

Both options are technically workable and the decision may be made for us by the existence of an external standard. If the system already exists, option 2 will be much easier to implement. But option 1 is more elegant, in that, for example, a single code will be used for all appendectomies. Queries of the form "list all operations that involved appendectomies" will therefore be simpler to specify and program.

Examining the relationship between the two tables led to thinking about the meaning of the tables themselves. Whatever decision we made about the relationship, we would need to document a clear definition of what was and wasn't a legitimate entry in the Operation Type table.

Redundant Lines

Look at the lines linking the Hospital, Operation, and Surgeon tables. There are lines from Hospital to Surgeon and from Surgeon to Operation. Also there is a line from Operation direct to Hospital. Does this third line add anything to our knowledge of the business rules supported by the model? It tells us that each operation must be performed at one hospital. But we can deduce this from the other two lines that specify each operation must be managed by a surgeon and each surgeon operates at a hospital. The line also shows that a program could "navigate" directly from a row in the Operation table to the corresponding row in the Hospital table. But our concern is with business rules rather than navigation. Accordingly, we can remove the "short-cut" line from the diagram, without losing any information about the business rules that the model enforces.

Figure 3-7 summarizes the rule for removing redundant lines, but the rule has some important caveats:

- If it were possible for an operation to be recorded without a surgeon (i.e., if the link to the Surgeon table were *optional*), we could not remove the short-cut line, which shows that *every* Operation is performed at a hospital, something we could no longer deduce from the other lines.

- If the line from Surgeon to Hospital was named (for example) "be trained at," then the direct link from Operation to Hospital would represent different information than the combined link. The former would tell at which hospital the operation was performed, the latter which hospital trained the surgeon who performed the operation.

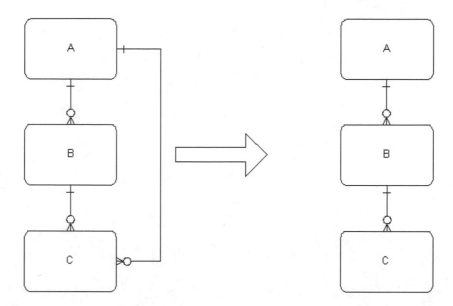

Figure 3-7. Removing Redundant Lines

The value of recording names and optionality on the lines should now be a little clearer – for one thing, they allow the correct decision to be made about which lines on the diagram are redundant and can be removed. Figure 3-8 shows the result of applying the redundant line rule to the whole model.

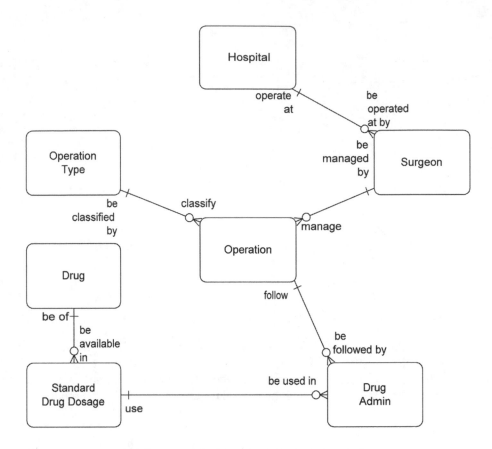

Figure 3-8. Drug Expenditure Model with Redundant Lines Removed

The Top-Down Approach: Entity-Relationship Modeling

In the preceding section, a reasonably straightforward technique was used to represent a data model in diagrammatic form. Although the diagram contains little new information, it communicates the principal rules so much more clearly that you should never review or present a model without drawing one. In the past, databases were often designed without the use of diagrams. It is interesting to prepare a diagram for such a database and show it to programmers and analysts who have been working with the database for some time. Frequently they have never explicitly considered many of the rules and limitations that the diagram highlights.

Developing the Diagram Top Down

The most interesting thing about the diagram is that it prompts a suspicion that normalization and subsequent translation into boxes and lines was not necessary at all. If instead we had asked the client "What things do you need to keep data about?" wouldn't we have received answers such as "hospitals, operations, and surgeons?" If we'd asked how they were related, might we not have been able to establish that each operation was managed by one surgeon only, and so forth? With these questions answered, couldn't we draw the diagram immediately, without bothering about normalization?

In fact, this is the approach most often taken in practice. The modeler develops a diagram that effectively describes which tables will be required, and how they will need to be related, and *then* allocates columns to the tables. Normalization becomes a final check to ensure that the "grammar" of the model is correct. For experienced modelers, the check becomes a formality, as they will have already anticipated the results of normalization and incorporated them into the diagram.

The reason we looked at normalization first is that in order to produce a normalized model, you need to know what one looks like, just as an architect needs to have examined some completed buildings before attempting to design one. Ultimately, we want a design made up of sound, fully normalized tables that meets our criteria of completeness, nonredundancy, stability, reusability, and elegance – not a mish-mash of business concepts. The frequently given advice to "ask what things the business needs to keep information about, and draw a box for each of these" is overly simplistic, although it indicates the general direction of the approach.

The need to produce a normalized model should be in the back of our minds, and we will therefore split out repeating groups and "look-up tables" as we discover them. For example, we might identify a table called "Aircraft." We recognize that some data will be the same for all aircraft of a particular type, and that normalization would produce an "Aircraft Type" look-up table for this data. Accordingly a box named Aircraft Type is drawn. We are actually doing a little more than normalization here, as we don't actually know that there is an existing determinant of Aircraft Type in the data (e.g., Aircraft Model Number). No matter – we reserve the right to define one if we need it!

In dealing with a Customer table, we may recognize that a customer may have more than one occupation, and that data about occupations therefore forms a repeating group that normalization would remove. We can anticipate this and define a separate Occupation table, again without knowledge of actual columns and determinants.

The top-down approach also overcomes most of the limitations of normalization used by itself. We do not need to start with a formidably complex single table, nor do we need to accept the tables implicitly defined by our historical choice of determinants. However, as we shift focus from the technical structure of the tables to the broader business requirements, it helps to introduce a more business-oriented terminology.

Terminology

The relational models were built on three basic concepts: tables, columns, and keys.

Our new terminology is more business-oriented. Again, there are three concepts:

1. **Entities** – things of interest to the business. Represented by boxes on the diagram, and implemented as tables.

2. **Attributes** – what we want to know about entities. Not usually shown on the diagram. They will be implemented as columns in tables.

3. **Relationships** – relationships between entities are represented by lines on the diagram and implemented through foreign keys.

The process of designing an appropriate set of entities and relationships to meet a business problem (i.e., getting as far as the diagram) is called, reasonably enough, **entity-relationship modeling** or E-R modeling for short. A data model in this format is often called an E-R model, and the diagram an E-R diagram (ERD).

Don't be daunted by the new terms. Broadly speaking, we have just introduced a less technical language, to enable us to talk about (say) "the relationship between a hospital and a surgeon," rather than "the existence of the primary key of Hospital as a foreign key in the Surgeon table."

In the following sections, these new terms and their representation are examined in more detail.

Entities

An entity is the "real world" class of things that a table represents, such as "Hospital." Strictly, we should distinguish between *entities*, such as "St. Vincent's Hospital" and *entity types* such as "Hospital." In practice, we tend to use the word entity loosely to mean entity type; and *entity instance* on those fairly rare occasions when we want to refer to a single instance (which would translate into a row in a table).

All entities will meet the criterion of being "a class of things we need to keep information about," as long as we are happy for "thing" to include more abstract concepts such as events (e.g., Operation) and classifications (e.g., Operation Type). However, the converse is not true – many classes that a user might nominate in response to the question "what do you need to keep information about?" would not end up as entities. Some concepts suggested by the user will be complex, and will need to be represented by more than one entity. For example, invoices would not usually be represented by a single Invoice entity, but by two entities – Invoice Header and Invoice Item (the result of removing the repeating group of invoice items to form a separate entity). Other user requirements will be derivable from more primitive data – for example "Quarterly Profit" might be derivable from sales and expense figures represented by other entities.

Still other "real world" classes will overlap, and would therefore violate our nonredundancy requirement. If our model already had "Personal Customer" and "Corporate Customer" entities, we would not add a "Preferred Customer" entity if such customers were already catered for by the original entities.

Finally, some concepts will be represented by attributes or relationships. There is a degree of subjectivity in deciding whether some concepts are best represented as entities or relationships: is a marriage better described as a relationship between two people, or as "something we need to keep information about?"

There is almost always an element of choice in how data is classified into entities. Should a single entity represent all employees or should we define separate entities for part-time and full-time employees? Should we use separate entities for insurance policies and cover notes or is it better to combine them into a single Policy entity? We'll discuss ways of generating and choosing alternatives in Chapter 4; for the moment, just note that such a choice does exist, even though it may not be obvious in these early examples.

Now, a few rules for representing entities. Recommending a particular set of conventions is one of the best ways of starting an argument among data modelers, and there was a time when there seemed to be as many diagramming conventions as modelers. In the last few years there has been greater standardization, thanks mainly to the influence of documentation tools, which enforce reasonably similar conventions. The rules for drawing entities and relationships presented in this chapter are typical of current practice.

Entity Diagramming Convention

In this book, entities are represented by boxes with rounded corners. We use the rounded corners to distinguish E-R diagrams from final logical database designs (square corners). The latter may include compromises required to achieve adequate performance or to suit the constraints of the implementation software. By using two conventions, we can quickly identify whether we are looking at what was specified (the model) or what was built (the final database design).

There are no restrictions, other than those imposed by your documentation tool, on the size or color of the boxes. If drawing a box larger or in another color aids communication, by all means do it. For example, you might have a Customer entity, and several associated entities resulting from removing repeating groups: Address, Occupation, Dependant, and so on. Just drawing a larger box for the Customer entity might help readers approach the diagram in a logical fashion.

Entity Naming

The name of an entity must be in the singular and refer to a single instance (in relational terms, a row) – not to the whole table. Thus collective terms like File, Table, Catalog, History and Schedule are inappropriate.

For example, we use:

1. Account rather than Accounts

2. *Customer* rather than *Customer File* or *Customer Table*, or even *Customer Record*

3. Product rather than Product Catalog

4. Historical Transaction rather than Transaction History

5. Scheduled Visit rather than Visiting Schedule

We do this for three reasons:

1. *Consistency* – it is the beginning of a naming standard for entities.

2. *Communication* – an entity is "something we want to keep information about," such as a customer rather than a customer file.

3. *Compatibility with Relationship Names* – which we'll look at in the following section.

A number of bad practices occur regularly:

One is to name the entity after the most "important" attribute – for example, Drug Cost rather than Standard Drug Dosage, or Specialty rather than Surgeon. This is particularly tempting when we have only one nonkey attribute. It looks much less reasonable later when we add further attributes, or if the original attribute is normalized out to another entity. You should also avoid giving an entity a name that reflects only a subset of the roles it plays in the business. For example, consider using Material Item rather than Component, Person rather than Witness, and Stock Item rather than Returned Item.

Another is to name one entity by prefixing the name of another, e.g., Employee and External Employee. The natural assumption is that an External Employee is a particular type of Employee. Such naming should therefore be limited to cases where one entity is a subtype of the other entity (we look at subtypes in Chapter 4). It would be wrong to have entities named Employee and External Employee where the Employee entity represented *only internal* employees, since it would be reasonable to infer that the Employee entity included external employees as well. If an entity representing only internal employees were required in this model it should be named Internal Employee.

Yet another is to abbreviate names unnecessarily. This is often done merely to save a few keystrokes. Analysts almost inevitably abbreviate inconsistently and without providing a list of abbreviation meanings. While the use of several abbreviations for the same word is perhaps more irritating than ambiguous, the opposite condition, of the same abbreviation being used for different words, is clearly ambiguous, yet it happens!

A list of abbreviation meanings might seem to be overkill, yet it is remarkable how much imagination is shown by analysts when choosing abbreviations, resulting in abominations that mean nothing to those attempting to understand the data structure. Some DBMSs impose stringent limits on the length of table and column names, requiring even more abbreviation. Given that developers and the writers of *ad hoc* queries may only have table and column names to go on, it is important that such name are unambiguous.

A good example of these perils occurred in a school administration system in which the names of the fields holding information about students' parents were prefixed by 'M' and 'F'. Was that 'mother' and 'father' or 'male' and 'female'? It depended!

Entity Definitions

Entity names must be supported by definitions.

In the early stages of data modeling, we work mainly with the diagram. But that is asking a lot of the entity names – they need to communicate without ambiguity exactly what real world data they represent. Does the Operation Type entity cover hybrid operations? Does Surgeon include a general practitioner who performs an operation, or only formally qualified specialists? What exactly qualifies as an "Operation?" The answers to these questions will affect the overall shape of the model, as we discovered when we discussed the definition of Operation Type earlier in this chapter.

Frequently in data modeling you need to decide on the best terminology to use. It may be that you need to discard familiar terms in favor of less widely used terms that do not carry the same diversity of meaning. This is particularly so for the most commonly used terms, which may have acquired all sorts of context-dependent meanings over a period of time. To a railroad company, the word "train" may mean a particular service (the 8.15 P.M. from Sydney to Melbourne), a physical object (Old Number 10), or perhaps a marketed product (the Orient Express).

But at some point in the development process (preferably sooner rather than later) we need to supplement the names in the boxes with more detailed and precise definitions. A good definition will clearly answer two questions:

1.   What distinguishes instances of this entity from instances of other entities?

2.   What distinguishes one instance from another?

Good examples of each, focusing on the marginal cases, are the best method of pinning this down. The primary key and a few other sample attributes can also do much to clarify the definition prior to the full set of attributes being defined.

Again a number of bad practices occur regularly, most often because entity definition is seen as a relatively meaningless chore rather than a key part of the modeling process:

- A glance at a thesaurus will reveal that many common words have many quite distinct meanings, yet these same words are often used without qualification in definitions. In one model, an entity named Role had the definition *'Part, task or function'*, which, far from providing the reader with additional information as to what the entity represented, widened the range of possibilities!

- Entity definitions often do not make clear whether instances of the entity are classes or individual occurrences. For example, does a Patient Condition entity with a definition *'A condition that a patient suffers'* have instances like 'Influenza' and 'Hangnail' or instances like 'Patient 123345's influenza that she presented with on 1/4/96'? This sort of ambiguity is often defended by assertions that the identifier or other attributes of the entity should make this clear. If the identifier is simply Patient Condition Identifier, we are none the wiser, and if the attributes are not well defined, as is often the case, we may still be in the dark.

- Another undesirable practice is using IT terminology and technical data modeling terms in entity definitions. Terms such as "intersection entity," "cardinality," "optionality," "many-to-many relationship" or "foreign key" mean nothing to the average businessperson, and should not appear in data definitions. If business users do not understand the definitions, their review of them will lack rigor."

Let's have a look at an example of a definition. We might define Drug as follows:

> An antibiotic drug as marketed by a particular manufacturer. Variants that are registered as separate entries in *Smith's Index of Therapeutic Drugs* are treated as separate instances. Excluded are generic drugs such as penicillin. Examples are: Maxicillin, Minicillin, Extracycline.

Note that there is no rule against using the entity name in the definition – we are not trying to write an English dictionary. However beware of using *other* entity names in a definition. When an analyst chooses a name for an entity, that entity is usually not intended to represent every instance of anything that conforms to the dictionary definitions of that name. For example, the name Customer may be used for an entity that only represents *some* of the customers of a business. If that entity name is then used in a definition of another entity, there is potential for confusion. Which meaning applies: the restricted meaning of that name implied by the definition of the original entity (e.g., loyalty program customers) or the more general meaning (*all* customers?)

I can't over-emphasize the importance of good entity definitions. From time to time, data modelers get stuck in long arguments without much apparent progress. Almost invariably, they have not put adequate effort into pinning down some working definitions, and are continually making subtle adjustments, which are never recorded. Modelers frequently (and, probably unwittingly) shift definitions in order to support their own position in discussion – "Yes, we could accommodate a patient who transfers hospitals while undergoing treatment by defining Hospital to mean the hospital where the treatment commenced," and later, "Of course we can work out how much each hospital spent on drugs – all the relevant hospitals are represented by the Hospital entity."

As well as helping to clarify the modelers' thinking, definitions provide guidance on the correct use of the resulting database. Many a user interrogating a database using a query language has been misled because of incorrect assumptions about what its tables contained. And many a programmer or user has effectively changed the data model by using tables to hold data other than that intended by the modeler. The latter constitutes a particularly insidious compromise to a model. If someone (perhaps the physical database designer) makes explicit changes to the logical database design, we can at least see the changes and raise the alarm. But bypassing a definition is far subtler, as the violation is buried in program specifications and logic. Because system enhancement cycles can be slow, users themselves may resort to re-use of data items for other purposes. In a typical case, a comment field was redefined by the users to hold a series of classification codes in the first line and the comment proper in the remaining lines!

The result can be inconsistent use of data by programmers, and consequent system problems ("I assumed that surgeons included anyone who performed an operation" or even "I used the Surgeon table for pharmacists – they're all prefixed with a 'P'.") The database may even be rendered unworkable because a business rule specified by the model does not apply under the (implicit) new definition. For example, the rule that each drug has only one manufacturer will be broken if the programmer uses the table to record generic drugs, in violation of a definition that allows only for branded drugs. Changes of this kind are often made after a database has been implemented, and fails to support a new requirement. A failure on the stability criterion leads to compromises in elegance and communication.

All of these scenarios are examples of degradation in data quality. If a database is to hold good quality data, it is vital that definitions are not only well written but *used*[16]. This, of course, implies that all participants in the system development process and all users of the resulting system have access to the same set of definitions, in a data dictionary or other form of controlled but accessible project documentation.

Sometimes we have a choice of either "tightening up" the definition of an existing term, or introducing a new term. The first approach produces a diagram that is more accessible to people familiar with the business, and apparently more meaningful; on the other hand, readers are less likely to look up the definition. Keep this in mind: "communication" must include an understanding of the meaning of entities as well as a superficial comfort with the diagram.

---

[16] See, for example, Witt, G.C., "The Role of Metadata in Data Quality," *Journal of Data Warehousing* Vol. 3 No. 4 (Winter 1998).

Relationships

In our drug expenditure model, the lines between boxes can be interpreted in "real world" terms as relationships between entities. There are relationships, for example, between hospitals and surgeons, and between operations and drug administrations.

Relationship Diagramming Conventions

We have already used a convention for annotating the lines to describe their meaning (relationship names), *cardinality* (the crow's foot can be interpreted as meaning "many," its absence as meaning "one"), and *optionality* (the circles and bars representing "optional" and "mandatory" respectively).

The convention is shown in Figure 3-9 and is typical of several in common use and supported by documentation tools. Figure 3-10 shows some variants, including UML, which is gaining in popularity. Use of this notation is discussed later in this chapter.

Figure 3-9. Relationship Notation

Note that we have named the relationship in both directions: "issue" and "be issued by." This enables us to interpret the relationship in a very structured, formal way:

"Each company may issue one or more shares"

and

"Each share must be issued by one company."

The value of this sentence form is in improving communication. While diagrams are great for conveying the big picture, they don't encourage systematic and detailed examination, particularly by business specialists. Generating the sentence is an *almost* entirely mechanical process (forming the plurals of the entity names can't be totally automated). Many documentation tools support this, using a more or less similar formula.

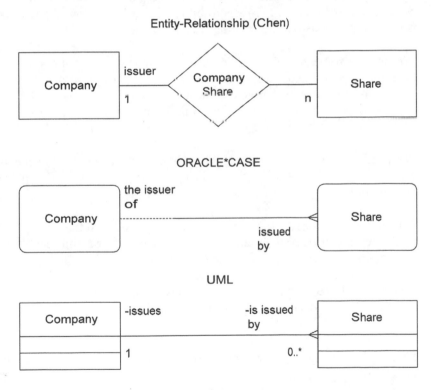

Figure 3-10. Alternative Relationship Notations

I like to use "one or more" rather than "many," which may have a connotation of "lots" ("Oh no, nobody would have *many* occupations, two or three would be the most.") I also like the "may" and "must" approach to describing optionality, rather than the "zero or more" and "one or more" wording used by some. "Zero or more" is an expression only a programmer could love, and our aim is to communicate with business specialists in a natural way without sacrificing precision.

An alternative to using "must" and "may" is to use "always" and "sometimes:" "Each company sometimes issues one or more shares" and "Each share is always issued by one company."

In order to be able to mechanically translate relationships into business sentences, a few rules need to be established.

We have to select relationship names that fit the sentence structure. It's worth trying to use the same verb in both directions ("hold" and "be held by," "be responsible for" and "be the responsibility of") to ensure that the relationship is not interpreted as carrying two separate meanings.

We have to name the relationships in both directions, even though this adds little to the meaning. I make a practice not only of placing each relationship name close to the entity that is the object of the sentence, but also of arranging the names above and below the line so they are read in a clockwise direction when generating the sentence (as, for example, in Figure 3-9).

We need to be strict about using singular names for entities. As mentioned earlier, this discipline is worth following regardless of relationship naming conventions.

Finally, we need to show the optional/mandatory symbol at the crow's foot end of the relationship, even though this will not usually be enforceable by the database management system (at the end without the crow's foot, "optional" is usually implemented by allowing the foreign key to be null i.e., empty). Despite this there are a number of situations, which we discuss in Chapter 12, in which the mandatory nature of a relationship at the crow's foot end is very important.

Figures 3-11 and 3-12 show some relationships typical of those we encounter in practice.

Note that:

- A crow's foot may appear at neither, one, or both ends of a relationship. The three alternatives are referred to as one-to-one, one-to-many, and many-to-many relationships, respectively.

- There may be more than one relationship between the same two entities.

- It is possible for the same entity to appear at both ends of a relationship – this is called a "self-referencing" or "recursive" relationship.

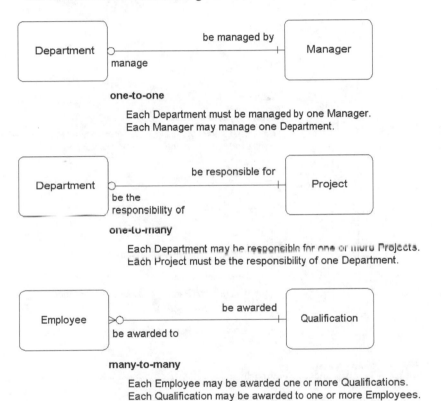

one-to-one

Each Department must be managed by one Manager.
Each Manager may manage one Department.

one-to-many

Each Department may be responsible for one or more Projects.
Each Project must be the responsibility of one Department.

many-to-many

Each Employee may be awarded one or more Qualifications.
Each Qualification may be awarded to one or more Employees.

Figure 3-11. Examples of Relationships

two relationships

Each Employee must hold one Position.
Each Position may be held by one Employee

and

Each Employee may act in one or more Positions.
Each Position may be acted in by one Employee

self-referencing one-to-many

Each Land Parcel may include one or more Land Parcels.
Each Land Parcel may be included in one Land Parcel.

self-referencing many-to-many

Each Manufactured Part may be an assembly of one or more
Manufactured Parts.

Each Manufactured Part may be a component of one or more
Manufactured Parts.

Figure 3-12. Examples of Relationships

When drawing one-to-many relationships, I suggest you orient the entities so that the crow's foot is nearer the bottom of the page. This means that hierarchies appear in the expected way, and diagrams are easier to compare. For horizontal relationship lines, the convention (by no means followed by all modelers) is to orient the crow's foot to the right. You won't always be able to follow these conventions, especially when you use subtypes, which we introduce in Chapter 4. Once again, don't sacrifice effectiveness of communication for blind adherence to a layout convention.

Similarly, in laying out diagrams, it usually helps to eliminate crossing lines wherever possible. But carrying this rule too far can result in large numbers of close parallel lines not dissimilar in appearance (and comprehensibility) to the tracks on a printed circuit board.

Another useful technique is to duplicate entities on the diagram to avoid long and difficult-to-follow relationship lines. You need to have a symbol (provided by some documentation tools) to identify a duplicated entity; a dotted box is a good option.

Many-to-Many Relationships

Many-to-many relationships crop up regularly in E-R diagrams in practice. But if you look again at the drug expenditure diagram in Figure 3-8 you will notice that it contains only one-to-many relationships. This is no accident, but a consequence of the procedure we used to draw the diagram from normalized tables. Remember that each value of a foreign key pointed to *one* entity instance, and that each value could appear *many* times; hence we only ever end up with one-to-many relationships when working from a relational model.

Look at the many-to-many relationship between Employee and Qualification in Figure 3-13.

Figure 3-13. Many-to-Many Relationship

How would we implement the relationship using foreign keys? The answer is that we can't in a standard relational DBMS[17]. We can't hold the key to Qualification in the Employee table, because an employee could have several qualifications. The same applies to the Qualification table, which would need to support multiple Employee keys. A normalized model cannot represent many-to-many relationships with foreign keys, yet such relationships certainly exist in the real world.

---

[17] At least one Object-Relational DBMS allows storage of open-ended arrays in row/column intersections. This provides an alternative mechanism for storage of a many-to-many relationship (admittedly no longer in 1NF).

A quick preview of the answer: although we can't represent the many-to-many relationship with a foreign key, we *can* represent it with a table. But let's tackle the problem systematically.

Applying Normalization to Many-to-Many Relationships

Although we can't capture the relationship in a fully normalized model using only Employee and Qualification tables, we can handle it with an *unnormalized* representation, using a repeating group (Figure 3-14).

EMPLOYEE (<u>Employee Number</u>, Employee Name, {Qualification ID, Qualification Name, Date Qualification Received})

Figure 3-14. Employee and Qualification Unnormalized

I've had to make up a few plausible columns to give us something to normalize!

Proceeding with normalization (Figure 3-15), we remove the repeating group, and identify the key of the new table as Employee Number + Qualification ID (if an employee could receive the same qualification more than once, perhaps from different universities, we would need to include Date Qualification Received in the key to distinguish them).

Looking at our 1NF tables, we note the following dependency:

Qualification ID =>> Qualification Name

Hence we provide a look-up table for qualification details. The tables are now in 3NF. You may like to confirm that we would have reached the same result if we had represented the relationship initially with a repeating group of employee details in the Qualification table.

Unnormalized:

> EMPLOYEE (<u>Employee Number</u>, Employee Name, {Qualification ID, Qualification Name, Date Qualification Received})

First Normal Form:

> EMPLOYEE (<u>Employee Number</u>, Employee Name)

> EMPLOYEE QUALIFICATION (<u>Employee Number*</u>, Qualification ID, Qualification Name, Date Qualification Received)

Second and Third Normal Forms:

> EMPLOYEE (<u>Employee Number</u>, Employee Name)

> EMPLOYEE QUALIFICATION RELATIONSHIP (<u>Employee Number*</u>, <u>Qualification ID*</u>, Date Qualification Received)

> QUALIFICATION (<u>Qualification ID</u>, Qualification Name)

Figure 3-15. Normalization of Employee and Qualification

Naming the tables presents a bit of a challenge. Employee and Qualification are fairly obvious, but what about the other table? "Employee-Qualification Relationship" is one option, and makes some sense because this less obvious table represents the many-to-many relationship between the other two. The result is shown diagrammatically in Figure 3-16.

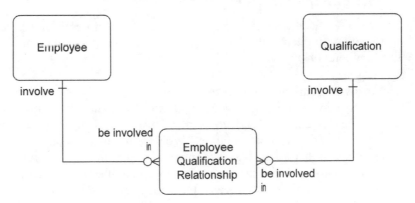

Figure 3-16. Many-to-Many Relationship Resolved

This example illustrates an important general rule. Whenever we encounter a many-to-many relationship between two entities, we can represent it with a new entity, linked to the two original entities. We call this process "resolving a many-to-many relationship" and the new entity a "resolution entity" (or "intersection entity.") There is no need to go through the normalization process each time – we simply recognize the pattern and handle it in a standard way.

Note the optional/mandatory nature of the new relationships and how they derive from the optional/mandatory nature of the original many-to-many relationship:

- The "one" ends of the new relationships will always be mandatory (since an instance of the relationship without both of the original participating entities – in this case, an Employee Qualification Relationship without both an Employee and a Qualification – does not make sense)

- The "many" ends of the new relationships will be optional or mandatory depending on the corresponding ends of the original relationship. The nature of that correspondence is best illustrated by reference to Figures 3-13 and 3-16. The nature of the relationship to Employee will correspond to the nature of the original relationship at the Qualification end and the nature of the relationship to Qualification will correspond to the nature of the original relationship at the Employee end. Thus, if an Employee had to have at least one Qualification (i.e., the original relationship is mandatory at the Qualification end), the relationship between Employee and Employee Qualification Relationship is also mandatory at the "many" end.

Choice of Representation

We are now faced with an interesting choice. We can represent the same real world situation either with a many-to-many relationship, or with an entity and two new relationships.

The many-to-many notation preserves consistency: we use a line to represent each real world relationship, whether it is one-to-many or many-to-many (or one-to-one, for that matter). But we now have to perform some conversion to get to a relational representation. Worse, the conversion is not totally mechanical, in that we have to determine the key of the resolution table. In our example, this key might simply be Employee Number plus Qualification ID; however if an employee can receive the same qualification more than once, the key of the resolution table must include Date Qualification Received. And how do we represent any nonkey attributes that might apply to the resolution entity – do we need to allow entities *and* relationships to have attributes?

On the other hand, if we restrict ourselves to one-to-many relationships, we seem to be stuck with the clumsy idea of an entity whose name implies that it is a relationship! And if this box actually represents a real world relationship rather than an entity, what about the two one-to-many "relationships" with the original entities? Can we really interpret them as real world relationships, or are they just "links" between relationships and entities?

The solution to this apparent mess lies in the fact that there is usually some choice as to whether to classify a particular concept as an entity or a relationship. For example, we could model the data relating prospective employees and job positions with either a relationship ("apply for/be applied for by") or an entity ("Application.") Here are some more examples:

Relationship	Resolution Entity
Students *enroll in* Subjects	Enrollment
Companies *employ* Persons	Employment
Employees *are responsible for* Assets	Responsibility

The name of the many-to-many relationship is usually a good source of an appropriate entity name. Perhaps we could use "Award" as an alternative to "Employee-Qualification Relationship."

Experienced data modelers take advantage of this choice, and are adept at selecting names that allow boxes to represent entities and lines to represent relationships. As a last resort, they would name the box representing a many to-many relationship as "entity-1 entity-2 Relationship" (e.g., Employee-Asset Relationship), and thereafter treat it as an *entity*. This practice is so universal that most data modelers refer to all boxes as entities and all lines as relationships. Many would be unaware that this is only possible because of choices they have made during the modeling process.

This may all sound a little like cheating! Having decided that a particular concept is going to be implemented by a foreign key (because of the way our database management system works), we then decide that concept is a relationship. Likewise, if a particular concept is to be implemented as a table, we decide to call that concept a real world entity! And we may change our view along the way, if we discover, for example, that a relationship we originally thought to be one-to-many is in fact many-to-many.

We come back to the questions of design, choice, and creativity. If we think of the real world as being naturally preclassified into entities and relationships, and our job as one of analysis and documentation, then we are in trouble. On the other hand, if we see ourselves as designers who can choose the most useful representation, then this classification into entities and relationships is a legitimate part of our task.

The Chen Convention for Relationships

Some in the academic world choose the first option: that there are entities and relationships "out there" that we need to document consistently. When reading the literature, watch out for this assumption – it isn't always explicitly stated. This leads to the argument that we need to use a consistent symbol for relationships, regardless of cardinality or the number of participating entities. The most common symbol is the diamond, introduced by Chen in his very important paper *The Entity-Relationship Model – Toward a Unified View of Data*[18].

Figure 3-17 shows the Employee-Asset example using the Chen convention. If we had started out thinking that the relationship was one-to-many, but on checking with the user found that it was many-to-many, we would only need to make a minor change to the diagram (changing the "1" to "n."). This seems more appropriate than introducing a Responsibility entity ("Fine," says the user, "but why didn't we need this entity before?")

Figure 3-17. Chen Convention for Relationships

Despite this, I don't recommend the convention, for three practical reasons.

First, it simply puts too many objects on the page. With our boxes and lines convention, we tend to look at the boxes first, then the lines, allowing us to come to grips with the model in two logical stages. In my experience, diamonds make this much harder, and practical Chen models can be quite overwhelming. Some academics even extend the convention to include attributes, shown as circles connected to the entities and relationships –

---

[18] *ACM Transactions on Database Systems* (March 1976).

excellent for illustrating simple examples, but even more unwieldy for practical problems.

Second, most documentation tools don't support the diamond convention. A few provide a special symbol for intersection entities, but still require one-to-many relationships to be documented using lines.

Third, many of the people who contribute to and verify the model will also need to see the final database design. End users may access it through query languages, and analysts will need to specify processes against it. If the final database design uses the same concepts as the verified model, these people don't have the problem of coming to grips with two different views of their data.

None of these problems need bother researchers, who typically work with fairly simple examples. A number of texts explain the Chen convention in detail[19]: they are worth reading if you want to pursue modeling theory further or to better understand some of the assumptions underlying the methods we use in practice.

In this book, we will steer a middle course, which will keep us in line with most documentation products. In the earlier stages of analysis, we will allow many-to-many relationships as a convenient and easily checked shorthand. But we will attach attributes only to entities (not to relationships), and the final model presented to the database designer will not contain any many-to-many relationships.

One-to-One Relationships

We'll leave a detailed discussion of one-to-one relationships until Chapter 7, as they are relatively uncommon (but nevertheless a legitimate and important structure in modeling). For the moment, note that you should not *automatically* combine the entities linked by a one-to-one relationship into a single entity, as is sometimes suggested.

---

[19] For example, Batini, Ceri, Navathe, *Conceptual Database Design*, Benjamin Cummings (1992).

Self-Referencing Relationships

Look at Figure 3-18. This type of relationship is sometimes called a "head scratcher," not only because of its appearance, but because of the difficulty many people have in coming to grips with the recursive structure it represents.

Figure 3-18. Self-Referencing One-to-Many Relationship

We interpret this in the same way as any other relationship, except that both participants in the relationship are the same entity:

"Each Employee may manage one or more Employees"

and

"Each Employee may be managed by one Employee."

The model represents a simple hierarchy of employees as might be shown on an organization chart. To implement the relationship using a foreign key, we would need to carry the key of Employee (say, Employee ID) as a foreign key *in the Employee table*. We would probably call it "Manager ID" or similar. We encountered the same situation in Chapter 2 when we discussed foreign keys, which pointed to the primary key of the same table.

Note that the relationship is optional in both directions. This reflects the fact that the organizational hierarchy has a top and bottom (some employees have no subordinates, one employee has no manager). A mandatory symbol on a self-referencing relationship should always raise your suspicions, but is not necessarily wrong if the relationship represents something other than a hierarchy.

Self-referencing relationships can also be many-to-many. Figure 3-19 shows such a relationship on a Manufactured Part entity. In business terms, we are saying that a part can be made up of parts, which themselves can be made up of parts and so on. Furthermore, we allow a given part to be used in the construction of more than one part – hence, the many-to-many relationship.

Figure 3-19. Self-Referencing Many-to-Many Relationship

This relationship, being many-to-many, cannot be represented by a single table with suitable foreign key(s). We can, however, resolve it in much the same way as a many-to-many relationship between two different entities.

Figure 3-20 shows an intuitive way of tackling the problem directly from the diagram. We temporarily split the Manufactured Part entity in two, giving us a familiar two-entity many-to-many relationship, which we resolve as described earlier. We then recombine the two parts of the split entity, taking care not to lose any relationships.

Figure 3-21 shows the same result achieved by representing the structure with a repeating group and normalizing.

The structure shown in Figure 3-20(d) can be used to represent any self-referencing many-to-many relationship. It is often referred to as the "Bill of Materials" structure, because in manufacturing, a bill of materials lists all the lowest level components required to build a particular product by progressively breaking down assemblies, subassemblies, and so forth. Note that the Manufactured Part Usage entity holds two foreign keys pointing to Manufactured Part (Assembly Manufactured Part Number and Component Manufactured Part Number) to support the two relationships.

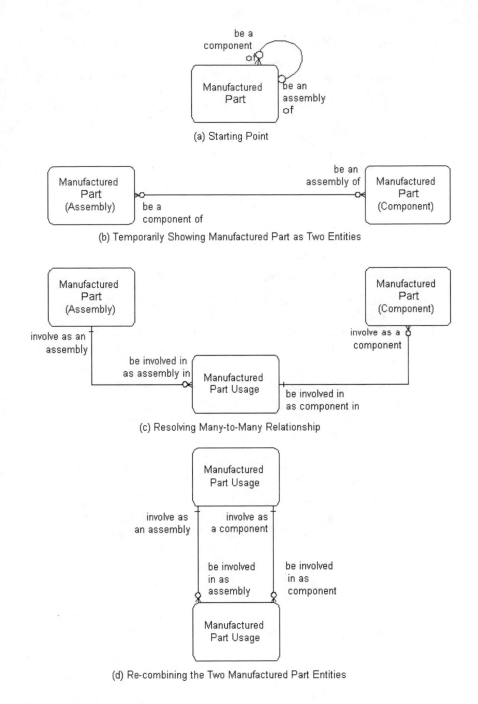

(a) Starting Point

(b) Temporarily Showing Manufactured Part as Two Entities

(c) Resolving Many-to-Many Relationship

(d) Re-combining the Two Manufactured Part Entities

Figure 3-20. Resolving a Self-Referencing Many-to-Many Relationship

**MANUFACTURED PART (<u>Manufactured Part Number</u>, Description,
{Component Manufactured Part Number, Quantity Used})**

Removing repeating group ...

MANUFACTURED PART (<u>Manufactured Part Number</u>, Description)

**MANUFACTURED PART USAGE (<u>Assembly Manufactured Part Number*</u>,
<u>Component Manufactured Part Number*</u>, Quantity Used)**

Figure 3-21. Using Normalization to Resolve a Self-Referencing Many-to-Many
Relationship

Relationships of Higher Degree

All our relationships so far have involved only two entities. How would we
handle a real world relationship involving three or more entities?

A welfare authority might need to record which services were provided by
which organizations in which areas. From a relational modeling viewpoint, our
three basic tables might be Service, Organization, and Area. The objective is to
record each allowable combination of the three. For example, the Service
"Child Care" might be provided by "Family Support Inc." in "Greentown." We
can easily do this by defining a table in which each row holds an allowable
combination of the three primary keys. The result is shown diagrammatically
in Figure 3-22, and it can be viewed as an extension of the technique used to
resolve two-entity many-to-many relationships. The same principle applies to
relationships involving four or more entities.

Once more, in modeling the real world using an E-R model, we find ourselves
representing a relationship with a box rather than a line. Modelers using the
Chen convention would use a diamond in this case. However, once again we
can change our perspective and view the relationship as an entity – in this case
we might name it Service Availability ("Allowed Combination" or similar is
often a good choice). We discuss relationships involving three or more entities
in Chapters 7 and 8.

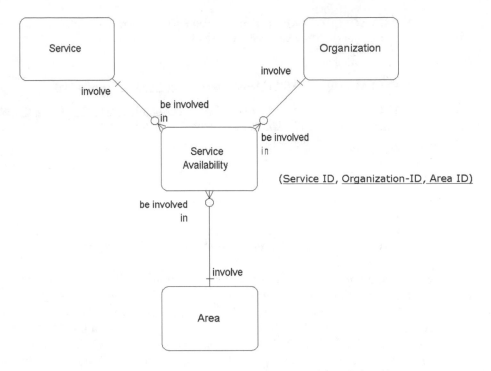

Figure 3-22. Resolution Entity Representing a Ternary (3-entity) Relationship

Relationship Names

Finally, a few words on one of the areas most often neglected in modeling – the naming of relationships. It is usual in the early stages of modeling to leave relationships unnamed. This is fine while the basic entities are still being debated, but the final model should always be properly annotated with meaningful relationship names – *not* "associated with" or "related to." The exception to this rule is the two relationships that arise from resolving a many-to-many relationship, because the name of the relationship has usually been used to name the new entity. I suggest "involve" and "be involved in" as workable names, as in Figure 3-16, but *only* for relationships that arise from resolving a many-to-many relationship.

A good example of the need for meaningful names is the relationship between Country and Currency, as might be required in a database to support foreign currency dealing. Figure 3-23 shows the two entities.

Figure 3-23. Unnamed Relationship

What is the relationship between these two entities? One to many? Many to many? We can't answer these questions until the meaning of the relationship has been clarified. Are we talking about the fact that currency is *issued* by a country? Or *legal tender* in the country? Or *able to be traded* in that country? The result of our investigation may well be that we identify more than one relationship between the same pair of entities.

There is another problem here that may affect cardinalities. What do we mean by "country?" Exactly what is a currency? Again these words can have many meanings. Does San Marino qualify as a country? It issues lire with the same value as Italian lire. Should they be considered the same currency?

Is the Euro a currency? If so, the "be issued by" relationship to Country may be optional. And so on.

The point is that definition of the relationship is closely linked to definitions of the participating entities. We focus on the entity definitions first, but our analysis of the relationships may lead us to revise these definitions.

Let's look at some further examples of the way in which entity and relationship definitions interact. Consider Figure 3-24: if the Customer entity represents *all* customers, the relationships are correct, since every purchase must be made by a customer but not every customer belongs to a loyalty program.

Figure 3-24. One Use of a Customer Entity

However, if the business is an airline or a retail store, it may not keep records of customers other than those in loyalty programs. In this case, not all purchases are made by customers (*as defined in the model*), but all customers (*as defined in the model*) belong to loyalty programs. The relationships should now look like those in Figure 3-25.

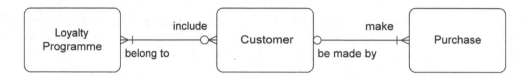

Figure 3-25. Another Use of a Customer Entity

An example of another type of entity that can cause problems of definition is a Position entity in a Human Resources model. Is a position a generic term like "Database Administrator," of which there may be more than one in the organization, or a specific budgeted position with a single occupant? We need to know before we can correctly draw the Position entity's relationships.

Attributes

I've left the easiest concept until last. Attributes in an E-R model correspond to columns in a relational model.

We sometimes show a few attributes, particularly keys, on the diagram for clarification of entity meaning, or to illustrate a particular point. But we don't generally show *all* of the attributes on the diagram, primarily because we would end up swamping our "big picture" with detail. They are normally recorded in simple lists for each entity, either on paper or in an automated documentation tool such as a data dictionary.

Attributes represent an answer to the question "what data do we want to keep about this entity?" The rules we applied to the definition of columns in Chapter 2 apply equally here: each attribute should represent a primitive fact, and no attribute value should be derivable from others.

In the process of defining the attributes we may find a repeating group, common information requiring a look-up table, or some other deviation from a fully normalized model. If so, we normalize, then modify the E-R model accordingly.

Recall that in a relational model, every table must have a key. In E-R modeling, we can identify entities prior to defining their keys. Ultimately (and better sooner than later), we will need to nominate a key for each entity, either drawn from existing attributes, or invented for the purpose. For example, we may already have a company-defined Employee ID. On the other hand, we would need to define a new one if the existing Employee ID didn't cover, for instance, casual employees.

We discuss attributes in more detail in Chapter 10, and the selection of keys in Chapter 9.

Using UML Object Class Diagrams

You may wish to use a UML Object Class Diagram to represent data requirements. I have observed two distinct approaches to the use of object modeling to model the data requirements of an information system:

1. Creating object classes which an E-R modeler would call entities, i.e., with attributes and relationships.

2. Creating object classes with operational behavior such as arithmetic values, geometrical figures, time objects, etc. and then designing tables in which instances of those objects can be held in row/column intersections.

Whereas the former approach allows for a very simple mapping of objects to entities (to the extent that the data modeling conventions of UML can be regarded as an alternative diagramming convention), the latter approach is the one that has been favored by Date, Stonebraker and other developers of Object-Relational DBMSs.

If you are following the first approach, the UML symbols shown in Figure 3-10 are appropriate as a representation of your entities and relationships (since each of your entities is treated as an object class). However, with the second approach, these symbols are not only used to represent entities and relationships but also attributes and entity/attribute associations respectively (since each attribute is also an object class and each entity/attribute association is a relationship).

Creativity and E-R Modeling

The element of choice is far more apparent in E-R modeling than in normalization, as we would expect. In E-R modeling we are defining our categories of data; in normalization these have been determined (often by someone else) before we start. The process of categorization is so subjective that even our broadest division of data, into entities and relationships, offers some choice, as we have seen.

It is helpful to think of E-R modeling as "putting a grid on the world:" we are trying to come up with a set of nonoverlapping categories so that each fact in our world fits into one category only. Different modelers will choose differently shaped grids to achieve the same purpose. Current business terminology is invariably a powerful influence, but we still have room to select, clarify, and depart from this.

Consider just one area of our drug expenditure model – the classification of operations into operation types. As discussed earlier, we could define Operation Type to either include or exclude hybrid operations. If we chose the latter course, we would need to modify the model as in Figure 3-26(a) to allow an operation to be of more than one operation type.

Alternatively, we could define two levels of operation type: Hybrid Operation Type and Basic Operation Type, giving us the model in Figure 3-26(b). Or we could allow operation types to be either basic or hybrid as in the original model, but record the component operations of hybrid operations, resulting in Figure 3-26(c).

Another option is to represent a hybrid operation as two separate operations, possibly an inelegant solution, but one we might end up adopting if we hadn't considered hybrid operations in our initial modeling Figure 3-26(d). This diagram looks the same as the original, but the definitions of Operation and Operation Type will be different. This gives us five solutions altogether (including the original one), each with different implications. For example, Figure 3-26(b), Figure 3-26(c), and the original model allow us to record standard hybrids, while the other options only allow their definition on an operation-by-operation basis. How many of these possibilities did you consider as you worked with the model?

Creativity in modeling is a progressively acquired skill. Once you make a habit of looking for alternative models, finding them becomes easier. You also begin to recognize common structures. The Operation Type example provides patterns that are equally relevant to dealing with customers and customer types or payments and payment types.

But we can also support the search for alternative models with some formal techniques. In the next chapter, we'll look at one of the most important of these.

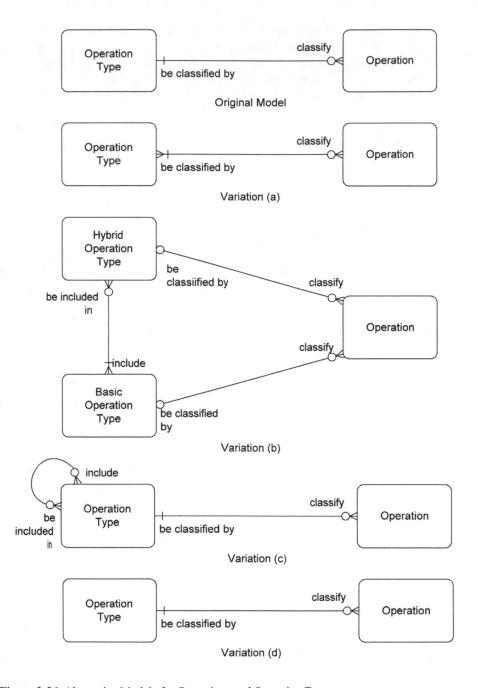

Figure 3-26. Alternative Models for Operations and Operation Types

Summary

Data models can be presented diagrammatically by using a box to represent each table and a line for each foreign key relationship. Further diagramming conventions allow the name, cardinality, and optionality of the relationships to be shown.

We can view the boxes as representing entities – things about which the business needs to keep information, and the lines as representing business relationships between entities. This provides a language and diagramming formalism for developing data models "top down" prior to identifying attributes. The resulting model is called an Entity-Relationship (E-R) model.

Many-to-many real world relationships cannot be directly implemented using foreign keys, but require the introduction of a "resolution" entity.

Entity identification is essentially a process of classifying data, and there is considerable room for choice and creativity in selecting the most useful classification.

Chapter 4

Subtypes and Supertypes

"A very useful technique ... is to break the parts down into still smaller parts and then recombine these smaller units to form larger novel units."

– Edward de Bono, The Use of Lateral Thinking

Introduction

In this chapter, we look at a particular, and very important, type of choice in data modeling. In fact, it is so important that we introduce a special convention – subtyping – to allow our diagrams to show several different options at the same time. We will also find subtyping useful for concisely representing rules and constraints, and for managing complexity.

Different Levels of Generalization

Suppose we are designing a database to record family trees. We need to hold data about fathers, mothers, their marriages, and children. I've presented this apparently simple problem many times to students and practitioners, and have been surprised by the sheer variety of workable, if sometimes inelegant, ways of modeling it. Figure 4-1 shows two of the possible designs.

Incidentally, the Marriage entity is the resolution of a many-to-many relationship "be married to" between Person and Person in (a) and Man and Woman in (b). The many-to-many relationships arise from persons possibly marrying more than one other person, usually over time rather than concurrently.

Note the optionality of the relationships "mother of" and "father of," particularly in the first model, where they are self-referencing. (Recall my advice in Chapter 3 to beware of mandatory self-referencing relationships). While the rule "every person must have a mother" may seem reasonable enough at first glance, it is not true of that subset of persons of interest to us, i.e., family members whom we can identify from historical records. Long before we need to face the real world problem of "who was the first woman?," we simply run out of data: we reach an ancestor whose mother we do not know.

The important issue, however, is our choice of entities. We can't use the nouns ("mother," "father," "child") given in the problem description, because these will overlap – a given person can be both a mother and a child, for example. Implementing Mother and Child entities would therefore compromise our objective of nonredundancy, by holding details of some persons in two places. We need to come up with another set of concepts, and in Figure 4-1 we see two different approaches to the problem: the first uses the person concept, the second the two nonoverlapping concepts of man and woman.

Aside from this difference, the models are essentially the same (although they need not be!) They appear to address our criterion of completeness equally well. Any person who can be represented by the first model can also be handled by the second, and vice versa. Neither model involves any redundant data. Although no attributes are shown, simple attributes such as Name, Date of Birth, and Place of Marriage could be allocated to either model without causing any normalization problems.

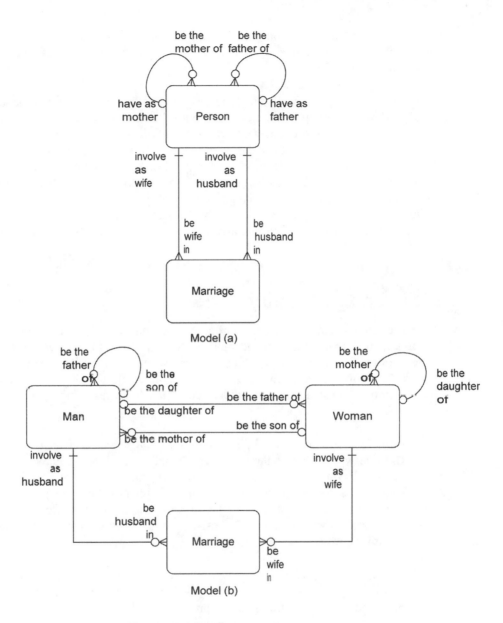

Figure 4-1. Alternative Family Tree Models

The difference lies in the level of generalization we have selected for the entities. Person is a *generalization* of Man and Woman, and, conversely, Man and Woman are *specializations* of Person. This helps us to understand how the two models relate, and raises the possibility that we might be able to propose other levels of generalization, and hence other models – perhaps specializing Man into Married Man and Unmarried Man, or generalizing Marriage to Personal Relationship.

It's important to recognize that our choice of level of generalization will have a profound effect not only on the database but on the design of the total system. The most obvious effect of generalization is to reduce the number of entities, and, on the face of it, simplify the model. Sometimes this will translate into a significant reduction in system complexity, through consolidating common program logic. In other cases, the increase in program complexity from combining the logic needed to handle quite different subtypes outweighs the gains. Estimates of system size based on function point counts tend to favor more generalized models, particularly if the estimates are based on the data model alone.

Rules versus Stability

To select the most appropriate level of generalization, we start by looking at an important difference between the models: the number and type of business rules (constraints) that each supports. The man-woman model has three entities and six relationships, whereas the person model has only two entities and four relationships. The man-woman model seems to be representing more rules about the data.

For example, the man-woman model insists that a marriage consists of one man and one woman, while the person model allows a marriage between two men or two women (one of whom would participate in the "wife of" relationship and the other in the "husband of" relationship, irrespective of gender!) The person model would allow a person to have two parents of the same gender; the man-woman model insists that the mother must be a woman, and the father a man.

The man-woman model is looking pretty good! But remember that we can enforce rules elsewhere in the system as well. If we adopt the person model, we only need to write a few lines of program code to check the gender of marriage partners and parents when data is entered, and return an error message if any rules are violated. We could even set up a table of allowed combinations, which was checked whenever data was entered. The choice, therefore, is not whether to build the rules into the system, but whether the database structure, as specified by the data model, is the best place for them.

Recall that one of the reasons we give so much attention to designing a sound data model is the impact of changing the database structure after it is implemented. On the other hand, changing a few lines of program code, or data in a table, is likely to be much less painful. Accordingly, we included stability as one of the criteria for data model quality. Stability is the counter balance to enforcement of constraints.

Put simply, the more likely it is that a rule will change during the life of the system, the less appropriate it is to enforce that rule by data structures rather than some other mechanism. In our example, we need to trade off the power of representing the rules about marriage in data structures against the risk that the rules may change during the life of the system. In some countries, the man-woman model would already be unworkable. Once again there is a need for some forward thinking and judgment on the part of those involved in the modeling process.

Let's just look at how strongly the man-woman model enforces the constraint on marriages. The Marriage entity contains, as foreign keys, a Man ID and a Woman ID. Programs will be written to interpret these as pointers to the Man and Woman tables, respectively. If we want to record a marriage between, say, two men without redesigning the database and programs, the most obvious "work around" is to record one as a man and one as a woman. What if both have previously been married to women? How will we need to modify reports such as "list all men?" Some complicated logic is going to be required, and our criterion of elegance is going to be severely tested.

We can express the flexibility requirement as a guideline:

> *Don't build a rule into the data structure of a system unless you are reasonably confident that the rule will remain in force for the life of the system.*

As a corollary, we can add:

> *Use generalization to remove unwanted rules from the data model.*

It's sometimes difficult enough to determine the *current* rules that apply to business data, let alone those that may change during the life of a system. Sometimes our systems are expected to outlast the strategic planning time frame of the business: "We're planning five years ahead, but we're expecting the system to last for ten." Chapter 12 includes some further discussion about the likelihood of rules changing.

The models developed by inexperienced modelers often incorporate too many rules in the data structures, primarily because familiar concepts and common business terms may themselves not be sufficiently general. Conversely, once the power of generalization is discovered, there is a tendency to overdo it. Very general models can seem virtually immune to criticism, on the basis that they can accommodate almost anything! This is not brilliant modeling, but an abdication of design in favor of the function modeler, or the user, who will now have to pick up all the business rules missed by the data modeler.

Representation of Subtypes and Supertypes

It is not surprising that many of the arguments that arise in data modeling are about the appropriate level of generalization, although they are not always recognized as such. We cannot easily resolve such disputes by turning to the rulebook, nor do we want to throw away interesting options too early in the modeling process. While our final decision might be to implement the "person" model, it would be nice not to lose the (perhaps unstable) rules we have gathered. Even if we don't implement them in our final database design, we can document them to be passed on to the function modeler.

So we defer the decision on generalization, and treat the problem of finding the correct level as an opportunity to explore different options. To do this, we allow two or more models to exist on top of one another on the same diagram. Figure 4-2 shows how this is achieved.

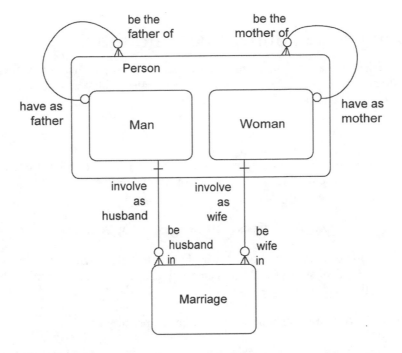

Figure 4-2. Different Levels of Generalization on a Single Diagram

The ability to represent different levels of generalization has cost us a new diagramming convention, the box-in-box. You should be very wary about overcomplicating diagrams with too many different symbols, but this one literally adds another dimension (generalization/ specialization) to our models.

We call the use of generalization and specialization in a model "subtyping."

Man and Woman are *subtypes* of Person.

Person is a *supertype* of Man and of Woman.

We'll now look at the main rules for using subtypes and supertypes.

Subtypes and Supertypes as Entities

Much of the confusion that surrounds the proper use of subtypes and supertypes can be cleared with a simple rule: subtypes and supertypes are *entities*.

Accordingly:

- We use the same diagramming convention (the box with rounded corners) to represent all entities, whether or not they are subtypes or supertypes of some other entity(ies).

- Subtypes and supertypes must be supported by definitions.

- Subtypes and supertypes can have attributes. Attributes particular to individual subtypes are allocated to those subtypes; common attributes are allocated to the supertype.

- Every subtype or supertype must have a primary key[20].

- Subtypes and supertypes can participate in relationships. Notice in our family tree model how neatly we have been able to capture our "mother of" and "father of" relationships by tying them to entities at the most appropriate level. In fact, this diagram shows most of the sorts of relationships that seem to worry modelers – in particular the relationship between an entity and its own supertype.

- Subtypes can themselves have subtypes. We need not restrict ourselves to two levels of subtyping. In practice, we tend to represent most concepts at one, two, or three levels of generality, although four or five levels are useful from time to time.

---

[20] Note that this does not mean that a supertype and its subtypes should have different primary keys. Choose a suitable primary key for the supertype and there should rarely be any reason to use some other attribute(s) for the primary key of any of its subtypes.

Diagramming Conventions

In this book, I use the "box-in-box" convention for representing subtypes. It's not the only option, but is compact, widely used, and supported by several popular documentation tools, including Oracle Designer from Oracle Corporation. Virtually all of the alternative conventions, including UML (see Figure 4-3), are based around lines between supertypes and subtypes. These are easily confused with relationships, and can give the impression that the model allows redundant data. (In our example, Person, Man, and Woman would appear to overlap, until we recognized that the lines joining them represented subtype-supertype associations, rather than relationships).

Some documentation tools do not provide a separate convention for subtypes at all, and the usual suggestion is that they be shown as one-to-one relationships. This is a pretty poor option, but better than ignoring subtypes altogether. If forced to use it, I suggest you adopt a relationship name, such as "be" or "is" which is reserved exclusively for subtypes (which one you use depends on your formula for constructing business rules, as discussed in Chapter 3). Above all, do not confuse relationships with subtype-supertype associations just because a similar diagramming convention is used. This is a common mistake, and the source of a great deal of confusion in modeling.

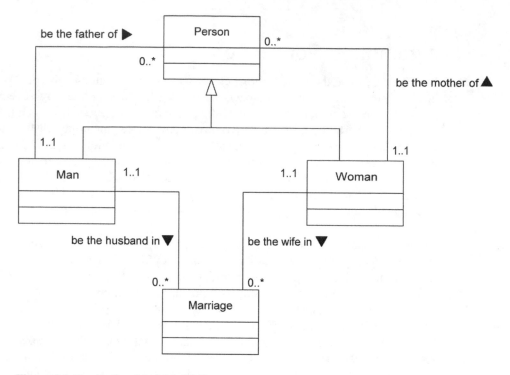

Figure 4-3. Family Tree Model in UML

Definitions

Every entity in a data model must be supported by a definition, as discussed in Chapter 3. To avoid unnecessary repetition, a simple rule applies to the definition of a subtype:

An entity inherits the definition of its supertype.

If the entity Job Position is subtyped into Permanent Position and Temporary Position, the definition of Permanent Position will be "a Job Position that ..." In effect we build a vocabulary from the supertypes, allowing us to define subtypes more concisely.

Attributes and Primary Keys of Supertypes and Subtypes

Where do we record the attributes of an entity that has been divided into supertypes and subtypes? In our example, it makes sense to document attributes that can apply to all persons against Person, and those that can apply only to men or only to women against the respective entities. So we would hold Date of Birth as an attribute of Person, and Maiden Name as an attribute of Woman. By adopting this discipline, we are actually modeling constraints: "Only a Woman can have a Maiden Name."

Sometimes we can add meaning to the model by representing attributes at two or more levels of generalization. For example, we might have an entity Contract, subtyped into Renewable Contract and Fixed-Term Contract. These subtypes could include attributes Renewal Date and Expiry Date, respectively. We could then generalize these attributes to End Date, which we would hold as an attribute of Contract. You can think of this as subtyping at the attribute level. It's vital that any differences in the meaning of a generalized attribute that apply to particular subtypes be documented.

In order for each level of subtyping to represent a valid implementation option, we need to be able to specify a primary key for every entity, regardless of whether it is a supertype or subtype. In fact, as long as all the entities have a primary key nominated at one level of subtyping, we can generate primary keys for the other levels. For example, if Person had a primary key of Person ID, we could use that attribute as the primary key for both Man and Woman. Similarly, if Man had a primary key of Man ID and Woman a primary key of Woman ID, we could use these, plus an attribute to distinguish men from women, as the primary key of Person. This provides a solution, but not always the most elegant one. The final choice of primary keys is discussed further in Chapter 9.

Conversion to a Relational Model

When we started with a set of tables, and used them to draw an E-R diagram, we didn't come up with any subtypes or supertypes. This is because relational data organization doesn't provide direct support for subtypes or supertypes. Therefore, at the end of the modeling process, we will need to produce a subtype-free model as a specification for the logical database design. I call this "leveling the model." However the version with the subtypes should be retained in case the leveling decisions need to be revisited in the light of new information (such as changes to transaction profiles or other changes to business processes) or if the system is ported to a DBMS that supports subtypes directly: the emerging SQL3[21] standard provides for direct support of subtypes and at least one object-relational DBMS provides such support.

Implementation at a Single Level of Generalization

One way of leveling the model is to select a single level of generalization from each hierarchy of subtypes. In our example, we can do this by discarding Person, in which case we implement only its subtypes, Man and Woman, or by discarding Man and Woman and implementing only their supertype, Person.

Actually, "discard" is far too strong a word. A model with subtypes describes rules and data that the system will need to implement somehow. Some will be retained in the final model. Others will be represented as data *values*, such as "Male" or "Female." We document what is left to be passed on to the function modelers to include in their specification.

We certainly won't discard any attributes. We need to *inherit* the attributes of any supertypes, and *roll up* the attributes of any subtypes. So if we implement Man and Woman, each entity will inherit all the attributes of Person. Conversely, if we implement Person, we need to roll up any attributes specific to Man or Woman. These attributes would become *optional* attributes of Person, i.e., null values would be permissible. In some cases, we might choose to combine attributes from different subtypes to form a single attribute. For example, in rolling up Purchase and Sale into Financial Transaction we might combine Price and Sale Value into Amount. This is generalization at the attribute level, and is discussed in more detail in Chapter 10.

---

[21] ANSI/ISO/IEC 9075.

If we implement at the supertype level, we also need to add "type" attributes to allow us to preserve any distinctions that the discarded subtypes represented and that cannot be derived from existing attributes of the supertype. In this example we would introduce a Gender attribute to allow us to distinguish those persons who are men from those who are women.

If we are rolling up two or more levels of subtypes, we have some choice as to how many "type" attributes to introduce. For a generally workable solution, I suggest you simply introduce a single "type" attribute based on the lowest level of subtyping. Look at Figure 4-4. If you decide to implement at the Customer level, add a single Customer-Type attribute, which will hold values of "Company," "Partnership," "Government Body," "High Net Worth Person," and "Ordinary Consumer." If you want to distinguish which of these are Persons and which are Organizations, you will need to introduce an additional look-up table with five rows as in Figure 4-5.

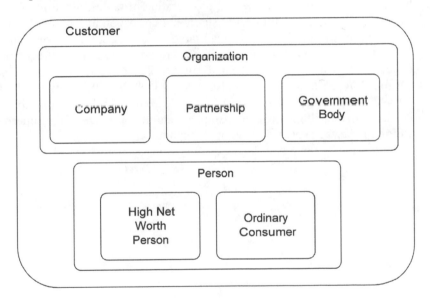

Figure 4-4. Customer Model with Three Levels of Generalization

Customer Type	Person/Organization Indicator
Company	Organization
Partnership	Organization
Government Body	Organization
High Net Worth Person	Person
Ordinary Consumer	Person

Figure 4-5. Look-Up Table of Customer Types

Implementation at Multiple Levels of Generalization

Returning to our family tree example, a third option is to implement all three entities in the Person hierarchy as tables (Figure 4-6). We link the tables by carrying the foreign key of Person in the Man and Women tables. The appeal of this option is that we don't need to discard any of our concepts. On the other hand, we can easily end up with a proliferation of tables, violating our aim of simplicity. And these tables will usually not correspond on a one-to-one basis with familiar concepts – the Woman table in this model does not hold all the attributes of women, but only those that are not common to all persons. The concept of woman is represented by the Person and Woman tables in combination. Note that we may also create a table for the supertype and tables for only *some* of the subtypes. This is quite common when some subtypes do not have any attributes or relationships in addition to those of the supertype, in which case those subtypes do not need separate tables.

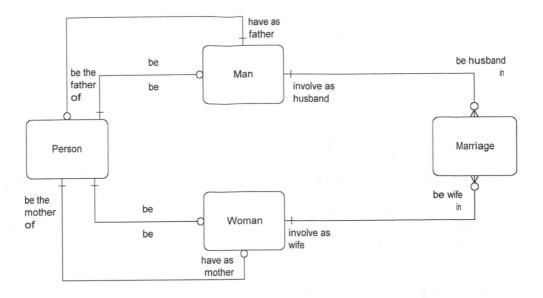

Figure 4-6. Direct Implementation of Person, Man, and Woman Entities

Construction of Views

As mentioned briefly in Chapter 1, we do not always access the tables of a relational database directly. Usually, we access them through *views*, which can consist of simple tables, or of tables combined or selected in various ways. We can use the standard facilities available for constructing views to present data at the subtype or supertype level, regardless of whether we have chosen to implement subtypes, supertype, or both. However, there are some limitations. Not all views allow the data presented to be updated. This is sometimes due to restrictions imposed by the particular database management system, but there are also some logical constraints on what types of views can be updated. These arise where data has been combined from more than one table, and it is not possible to unambiguously interpret a command in terms of which underlying tables are to be updated. It is beyond the scope of this book to discuss view construction and its limitations in any detail. Broadly, the implications for the three implementation options described above are:

1. Implementation at the supertype level. If we implement a Person table, a simple selection operation will allow us to construct Man and Woman views. These views will be logically updateable.

2. Implementation at the subtype level. If we implement separate Man and Woman tables, a Person view can be constructed using the "union" operator. Views constructed using this operator are not updateable.

3. Implementation of both supertype and subtype tables. If we implement Man, Woman, and Person tables, full views of Man and Woman can be constructed using the "join" operator. Most views using this operator are not updateable. They can be combined using the "union" operator to produce a Person view, which again will not be updateable.

Nonrelational database management systems offer different facilities, and may make one or other of the options more attractive. The ability to construct useful, updateable views becomes another factor in selecting the most appropriate implementation option.

The important thing, however, is to recognize that views are not a substitute for careful modeling of subtypes and supertypes, and consideration of the appropriate level for implementation. Identification of useful data classifications is part of the data modeling process – not something that should be left to some later task of view definition. If subtypes and supertypes are not recognized in the modeling stage, we cannot expect the function specification to take advantage of them. There is little point in constructing views unless we have planned to use them in our programs.

What Happens to Relationships?

When we select a level for implementation, we need to do something about relationships involving discarded subtypes and supertypes. The approach is the same as for attributes (after all, one-to-many relationships are implemented using attributes). We inherit relationships from discarded supertypes and roll up relationships from discarded subtypes. In rolling up, we will make some relationships "optional," and may generalize or aggregate two or more to a single relationship, as we did with attributes. Figures 4-7(a), (b), and (c) show some examples. We discuss the handling of relationships in more detail in Chapter 7.

Figure 4-7(a). Relationship Generalization

Figure 4-7(b). Relationship Generalization

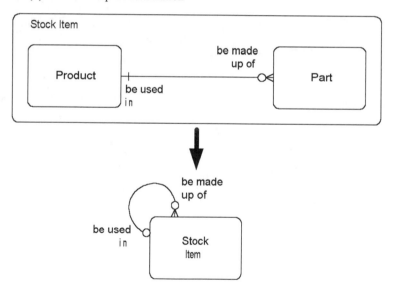

Figure 4-7(c). Relationship Generalization

Nonoverlapping and Exhaustive

The subtypes in our family tree model obeyed two important rules:

1. They were *nonoverlapping* – a given person cannot be both a man and a woman.

2. They were *exhaustive* – a given person must be either a man or a woman, nothing else.

In fact, these two rules are necessary in order for each level of generalization to be a valid implementation option in itself. Consider a model in which Trading Partner is subtyped into Buyer and Seller. If a buyer can also be a seller, then the subtypes overlap. If we were to discard the supertype and implement the two subtypes, our database would hold redundant data: those trading partners who were both buyers and sellers would appear in both tables.

Now look again at the family tree model. In the real world, it may be true that all people are either men or women, but sometimes our *data* about the real world is incomplete, and we may not have enough information to classify all persons whom we want to record. Implementing Man and Woman tables only would result in a database that was not able to hold an important category of persons – those whose gender was unknown.

To summarize: in order to allow each level to represent a sound option for implementation, subtypes must be nonoverlapping and exhaustive. This makes the final leveling of the model considerably easier, but restricts our choice in selecting subtypes, and consequently our ability to represent rules applying to specific subtypes. Whether the sacrifice is worth it is a contentious issue.

The most common argument against restrictions on subtyping is that we should not allow the facilities available for implementation (i.e., simple tables) to limit the power of our data modeling language. This is a nice idea in theory, but there are many facts about data that cannot be represented even by overlapping, nonexhaustive subtypes. Genuine observance of this principle would seriously complicate our data modeling language and conventions with constructs that could not be translated into practical database designs using available technology. This has not stopped researchers from developing richer languages, for example, Nijssen and Halpin's fact-based approach[22], but

---

[22] Nijssen, G.M. and Halpin, T.A., *Conceptual Schema and Relational Database Design – A Fact Based Approach*, Prentice Hall (1989).

practitioners have been reluctant to extend their modeling much beyond that needed to specify a database design. Indeed, many practitioners do not even use subtypes.

Another, more convincing, argument is that the value of our models is reduced (particularly in the areas of communication and representation of constraints) if we cannot represent common but overlapping business concepts. This happens most often when modeling data about people and organizations. Typical businesses deal with people and organizations in many roles: supplier, customer, investor, account holder, guarantor, and so forth. Almost invariably the same person or organization can fill more than one of these roles; hence we cannot subtype the entities Person and Organization into these roles without breaking the "no overlaps" rule. But leaving them out of the model may make them difficult to understand ("where is Customer?") and will limit our ability to capture important constraints ("only a customer can have a credit rating.") This is certainly awkward, but in practice is seldom a problem outside the domain of persons and organizations. I once supervised a graduate student who was investigating the issues of modeling roles, and he encountered great difficulty finding further real world examples. Some tactics for dealing with situations that seem to demand overlapping subtypes are discussed in the next section.

It's worth comparing the situation with function modeling. The rules for function decomposition and data flow diagrams do not normally allow functions at any level to overlap. Most of us don't even stop to consider this, but happily model nonoverlapping functions without thinking about it. Much the same applies in data modeling: we are used to modeling nonoverlapping entities in a level (subtype-free) model, and we tend to carry this over into the modeling of subtypes.

Some of the major documentation tool manufacturers have chosen the restrictive route, in part, no doubt, because translation to relational tables is simpler. If you're using these tools, the choice will be made for you. The academic community has tended to allow the full range of options, in some cases recommending diagramming conventions to distinguish the different possible combinations of overlap and completeness.

On balance, my recommendation is that you discipline yourself to use only nonoverlapping, exhaustive subtypes, as I do in practice and in the remainder of this book.

Overlapping Subtypes and Roles

Having established a rule that subtypes must not overlap, we are left with the problem of handling certain real world concepts and constraints that seem to require overlapping subtypes to model. As mentioned earlier, the most common examples are the various roles played by persons and organizations. Many of the most important terms used in business (Client, Employee, Stockholder, Manager, etc). describe such roles, and we are likely to encounter at least some of them in almost every data modeling project.

There are several tactics we can use to model these roles without breaking the "no overlaps" rule.

Ignoring Real World Overlaps

Sometimes it is possible to model as if certain overlaps did not exist. We have previously distinguished real world rules ("every person must have a mother") from rules about the data that we need to hold or are able to hold about the real world ("we only know some peoples' mothers"). Similarly, while a customer and a supplier may in fact be the same person, the business may be happy to treat them as if they were separate individuals. Indeed, this may be legally required. In such cases, we can legitimately model the roles as nonoverlapping subtypes. In the absence of such a legal requirement, we will need to look at the business value of knowing that a supplier and customer may be the same person or organization. One organization sued a customer for an outstanding debt unaware that the same party (in their other role as a supplier) was withholding funds because the organization owed them money.

You obviously need to be careful in using this approach. Its inappropriate application is one of the most common faults in older database designs, and it is most unlikely that it will provide a complete solution to the role problem. Its value is in excluding a few key entities from the problem. Often these are entities that are handled quite differently by the business, so useful gains in simplicity and elegance can be achieved. A banking model is unlikely to treat borrowers, guarantors, and depositors as separate entities, but may well separate stockholders and suppliers.

Data modelers are inclined to reject this approach on the grounds of infidelity to the real world, rather than any negative impact on the resulting database or system. This is a simplistic argument, and not likely to convince other stakeholders in the database design.

Modeling Only the Supertype

One of the most common approaches to modeling the roles of persons and organizations is to use only a single supertype entity to represent all possible roles. If subtyping is done at all, it is on the basis of some other criterion, such as "legal entity type" – partnership, company, individual, etc. Naming the supertype entity presents a challenge, but Party, Involved Party, and Legal Entity are regularly used.

The problem of communicating this high-level concept to business people has been turned into an opportunity to influence thinking and terminology in some organizations. In particular, it can encourage a move from managing "customer" relationships to managing the total relationship with persons and organizations. A database that includes a table of parties rather than merely those who fulfill a narrower definition of "customer" provides the data needed to support this approach.

The major limitation of the approach is the inability to model relationships specific to particular roles. These can still be documented, of course, along with other rules constraining the data, in textual form, e.g., "Market Segment must be nonnull if this Party interacts with the organization in the role of Customer," but such relationships will not appear in the Entity-Relationship Diagram.

Modeling the Roles as Participation in Relationships

In the supertype-only model described above, roles can often be described in terms of participation in relationships. For example, we can describe a customer as a party who maintains an account, and a supplier as a party who participates in a contract for supply. Chen[23] actually describes a convention to support this (Figure 4-8).

---

[23] Chen, "The Entity-Relationship Model – Toward a Unified View of Data," *ACM Transactions on Database Systems*, Vol. 1, No. 1 (1976), pp. 9-36.

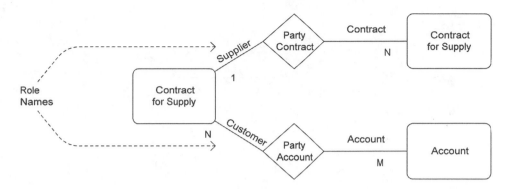

Figure 4-8. Chen Convention for Roles

Rather than further complicate relationship notation for the sake of one section of a model, I suggest you document such rules within the definition of the main entity. For example, "A guarantor is a party who participates in the (guarantee) relationship with Loan."

Using Role Entities and One-to-One Relationships

An approach that allows us to record the business terminology as well as the specific attributes and relationships applicable to each role is shown in Figure 4-9. The role entities can be supertyped into Party Role to facilitate communication, although we would be most unlikely to implement at this level – we would then lose the distinction among roles that the role entities were designed to provide. However, intermediate supertyping is often useful. For example, we might decide that a single Customer Role would cover all roles involving participation in insurance policies, regardless of the type of policy or participation.

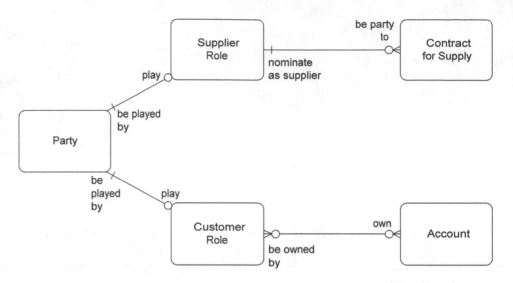

Figure 4-9. Role Entities and One-to-One Relationships

Note the entity names. The word "role" is included to indicate that these entities do not hold the primary data about customers, suppliers, etc. There is a danger here of blurring the distinction between subtypes and one-to-one relationships.

Despite this inelegance in distinguishing relationships from subtypes, the role entity approach is usually the neatest solution to the problem when there are significant differences in the attributes and relationships applicable to different roles.

Multiple Partitions

At least one documentation tool (Information Engineering Facility, originally from Texas Instruments) supports a partial solution to overlapping subtypes by allowing multiple breakdowns (*partitions*) into complete, nonoverlapping subtypes (Figure 4-10). In the example, the two different subtypings of Company enable us to model the constraints that, for example:

- Only a public company can be listed on a stock exchange.

- Only an overseas company can be represented by a local company.

If a given company could be both public and local, for example, it would be difficult to model both of these constraints if we were restricted to a single partition.

Figure 4-10. Multiple Partitions

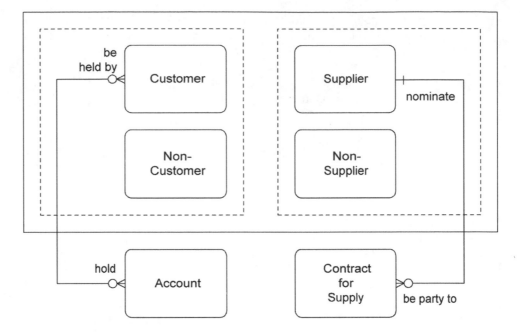

Figure 4-11. Representing Roles Using Multiple Partitions

The multiple partition facility is useful when we have two or three alternative ways of subtyping according to our rules. It is less helpful in handling the roles problem, as we end up with the less-than-elegant partitioning shown in Figure 4-11. Translation to relational database design is also more difficult. We can either:

1. Implement only the highest level supertype as a table (straightforward, but not always the best choice)

2. Implement multiple levels (as we did for the Marriage model in Figure 4.5) selecting only some of the partitions, e.g., implement only Company, Private Company and Public Company as tables, or

3. Implement multiple levels and multiple partitions, e.g., implement Company, Local Company, Overseas Company, Private Company and Public Company all as tables.

If we choose option 2, we need to ensure that relationships and attributes from the other partitions are reallocated to the chosen subtypes.

Hierarchy of Subtypes

I have already used the term "subtype hierarchy." Each subtype can have only one immediate supertype (in a hierarchy, everybody has one immediate boss only – except the person at the top who has none). This follows from the "no overlap" requirement, as two supertypes that contained a common subtype would overlap. Again, adherence to this rule produces a model that is more readily translated into an implementable form with each fact represented in one place only.

Few conventions or tools support multiple supertypes for an entity, possibly because they introduce the sophistication of "multiple inheritance," whereby a subtype inherits attributes and relationships directly from two or more supertypes. Multiple inheritance is a major issue in object-oriented design. The object-oriented designers' problem is almost the opposite of ours: their programming languages provide the facilities, but the questions of how and where they should be used, if at all, are still contentious.

Benefits of Using Subtypes and Supertypes

We've introduced subtypes and supertypes as a means of comparing many possible options on the one diagram. Each level in each subtype hierarchy represents a particular option for implementing the business concepts embraced by the highest-level supertype. But subtypes and supertypes offer benefits not only in presenting options, but also in supporting creativity and handling complexity.

Creativity

Our use of subtypes in the creative process has been a bit passive so far. We have assumed that two or more alternative models have already been designed, and used subtypes to compare them on the same diagram. This is a very useful technique when different modelers have been working on the same problem and (as almost always happens) produced different models. Generally, though, we use these conventions to enhance creativity in a far more active way. Rather than design several models and attempt to bring them together, we work with one multilevel model. As we propose entities we ask:

"Can this entity be subtyped into more specific entities that represent distinct business concepts?" and

"Are any of the entities candidates for generalization into a common supertype?"

The first question is usually reasonably straightforward to answer, although it may require some research and perhaps some thinking as to the best breakdown. However, the second frequently prompts us to propose new supertype entities that represent novel but useful classifications of data. Let's assume we already have a model that is complete and nonredundant. Experimenting with different supertypes will preserve these properties, and we can focus on other objectives, such as simplicity and elegance. "Taking the model down another level" by further subtyping existing entities will give us more raw material to work with. We'll look at this technique more closely in Chapter 5. For the moment, take note that the use of subtyping and supertyping is one of the most important aids to creativity in modeling.

Presentation – Level of Detail

Subtypes and supertypes provide a mechanism for presenting data models at different levels of detail. This can make a huge difference to our ability to communicate and verify a complex model. If you are familiar with function modeling techniques, you will know the value of leveled data flow diagrams in communicating first the "big picture," then the detail as required. The concept is applied in many, many disciplines, from the hierarchy of maps in an atlas, to the presentation of a company's accounts. Subtypes and supertypes form the basis of a similar *structured* approach to data modeling[24].

We can summarize a data model simply by removing subtypes, choosing the level of summarization by how many levels of subtyping we leave. We can even vary this across the model, to show the full detail in an area of interest, while showing only supertypes outside that area. For example, our model might contain (among other things) details of contracts and the employees who authorized them. The human resources manager might be shown a model in which all the subtypes of Employee were included, with a relationship to the simple supertype entity Contract. Conversely, the contract manager might be

---

[24] Described in Simsion, G.C., "A Structured Approach to Data Modelling," *Australian Computer Journal* (August 1989).

shown a full subtyping of contracts, with a relationship to the supertype entity Employee (Figure 4-12).

Each sees only what is of interest to them, without losing the context of external data.

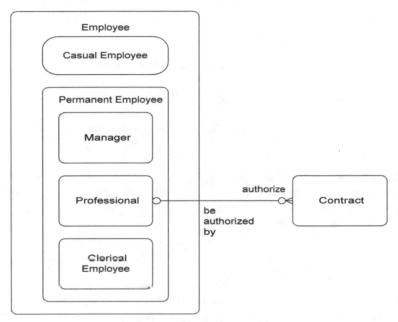

View (a) Human Resources Focus

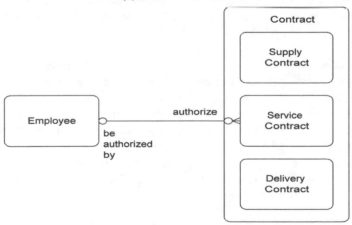

View (b) Contract Management Focus

Figure 4-12. Different Views of a Model

In practice, when presenting a very high-level model, I often selectively delete those entities that do not fit into any of the major generalizations, and that are not critical to conveying the overall "shape" of the model. In doing this, I lose the completeness of coverage that a strict supertype model provides. While the model no longer specifies a viable design, it serves as a starting point for understanding. Anyone who has tried to explain a data model for even a medium-sized application to a non-technical person will appreciate the value of such a high-level starting point.

Specific techniques for simplifying a high-level model include:

- Removal of classification entities ('type tables')

- Retention of many-to-many relationships as such rather than resolving them.

Documentation tools that can display and/or print multiple views of the same model by selective removal of entities and/or relationships are useful in this sort of activity. A more formal approach to presenting complex models is described in Appendix B.

Communication

Communication is not only a matter of dealing with complexity. Terminology is also frequently a problem. A vehicles manager may be interested in trucks, but the accountant's interest is in assets. Our subtyping convention allows Truck to be represented as a subtype of Asset, so both terms appear on the model, and their relationship is clear.

This is particularly useful to the creative modeler, who may want to introduce or use a less-familiar concept. By showing a new entity in terms of old, familiar entities, the model can be verified without business people becoming stuck on the unfamiliar term. Perhaps our organization trades in bonds and bills, and we are considering representing both by a single entity type Financial Instrument. To the organization, they are separate and have always been treated as such. By showing Financial Instrument subtyped into Bond and Bill, we provide a starting point for understanding. If they prefer, the business specialists need never use the new word, but can continue to talk about "bonds or bills."

In one organization, senior management wanted to develop a consolidated asset management system, but divisional management wanted local systems, arguing that their own requirements were unique. Rather than try to develop a consolidated model straight away (with little cooperation), I developed two separate models, using local terminology, but with one eye on consistency. I then combined the models, preserving all the local entities, but introducing supertypes to show the commonality. With the understanding that their specific needs had been accommodated (and the differences – and there were some – recognized), the managers agreed to proceed with the consolidated system.

When using subtypes and supertypes to help communicate a model, remember that we need have no intention of implementing them as tables: communication is a sound enough reason in itself for including them.

Classifying Common Patterns

We can also use supertypes to help us classify and recognize common patterns. In the later chapters of this book, we look at a number of structures that appear again and again in models. In most cases, we first look at an example of the structure (such as the different ways of modeling Operation Type and Operation in Chapter 3), then apply what we have learned to the general case (Thing and Thing Type, if you like). *Without generalization, we cannot apply what we learn in designing one model to the design of another.* Supertypes and subtypes provide a formal means of doing this.

I once had to review several models covering different stages in the brewing of beer. The models had been produced independently, but some common patterns began to emerge, so that I developed a mental generic model roughly applicable to any stage. I could then concentrate on how the models differed. Reviewing one model, I asked why no samples were taken at this stage (since my high-level model included a Sample entity). Later investigation showed that this was an oversight by the modeler, and I was congratulated on my knowledge of brewing! The other modelers had not noticed the omission, because without a high-level model, they were "too close to the problem" – unable to see the pattern for the detail.

Divide and Conquer

The structured approach to modeling gives us the ability to attack a model from the top down, the middle out, or the bottom up.

The top-down option is particularly important as it allows us to break a large modeling problem into manageable parts, then address the question: "What types of ... do we need to keep information about?" Our early analysis of a finance company might suggest the entities Customer and Loan (nothing terribly creative here!) We could then tackle the questions: "What types of loan are we interested in (and how do they differ?)" and "What type of customers are we interested in (and how do they differ?)" Alternatively, we might model the same business problem in terms of Agreements and Parties to Agreements. Again we can then proceed with more detailed analysis, *within the high-level framework we have established.*

In developing large models, we may allocate different areas to different modelers, with some confidence that the results will all fit together in the end. This is much harder to achieve if we divide the task based on function or company structure rather than data ("Let's model the data for commercial lending first, then retail lending.") Because data is frequently used by more than one function or area, it will be represented in more than one model, usually in different ways. Often the reconciliation takes much longer than the initial modeling!

From a creative modeling perspective, a top-down approach based on specialization allows us to put in place a set of key concepts at the supertype level, and fit the rest of our results into this framework. There is a good analogy with architecture here: the basic shape of the building determines how other needs will be accommodated.

When Do We Stop Supertyping and Subtyping?

I once encountered a data model that contained more than 900 entities, and took up most of a sizeable wall. The modelers had adopted the rule of "keep subtyping until there are no optional attributes," and had in fact run out of wall space before they ran out of optional attributes.

There is no absolute limit to the number of levels of subtypes that we can use to represent a particular concept. We therefore need some guidelines as to when to stop subtyping. The problem of when to stop supertyping is easier. We can't go any higher than a single entity covering all the business data – the "Thing" entity. In practice, we'll often go as high as a model containing only five to ten entities, if only for the purpose of communicating broad concepts.

Very high levels of supertyping are actually implemented sometimes. As we should expect, they are used when flexibility is paramount. Data Dictionaries that allow users to define their own contents (or "meta models" as they are often called) are one example.

No single rule tells us when to stop subtyping, because we use subtypes for several different purposes. We may, for example, show subtypes that we have no intention of implementing as tables, in order to better explain the model. Instead, there are several guidelines. In practice, you will find that they seldom conflict. When in doubt, include the extra level(s).

Differences in Keys

If an entity can be subtyped into entities that are identified by different keys, show the subtypes.

For example, we might subtype Equipment Item into Vehicle and Machine, because vehicles were identified by registration number and machines by serial number. Conversely, if we have two entities that are identified by the same key we should consider a common supertype.

Be careful of circular thinking here! I am not talking about keys you have allocated yourself, but keys that have some existing standing within or outside the organization.

Different Attribute Groups

If an entity can be subtyped into entities that have different attributes, consider showing the subtypes.

For example, Insurance Policy may be subtyped into House Policy (with attributes Type of Construction, Floor Area, etc.), and Motor Vehicle Policy (with attributes Make, Model, Color, Engine Capacity, Modifications, Garaging Arrangements, etc.).

In practice, optional attributes are so common that strict enforcement of this rule will result in a proliferation of subtypes – we shouldn't need to draw two boxes just to show that a particular attribute can take a null value. However, if *groups of attributes* are always null or nonnull together, show the corresponding subtypes.

Different Relationships

If an entity can be divided into subtypes such that one subtype may participate in a relationship while the other never participates, show the subtype.

Don't confuse this with a simple optional relationship. You need to look for groups that can never participate in the relationship. For example, a machine can never have a driver but a vehicle may have a driver (Figure 4-13).

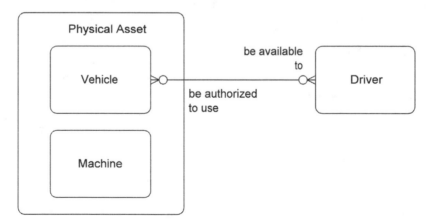

Figure 4-13. Subtyping Based on Relationship Participation

Different Processes

If some instances of an entity participate in important processes, while others don't, consider subtyping. Conversely, entities that participate in the same process are candidates for supertyping.

Be very wary of supertyping entities that are not treated in a similar way by the business, regardless of superficial similarity of attributes, relationships, or names. For example, a wholesaler might propose entities Supplier Order (placed by the wholesaler) and Customer Order (placed by the customer). The attributes of both types of order may be similar, but the business is likely to handle them in quite different ways. If so, it is unlikely that there will be much value in introducing an Order supertype.

Migration from One Subtype to Another

We do not usually subtype to a level where an entity occurrence may migrate from one subtype to another. For example, we would not subtype Account into Account-in-Credit and Overdrawn-Account, because an account could move back and forth from subtype to subtype.

If we were to implement a database based on such subtypes, we would need to transfer data from table to table each time the status changed. This would complicate processing, and make it difficult to keep track of accounts over time.

Communication

As mentioned earlier, we may add both subtypes and supertypes to help explain the model. Sometimes it is useful to show only two or three illustrative subtypes. To avoid breaking the completeness rule, we then need to add a "miscellaneous" entity. For example, we might show Merchant Event (in a credit card model) subtyped into Purchase Authorization, Voucher Deposit, Stationery Delivery, and Miscellaneous Merchant Event.

Capturing Meaning and Rules

In our discussions with users, we are often given information that can conveniently be represented in the data model, even though we would not plan to include it in the final level model. For example, the business specialist might tell us "only management staff may take out staff loans." We can represent this rule by subtyping Staff Member into Manager and Non-manager, and tying the relationship to Staff Loan to Manager only (Figure 4-14). We would anticipate that this subtyping would not be retained in the level model (the subtyping is likely to violate the "migration" rule), but we've captured an important rule to be included elsewhere in the system.

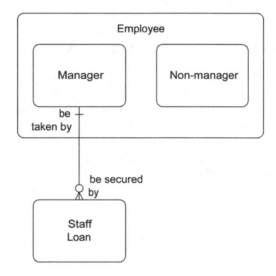

Figure 4-14. Using Subtypes to Represent Rules

Summary

Subtypes and supertypes are tools we use in the data modeling *process*, rather than structures that appear in the final model, at least as long as our database management systems are unable to implement them directly. Therefore, we use them whenever they can help us produce a better final product, rather than according to a rigid set of rules. No subtyping or supertyping is invalid if it achieves this aim, and obeys the very simple rules of completeness and overlap. In particular, there is nothing intrinsically wrong with subtypes or supertypes that do not have any attributes other than those inherited or rolled-up, if they contribute to some other objective, such as communicating the model.

Theoretical Background

In 1977 Smith and Smith published an important paper titled *Database Abstractions: Aggregation and Generalization*[25], which recognized that the two key techniques in data modeling were aggregation/disaggregation and generalization/specialization.

Aggregation means "assembling component parts," and disaggregation means "breaking down into component parts." In data modeling terms, examples of disaggregation include breaking up Order into Order Header and Ordered Item, or Customer into Name, Address, and Date of Birth. This is quite different from specialization and generalization, which are about classifying, rather than breaking down. I find it helpful to think of disaggregation as "widening" a model, and specialization as "deepening" it.

Most texts and papers on data modeling focus on disaggregation, particularly through normalization. Decisions about the level of generalization are often hidden or dismissed as "common sense." We should be very suspicious of this; before the rules of normalization were formalized, that process too was regarded as just a matter of common sense.

In this book, and in day-to-day modeling, I try to give similar weight to the generalization/specialization and aggregation/disaggregation dimensions.

---

[25] *ACM Transactions on Database Systems*, Vol. 2, No. 2 (1977).

Summary

Subtypes and supertypes are used to represent different levels of entity generalization. They facilitate a top-down approach to the development and presentation of data models, and concise documentation of business rules about data. They support creativity by allowing alternative data models to be explored and compared.

Subtypes and supertypes are not directly implemented by relational database management systems. The final data model therefore needs to be subtype-free, although the version with supertypes and subtypes should be retained in case of future developments. This can be achieved by selecting a single level of generalization from each subtype hierarchy, or by implementing both subtype and supertype entities, linked by one-to-one relationships.

By adopting the convention that subtypes are nonoverlapping and exhaustive, we can ensure that each level of generalization is a valid implementation option. The convention results in the loss of some representational power, but is widely used in practice.

Chapter 5

Putting It All Together

"The crux of creativity resides in the ability to manufacture variations on a theme."

– Douglas R. Hofstadter, *Metamagical Themas*.

Designing Real Models

So far, we have established a set of diagramming conventions for documenting data models, and some basic rules of good design. We are in a position not unlike that of the budding architect who has learned only the drawing conventions and a few structural principles. The real challenge of taking a set of requirements and producing a sound data model to meet them is still in front of us.

In common with other design processes, development of a data model involves three main stages.

1. Identification of requirements

2. Design of solutions

3. Evaluation of the solutions

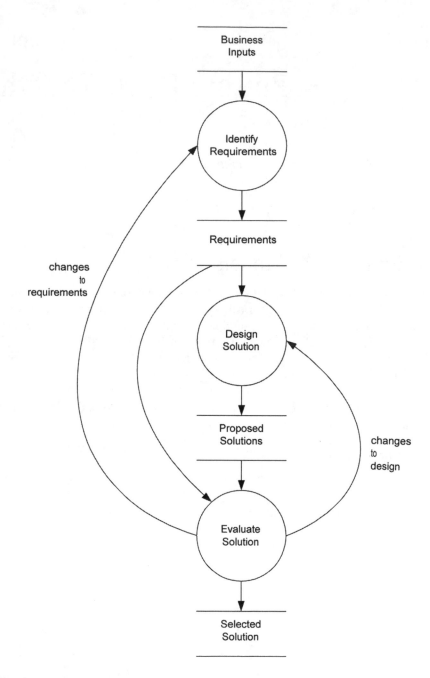

Figure 5-1. Data Modeling as a Design Activity

This is an iterative process (Figure 5-1). In practice, the initial requirements are never comprehensive or rigorous enough to constrain us to only one possible design. Draft designs will prompt further questions, which will in turn lead to new requirements being identified. The architecture analogy is again appropriate: as users, we do not tell an architect the exact dimensions and orientation of each room. Rather we specify broader requirements such as "we need space for entertaining" and "we don't want to be disturbed by the children's play when listening to music." If the architect returns with a plan that includes a wine cellar, prompted perhaps by his or her assessment of our lifestyle, we may decide to revise our requirements to include one.

In this chapter, we focus on the design stage, which is the most difficult to describe and to learn. Designing a candidate solution from first principles involves conceptualization, abstraction, and possibly creativity, skills that are hard to invoke on a day-to-day basis without considerable practice. Teachers of data modeling frequently find that students who have understood the theory (sometimes in great depth) become "stuck" when faced with the job of developing a real model.

If there is a secret to getting over the problem of being stuck, it is that data modeling practitioners, like most designers, seldom work from first principles, but adapt solutions that have been used successfully in the past. The development and use of a repertoire of standard solutions ("patterns") is so much a part of practical data modeling that I have devoted a large part of this chapter to it.

Getting Started – Identifying Entities

Despite the availability of documentation tools, the early work in data modeling is usually done with whiteboard and pen. Most experienced data modelers initially draw only entities and partly annotated relationships. Crow's feet are usually shown, but optionality and names are only added where they serve to clarify an obviously difficult or ambiguous concept. The idea is to keep the focus on the big picture, moving fairly quickly and exploring alternatives, rather than becoming bogged down in detail.

We cannot expect our users to have the data model already in their minds, ready to be extracted with a few well-directed questions ("What things do you want to keep data about?; what data do you want to keep about them?; how are they related?") Unfortunately, much that is written and taught about data modeling makes this very naive assumption. In practice, experienced data modelers do not try to solicit a data model directly, but take a holistic approach. They first establish a broad understanding of the client's requirements, and then propose designs for data structures to meet them.

This puts the responsibility for coming up with the entities squarely on the data modeler's shoulders. In the first four chapters, we looked at a number of techniques which generated new entities: normalization produces new tables by disaggregating existing tables, and supertyping and subtyping produce new entities through generalizing and specializing existing entities. But we have to start with something!

To design a data model from "first principles," we generalize (more precisely, *classify*) instances of things of interest to the business into entities. We have a lot of choice as to how we do this, even given the constraint that we do not want the same fact to be represented by more than one entity type. Some classification schemes will be much more useful than others, but, not surprisingly, there is no rule for finding the *best* scheme, or even recognizing it if we do find it. Instead, we have a set of guidelines that are essentially the same as those we use for selecting good supertypes. The most important of these is that we group together things that the business handles in a similar manner (and will therefore need to keep similar data about).

This might seem a straightforward task. On the contrary, "similarity" can be a very subjective concept, often obscured by the organization's structure and procedures. For example, an insurance company may have assigned responsibility for handling personal accident and life insurance policies to separate divisions, which have then established quite different procedures and terminology for handling them. It may take a considerable amount of investigation to determine the underlying degree of similarity.

Patterns and Generic Models

Using Patterns

Experienced data modelers rarely develop their designs from first principles. Like architects, they draw on a "library" of proven structures and structural components. We already have a few of these from the examples in earlier chapters. For example, we know the general way of representing a many-to-many relationship or a simple hierarchy.

Until relatively recently (as recently as the first edition of this book) there was little acknowledgment of the importance of patterns. Most academic texts treated data modeling as something to be done from first principles, and there were virtually no published libraries of data modeling patterns for practitioners to refer to. What patterns there were tended to exist in the minds of experienced data modelers – sometimes without the data modelers being aware of it!

That picture has since changed substantially. A number of detailed data models, generally aimed at particular industries such as banking, health care or oil, can now be purchased – or in some cases have been made available free of charge through industry bodies. Some useful books of more general data modeling patterns have been published[26]. And the object-oriented theorists and practitioners, with their focus on reuse, have contributed much to the theory and body of experience around patterns[27].

It is worth distinguishing some different types of patterns:

- A **standard structure** is a reusable application-independent component of a data model, such as a hierarchy or a standard way of modeling historical transactions. We use standard structures, modified if necessary, as building blocks for specific areas of a total model. We will see plenty of examples in the chapters of this book covering data warehousing and the time dimension.

- A **generic model** is a model covering a complete business or major business activity, usually at a high level of generalization. We might, for example, have a generic accounting or asset management model. Generic models provide a framework for more detailed modeling. They can also be useful in establishing the scope of a modeling exercise.

- A **detailed application model** or business model is more like a prepackaged solution, typically including detail right down to attribute definitions, formats and code sets. It may be borrowed from an earlier application, or purchased from a model vendor. In some cases, such models are used only as a starting point or "straw man;" in others they are

---

[26] Silverston, L., Graziano, K., Inmon, W. H., *The Data Model Resource Book: A Library of Logical Data and Data Warehouse Design*, John Wiley & Sons (1997). Hay, D. C., Data Model Patterns: Conventions of Thought, Dorset House (1995).
[27] Fowler, M., Analysis Patterns: Reusable Object Models, Addison-Wesley (1997).

intended to be rigorously adhered to promote common data standards across an industry.

Using a Generic Model

In practice, we usually try to find a generic model that broadly meets the users' requirements, and then tailor it to suit the particular application, drawing on standard structures and adapting structures from other models as opportunities arise. For example, we may need to develop a data model to support human resource management. Suppose we have seen successful human resources models before, and (explicitly or just mentally) generalized these to produce a generic model, shown in part in Figure 5-2.

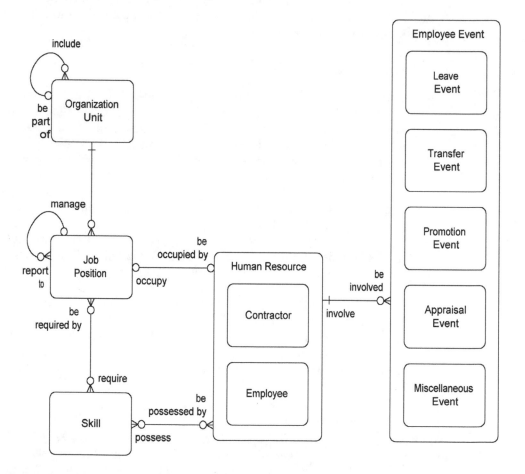

Figure 5-2. Generic Human Resources Model

The generic model suggests some questions, initially to establish scope (and our credibility as modelers knowledgeable about the data issues of human resource management). For example:

> "*Does your organization have a formally-defined hierarchy of job positions?*" "*Yes, but they're outside the scope of this project.*" We can remove this part of the model.

> "*Do you need to keep information about leave taken by employees?*" "Yes, and one of our problems is to keep track of leave taken without approval, such as strikes." We will retain Leave Event, possibly subtyped, and add Leave Approval. Perhaps Leave Application – with a status of approved or not approved would be better – or should this be an attribute of Leave Event? Some more focused questions will help with this.

> "*Could Leave be approved but not taken?*" "Certainly." "*Can one application cover multiple periods of leave?*" "Not currently – could our new system support this?"

And so on. Having a generic model in place as a starting point helps immensely, just as architects are helped by being familiar with some generic "family home" patterns. Incidentally, asking an experienced modeler for his or her set of generic models is likely to produce a blank response. Experienced modelers generally carry their generic models in their heads rather than on paper, and are often unaware that they use such models at all.

Adapting Generic Models from Other Applications

Sometimes we don't have an explicit generic model available, but can draw an analogy with a model from a different field. Suppose we are developing a model to support the management of public housing. The users have provided some general background on the problem in their own terms. They are in the business of providing low cost accommodation, and their objectives include being able to move applicants through the waiting list quickly, providing accommodation appropriate to clients' needs, and ensuring that the rent is collected.

We haven't worked in this field before, so we can't draw on a model specific to public housing. In looking for a suitable generic model, we might pick up on the central importance of the rental agreement. We recall an insurance model in which the central entity was Policy – an agreement of a different kind, but nevertheless one involving clients and the organization (Figure 5-3). This model suggests an analogous model for rental agreement management (Figure 5-4).

Figure 5-3. Insurance Model

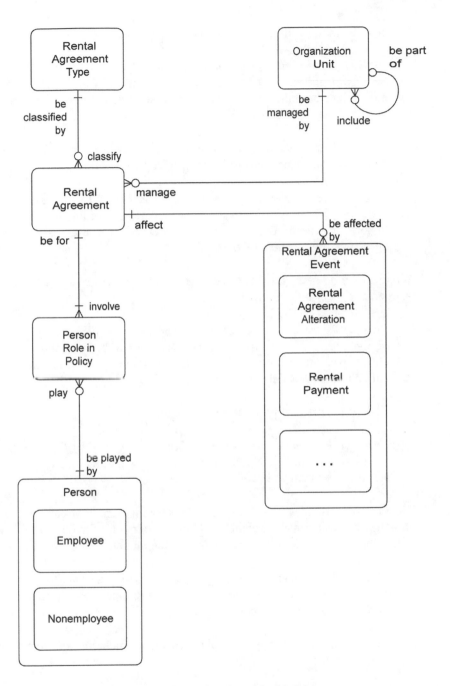

Figure 5-4. Rental Agreement Model Based on Insurance Model

We proceed to test and flesh out the model with the business specialist:

> *"Who are the parties to a rental agreement? Only persons? Or families, or organizations?"* "Only individuals (tenants) can be parties to a rental agreement, but other occupiers of the house are noted on the agreement. We don't need to keep track of family relationships."

> *"Are individual employees involved in rental agreements? In what role?"* "Yes, each agreement has to be authorized by one of our staff."

> *"How do we handle changes to rental agreements? Do we need to keep a history of changes?"* "Yes, it's particularly important that we keep a history of any changes to rent. Sometimes we establish a separate agreement for payment of arrears."

What do we do here? Can we treat a rental arrears agreement as a subtype of Agreement? We can certainly try the idea.

> *"How do rental arrears agreements differ from ordinary rental agreements?"* "They always relate back to a basic rental agreement. Otherwise, administration is much the same – sending the bill and collecting the scheduled repayments."

Let's check the cardinality of the relationship:

> *"Can we have more than one rental arrears agreement for a given basic rental agreement?"* "No, although we may modify the original rental arrears agreement later."

The answer provides some support for treating rental arrears agreements similarly to basic rental agreements. Now we can look for further similarities to test the value of our subtyping and refine the model.

> *"Do we have different types of rental arrears agreements? Are people directly involved in rental arrears agreements or are they always the same as those involved in the basic rental agreement?"*

And so on. Figure 5-5 shows an enhanced model including the rental arrears agreement concept.

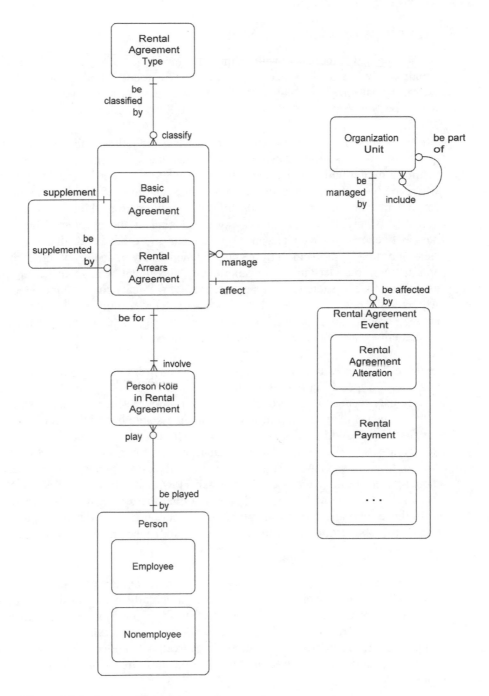

Figure 5-5. Inclusion of Rental Arrears Agreement

Developing a Generic Model

As we gained experience with using this model in a variety of business situations, we would develop a generic "agreement" model, rather than drawing analogies, or going through the two stage process of generalizing from Policy to Agreement, then specializing to Rental Agreement.

With this model in mind, we can approach data modeling problems with the question: "What sort of agreements are we dealing with?" In some cases, the resulting model will be reasonably conventional, as with our housing example, where perhaps the only unusual feature is the handling of arrears repayment agreements. In other cases, approaching the problem from the perspective of agreements might lead to a new way of looking at the problem. The new perspective may offer an elegant approach; on the other hand, the result of "shoe-horning" a problem to fit the generic model may be inelegant, inflexible, and difficult to understand. For example, the "agreement" perspective could be useful in modeling foreign currency dealing, where deals could be modeled as Agreements, but less useful in a retail sales model. Certainly a sale constitutes an agreement to purchase, but the concepts of alterations, parties to agreements, etc. may be less relevant in this context.

Generic models can also be suggested by answers to the "what is our business?" type of question. Business people addressing the question are consciously trying to cut through the detail to the "essence" of the business, and the answers can be helpful in establishing a stable generic model. I recall the first time I attempted to model the complexities of money market dealing. A business specialist offered the explanation that the fundamental objective was to "trade cash flows." This very simple unifying idea suggested a generic model based on the entities Deal and Cash Flow, and ultimately provided the basis for a flexible and innovative system. Often these insights will come not from those who are close to the problem and burdened with details of current procedures, but from more senior managers, staff who have recently learned the business, consultants, and even textbooks.

Even amongst very experienced modelers, there is a tendency to adopt an "all purpose" generic model. I have seen some particularly inelegant data models resulting from trying to force such a model to fit the problem. In our housing model, for example, there is unlikely to be much value in including Employment Agreement and Supplier Agreement under the Agreement supertype, unless we can establish that the business treats these entities in a common way.

Sometimes an organization will develop a generic model of its primary business activities, with the intention of coordinating data modeling at the project level (data models of this kind are discussed in Chapter 14). Such a model may be an excellent representation of the core business, but inappropriate for support functions such as personnel management or inventory control.

The best approach is to consciously build up your personal library of generic models, and to experiment with more than one alternative when tackling problems in practice. This is not only a good antidote to the "shoe-horning" problem; it also encourages exploration of different approaches, and often provides new insights into the problem. Frequently, the final model will be based primarily on one generic model, but will include ideas resulting from exploring others.

When There Isn't a Generic Model

From time to time, we encounter situations for which none of our generic models is a good fit. Such problems should be viewed as opportunities to develop new generic models. There are essentially two approaches, the first "bottom up" and the second "top down." We look at these in the following sections.

Bottom-Up Modeling

With the bottom-up approach, you initially develop a very "literal" model, based on existing data structures and terminology, then use subtyping and supertyping to move towards other options.

We touched on this technique in Chapter 4, but it is so valuable that it's worth working through an example that is complex enough to illustrate it properly. Figure 5-6 shows a form containing information about products sold by an air conditioning systems retailer.

Product No.:	450TE	**Volume**	2-4		5%
Type:	Air Conditioning Unit – Indust.	**Discount**	5-10		10%
Unit Price:	$420		Over 10		12%
Sales Tax:	3% (except Vic/NSW: 2%)	**Service**	09	Install	$35
Delivery Charge:	$10	**Charges**	01	Yearly Service	$40
Remote Delivery:	$15		05	Safety Check	$10
Insurance:	5%				

Figure 5-6. Air Conditioning Product Form

Figure 5-7 is a straightforward model produced by normalizing the repeating groups contained in the form (note that we have already departed from strictly literal modeling by generalizing the specific types of tax, delivery, and service charges).

Figure 5-7. Literal Model of Air Conditioning Products

There is a reasonably obvious opportunity to generalize the various charges and discounts into a supertype entity "Additional Charge or Discount." In turn, this decision would suggest separating Insurance Charge from Product, even though it is not a repeating group, in order to represent all price variations consistently (Figure 5-8).

Figure 5-8. Generalizing Additional Charges

We could also consider including Unit Price, and renaming the supertype "Price Component," depending on how similarly the handling of Unit Price was to that of the price variations.

Looking at the subtypes of Additional Charge or Discount, we might consider an intermediate level of subtyping, to distinguish charges and discounts directly related to sale of the original product from stand-alone services (Figure 5-9).

Figure 5-9. Separating Service Charges

This in turn might prompt a more adventurous generalization: why not broaden our definition of Product to embrace services as well? We would then need to change the name of the original Product entity to (say) Physical Product. Figure 5-10 shows the result.

Figure 5-10. Redefining Product to Include Services

Note that we started with a very straightforward model, based on the original form. This is the beauty of the technique – we don't need to be creative "on the fly," but can concentrate initially on getting a model which is complete and nonredundant, and clarifying how data is currently represented. Later we can break down the initial entities, and reassemble them to explore new ways of organizing the data. The approach is particularly useful if we are starting from existing data files.

Note also that we ended up with a new definition of Product. Ideally, we would never give more than one meaning to the same word. However the desire to keep the model reasonably approachable through use of familiar terminology often means that a term will need to change meaning as we develop it. We could have encountered the same situation with Service, had we decided to regard delivery as a type of service. Just remember to keep the definitions up to date!

Top-Down Modeling

The top-down approach to an unfamiliar problem is an extreme version of the generic model approach; we simply use a model that is generic enough to cover at least the main entities in any business or organization. The ultimate extreme is that suggested in many texts: by asking "what `things' are of interest to the business?" we are effectively starting from the single entity Thing, and looking for subtypes. We can usually be a little more specific than this!

I find the following high-level supertypes useful as a starting point:

Party – Who is involved in this business activity? Persons and organizations in various roles – suppliers, customers, internal organization units, employees, etc.

Contract or *Agreement* – What types of contracts or agreements do we enter into? Contracts for supply, purchase, employment, etc.

Product – What products or services do we provide? What does this business activity produce?

Resource – What resources do we need to manage? Physical, human, financial, etc.

Event – What events do we need to record? Customer transactions, internal activities, payments, receipts, etc.

Location – What geographic areas or points are we interested in? Regions, states, countries, nodes, delivery points etc.

Account – What type of accounts need to be set up or used to keep track of the financial position?

Be aware that using a first-cut classification like this is still only one step removed from asking "What things are we interested in?" and will produce a very literal and often incomplete picture if not used in conjunction with other techniques and views of the business. In particular, you should use these supertypes only as a starting point, and be prepared to regroup entities as the model develops.

When the Problem is Too Complex

Sometimes it is possible to be overwhelmed by the complexity of the business problem. Perhaps we are attempting to model the network managed by a large and diverse telecommunications provider. Unless we are very experienced in the area, we will be quickly bogged down in technical detail, terminology, and traditional divisions of responsibilities. A useful strategy in these circumstances is to develop a first-cut generic model as a basis for classifying the detail.

Paradoxically, a good way to achieve this is by initially *narrowing* our view. We select a specific (and, as best as we can judge) typical area and model it in isolation. We then generalize this to produce a generic model that we use as a basis for investigating other areas. In this way we are able to focus on similarities and differences, and on modifying and fleshing out our base model.

Obviously the choice of initial area is important. We are looking for business activities that are representative of those in other areas – in other words we anticipate that when generalized they will produce a useful generic model. There is a certain amount of circular thinking here, but in practice, selection is not too difficult. Many organizations are structured around products, customer types or geographic locations. Often, each organization unit has developed its own procedures and terminology. Selecting an organizational unit, then generalizing out these factors is usually a good start. Often the *second* area that we examine will provide some good pointers on what can usefully be generalized.

In our telecommunications example, we might start by modeling the part of the network which links customers to local exchanges, or perhaps only that part administered by a particular local branch. Part of an initial model is shown in Figure 5-11.

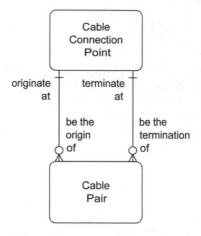

Figure 5-11. Local Exchange Network Model

Testing this model against the requirements of the Trunk Network Division, which has an interest in optical fibers and their termination points, suggests that Cable Pair can usefully be generalized to Physical Bearer, and Cable Connection Point generalized to Connection Point to take account of alternative technologies (Figure 5-12).

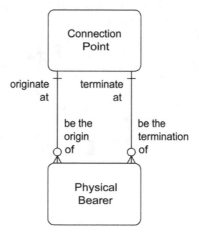

Figure 5-12. Generalized Network Model

But we are now able to ask some pointed questions of the next division: "What sort of bearers do you use? How do they terminate or join?"

This is a very simple generic model, but no simpler than many which I have found invaluable in coming to grips with complex problems. And its use is not confined to telecommunications networks. What about other networks, such as electricity supply, railways, or electrical circuits? Or, more creatively, could the model be applied to a retail distribution network?

Developing Entity Definitions

Definitions, even if initially very rough, should be noted as entities are identified and written up more fully at the end of each session or day. It's surprising how much disagreement can arise overnight!

One useful way of getting to a first-cut definition is to write down a few candidate subtypes or examples, some of which are expected to fit the ultimate definition, and some of which are expected to be outside the definition or "borderline." Then take a vote of participants in the modeling session: "include" or "exclude." This is a very effective way of highlighting areas of agreement and disagreement, and often produces some surprises. For the entity Asset we might suggest Building, Vehicle, Consumable, Employee, Cash on Hand, and Bank Account Balance as potential subtypes. A vote might unanimously support inclusion of Building, Vehicle, Cash and Bank Account Balance and exclusion of Employee, but indicate disagreement on Consumable. Further discussion might indicate that some participants were assuming a strict accounting definition of asset, while others (perhaps unfamiliar with accounting!) had taken a more flexible view. Once any disagreements are resolved, the examples can be included permanently in the definition.

Handling Exceptions

One of the frustrations of data modeling is to produce a model that seems to handle every case – except one or two. In general we should welcome these exceptions. Better to discover them now than to have them appear as new requirements after the database is built. Usually we face a choice:

1. Make the model more flexible, by generalizing the structures to accommodate the exceptions. This often makes the model more difficult to understand by introducing obscure terminology, and may make the common cases more complicated to specify and process.

2. Add new structures specifically to cope with the exceptions. The result may be a more complex structure, and less elegant processing when common cases and exceptions need to be handled together (e.g., in calculating totals).

3. Optimize for the common situation and accept that exceptions will not be as well handled. Perhaps most wine can be classified as being from one vintage only or from unspecified vintages ("non vintage"), but a very few wines are blends from specific years. We could record these exceptions with a vintage year of (say) "1995/1997" – possibly a reasonable compromise between complexity of structure and processing.

But sometimes the exceptions are historical, and unlikely to recur. In these situations, the best decision sometimes requires intervention at the business level. Perhaps those few unusual insurance policies can be paid out at less cost to the business than that of accommodating them in the information system. Another possibility is to handle them outside the system. This may be attractive from an operational, day-to-day processing perspective, but can play havoc with reporting and executive information, as the exceptions have to be "added in." It is the data modeler's duty to suggest these options, rather than assuming that every problem requires a data modeling solution.

The option of deferring the exceptions to a later stage of systems development is usually unrealistic, though often proposed as an easy way of avoiding facing the problem. If the data model cannot accommodate the exceptions from the outset, we will not be able to handle them later without database changes, and probable disruption to existing programs.

The Right Attitude

We finish this chapter with a look at "attitude." In a design discipline it does make sense to look at the personal strengths, habits[28],or "baggage" that the individual modeler brings to the task. After all, we are comfortable describing an architect as "innovative," "unimaginative," or "derivative" – data modelers can be all of these!

I'm indebted to Clare Atkins of Massey University in New Zealand, who has taught data modeling to many students, for suggesting some of the factors that make up a good attitude to the data modeling task.

Being Aware

A big part of improving your modeling skill, and being able to explain your decisions, is simply being conscious of what you are doing. As you model, it's worth asking:

1. What process am I following?

2. Why heuristics am I using?

3. What patterns am I using?

4. What don't I know yet? Where am I guessing?

5. What have I done that I could use again? (Write it down!)

6. How did I do? What would I do differently next time?

If you want to be forced to do all of these things, take any opportunity to teach an "apprentice" modeler and explain to him or her what you're doing as you go. Meetings with a mentor or experienced modeler in a quality assurance role can also help.

---

[28] My colleague Daniel Moody published a paper and has presented widely on the "habits" of effective data modelers, in the spirit of Stephen Covey's best-selling *Seven Habits of Highly Effective People,* Fireside (1990).

Being Creative

If I haven't stressed it enough already, modeling is a creative process. You need to ask:

1. Am I deliberately creating alternative models – or am I getting "anchored" on one design?

2. Have I stepped back from the problem – or am I still modeling the traditional view?

3. Have I "fallen in love" with a particular design at the expense of others?

4. Am I trying to force this model to fit a pattern?

5. Why do I prefer this design to another?

6. Have I asked for a second or third opinion – and opened my mind to it?

Analyzing or Designing

Data modeling is, overall, a design activity, but it includes the task of understanding requirements. There's a time to ask – and listen, and a time to propose – and even persuade. What is important is recognizing which you are doing, to ensure that adequate attention is given to both. Literal modeling (the model *is* the user requirement) is one extreme; uninformed design (the model *ignores* the user requirement) is the other. The key questions are:

1. Am I balancing analysis and design?

2. Am I analyzing or designing right now?

Being Brave

Designers, particularly if they are proposing an unfamiliar or radical solution, need to have a level of self-confidence. The requirement to get others' agreement to a model should not cause you to neglect your professional duty to produce the highest quality model (and I use the word "quality" in the sense of "fit for purpose.") Rather, it should alert you to the need to present the model and its rationale clearly and persuasively.

You need to ask:

1. Do I believe in the model?

2. Are there areas that I'm unsure of – and am I prepared to admit this?

3. Can I explain how the model works?

4. Can I explain the design decisions?

5. Can I explain how the model provides a better solution than alternatives?

6. Am I prepared to modify the model in the face of sound criticism?

Having a Plan

We look more at the organization and practicalities of the modeling process in Chapter 6. The data modeler is virtually always part of a larger project, and has to work to deadlines – and hence to a plan. You should check:

1. Do I have a plan in place, including time for participation of all stakeholders?

2. Do I have a starting point – beyond "waiting for inspiration."

3. Have I allowed time to explore different options – and review these with stakeholders?

4. Am I prepared to change the plan if things don't turn out as expected?

Being Understanding and Understood

Many a data modeler has been frustrated to see a quality solution or approach rejected in favor of one proposed by someone with more power or persuasive skills. (This doesn't just happen to data modelers!) Data modelers need to be aware of the context in which they are operating. If you're a student studying data modeling and this sounds irrelevant to you, take note that one of my very experienced colleagues helped a student with an assignment and was failed. The model was too sophisticated for the context, and by the time the professional modeler entered into an argument with the professor, there was too much "face" at stake!

You should be asking:

1. How will this model be used? Who will use it?

2. Have I involved all stakeholders? Will anyone say "why wasn't I asked?"

3. Can I communicate the model to all stakeholders?

4. Will anyone have reasons for not liking the model (too hard to program against, difficult to understand ...?)

5. Is there any history in the organization or project of data models being misunderstood, ignored or rejected?

6. Will the model surprise anyone? Will anyone have to change their plans?

Summary

Data modeling is a design discipline. Data modelers tend to adapt generic models and standard structures, rather than work from first principles. Innovative solutions may result from employing generic models from other business areas. New problems can be tackled top-down from very generic supertypes, or bottom-up by modeling representative areas of the problem domain and generalizing.

Chapter 6

Organizing the Data Modeling Task

*"An expert is someone who knows everything
about the topic except for its place in the world."*

--Anonymous

Data Modeling in the Real World

In the preceding chapters we have tackled the challenge of designing a data model without giving much attention to the practicalities of modeling in a real business environment.

In particular, we have not looked in any detail at:

- Who should be involved

- How business requirements are determined

- What documentation should be produced

- What happens to the model after the modeling task is formally completed

These questions are of relatively little importance to the student learning the techniques of data modeling, but they are crucial for the data modeling practitioner contributing to information systems development in an organization of any real complexity.

Roles and Responsibilities

There is some debate about how many and what sort of people should participate in the development of a data model. The extremes are the specialist data modeler working largely alone and gathering information from documentation and one-to-one interviews, and the joint applications development (JAD) style of session that brings business people, data modelers, and other systems staff together in facilitated workshops.

We need to keep in mind two key objectives: we want to produce the best possible model, and we need to have it accepted by all stakeholders. Both objectives suggest the involvement of a fairly large group of people, firstly to maximize the "brainstorming" power, and secondly to build commitment to the result. On the other hand, involvement need not mean *constant* involvement. Good ideas come not only from brainstorming sessions, but from reflection by individuals outside the sessions. Time outside group sessions is also required to ensure that models are properly checked for technical soundness (normalization, nonoverlapping subtypes, conformity to naming standards, etc). And some tasks are best delegated to one or two people, with the group being responsible for checking the result. These tasks include diagram production, detailed entity and attribute definition, and follow-up of business issues outside the expertise of the group.

One of the most important decisions in data modeling is the division of business rules between program logic, data content, and database design (covered in more detail in Chapter 12). Fairly obviously, this decision should not be taken by the data modeler in isolation, but in conjunction with the function designer/modeler. Similarly, a physical database designer may be able to determine that one option has a strong performance advantage over another. Another key player may be the data administrator or data manager, who will be interested in maintaining consistency in data definition across systems. However we organize the modeling task, we must ensure the involvement of these professionals.

My own preference is to nominate a small core team, usually consisting of a specialist data modeler, a senior function modeler (systems analyst) from the project team, and one of the system owners. If performance is likely to be a critical factor, I would consider including a member of the physical database design team. Another, larger team is made up of representatives of other stakeholders, always including further owner/user representatives, someone from the physical database design team, and at least one other specialist modeler. Other participants may include subject area specialists (who may not actually be users of the system), the project manager(s), and the data administrator. The larger team meets regularly to discuss the model. In the initial stages, their focus is on generating ideas and exploring major alternatives. Later, the emphasis shifts to review and verification. The smaller team is responsible for managing the process, developing ideas into workable candidate models, ensuring that the models are technically sound, preparing material for review, and incorporating suggestions for change.

Support for the model by all stakeholders, particularly the function modelers and physical database designers, is critical. Many good data models have been the subject of long and acrimonious debate, and sometimes rejection, after being forced upon systems analysts and physical database designers who have not been involved in their development. This is particularly true of innovative models resulting from a creative modeling approach. Other stakeholders may not have shared in the flashes of insight that have progressively moved the model away from familiar concepts, nor may they be aware of the problems or limitations of those concepts. Taking all stakeholders along with the process stage by stage is the best way of overcoming this. My rule is to involve anyone likely to be in a position to criticize or reject the model and anyone likely to ask "why wasn't I asked?" If this seems to be excessive, be assured that the cost of doing so is likely to be far less than that of trying to force the model on these people later.

Be particularly careful in using methodologies that allow for stage-by-stage development of the model and logical database design with "hand-offs" from one group to another. Certainly there is value in having clear interim deliverables and responsibilities, but too often the serial involvement of different stakeholders results in a model that favors one group's requirements over another's. If control over change is tight, we find the later participants constrained in suggesting alternatives; if it is loose, the original set of requirements may be overridden. The classic example of this is in the hand-off from data modeler to physical database designer, and the propensity for change to the model following the change of custody. Follow the formal stages and sign-offs, but involve all the players.

Sequence

Larger applications are often partitioned and designed in stages.

There are essentially two approaches:

1. Design the functions that create entity instances before those that read, update, and delete them. Achieving this is not quite as simple as it might appear, as some entity instances cannot be created without referring to other entities. In the data model of Figure 6-1, we will not be able to create an instance of Contribution without checking Employee and Fund to ensure that the contribution refers to valid instances of these. We would therefore address these "reference" entities and associated functions first.

   Generally, this approach leads to us commencing at the top of the hierarchy and working down. In Figure 6-1 we would commence detailed modeling around Fund Type and Fund, Employer, or Account, at the top of the hierarchy, moving to Person only when Fund and Fund Type were completed, and Account Entry only when all the other entities were fully specified.

   The attraction of the approach is that it progressively builds on what is already in place and (hopefully) proven. If we follow the same sequence for *building* the system (as we will have to do if we are prototyping), we should avoid the problems of developing transactions that cannot be tested because the data that they read cannot be created.

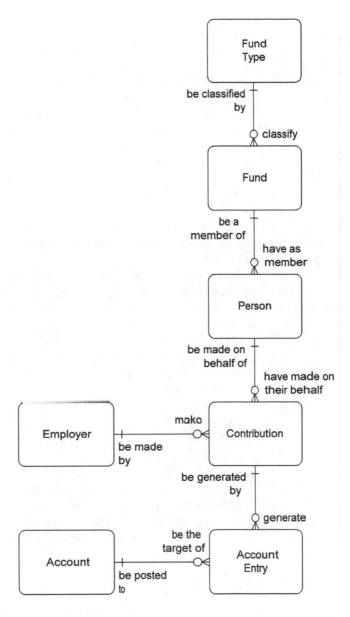

Figure 6-1. Pension Fund Model

2. Design core functions first, and put in place the necessary data structures to support them. In Figure 6-1, we might commence with the "Record Contribution" function, which could require virtually all of the entities in the model. This puts pressure on the data modeler to deliver quite a complete design early (and we need to plan accordingly), but also provides considerable input on the workability of the high level model. If we follow the same sequence for development, we may have to use special programs (e.g., database utilities) to populate the reference tables for testing. While this approach is less elegant, it has the advantage of addressing the more critical issues first, leaving the more straightforward handling of reference data until later. As a result, rework may be reduced.

There are as many variations on these broad options as there are systems development methodologies. Some rigorously enforce a sequence derived from "Create, Read, Update, Delete" dependencies, whilst others allow more flexibility to sequence development to meet business priorities. As a data modeler, my own preference is for the second approach, which tends to raise critical data modeling issues early in the process, before it is too late or expensive to address them properly. Whichever approach you use, the important thing is to be conscious of the quality and reliability of the data model at each stage, and to ensure that the function modeler understands the probability of change as later requirements are identified.

Inputs to the Modeling Task

We use a variety of sources to identify requirements. Interviews are essential, but should be used tactically, rather than as the sole input. Other important sources of information include existing systems and files, requests for system enhancements, system proposals and functional specifications, mission and job position statements, policy and procedure manuals, and the full variety of documentation that exists around any business function or existing system.

Interviews and Workshops

Interviews and workshops are expensive and sometimes unreliable sources of information. Be particularly wary of the "user representative" – the single person charged with answering all the modeler's questions about the business. One sometimes wonders why this all-knowing person is so freely available! You need to mix interviews with senior managers and staff at the "coal-face." Essentially, the former provide broad direction while the latter fill in the detail - but don't expect that rule to apply without exception, and don't go into an interview with a senior manager without a working knowledge of the process. If consultants or internal staff are reviewing or reengineering the business processes (as should happen prior to any major application replacement), be sure to get their take on the business. There is little point in developing a data model for a business area that is about to be radically changed.

Should You Model in the Interview?

Be very, very careful about drawing data models during interviews or workshops. In fact, use anything *but* data models – plain text, data flow diagrams, event diagrams, functional hierarchies, report layouts, object models – unless you are very certain that the data model you draw will be incorporated in the final design. Data models are *not* a comfortable language for most business people, who tend to think more in terms of activities. And by drawing them in a session, you are making it harder (both cognitively and politically) to experiment with other options later.

Expressing the requirements in a form other than a data model provides a degree of *traceability*, and a basis for comparing alternative models. If only a data model is produced, the opportunity to experiment with other options is effectively lost: the initial data model effectively *becomes* the business requirement.

Interviews with Senior Managers

Senior managers may not be familiar with the details of process and data, but are usually best placed to paint a picture of future directions. Many a model has failed the stability test (which is a polite way of saying that the system has been rendered prematurely obsolete) because information known to senior management was not communicated to the modeler.

Getting to these people can be an organizational and political problem, but one which must be overcome. Keep time demands limited; if you are working for a consultancy, bring in a senior partner for the occasion; explain in concise terms the importance of their contribution to the success of the system. Approach the interview with top management forearmed. Ensure that you are familiar with their area of business, and focus on future directions. What types of regulatory and competitive change does the business face? How does the business plan to respond to these challenges? What changes may be made to product range and organizational structure? Are there plans to radically reengineer processes? What new systems are likely to be required in the future? By all means ask if their information needs are being met, but don't make this the focus of the interview. Most senior managers are far less driven by structured information than the vendors of executive information systems would have us believe.

And above all, be aware of what the project as a whole (of which the data model is usually only a part) will do for them. Self-interest is a great motivator! I recall one consultant being summarily thrown out by the chief executive of a major organization when he commenced an interview with the question: "What information do you need to run your business?" (To be fair, this is an important question, but many senior managers have been asked it one too many times without seeing much value in return).

Interviews with Subject Matter Experts

Business experts, end users, and "subject matter experts" are the people we speak to in order to understand the data requirements in depth. Don't let them design the model! Rather encourage them to talk about the processes and the data they use, and to look critically at how well their needs are met. The challenge is often to get them to think at least a little "outside the square." I remember interviewing a bank manager to identify the optimum set of reports to meet his needs. He kept insisting that the current reports were close to perfect, because they supported his processes, which in turn had been designed around responding to the information in the reports.

A goal and process based approach is often the best way of structuring the interview. "What is the purpose of what you do?" is not a bad opening question, leading to an examination of how the goals are achieved and what data is (ideally) required to support them.

Workshops

Facilitated workshops are a powerful way of bringing people together to identify requirements and test alternative designs. They can be an excellent forum for brainstorming, for ensuring that a wide range of stakeholders have an opportunity to contribute, and for identifying and resolving conflicts.

Here are a few basic guidelines:

- Use an experienced facilitator if possible, and spend time with them explaining what you want from the workshop.

- Don't facilitate it yourself unless you are an experienced facilitator or cannot find one whom you can rely on to do the job well.

- Have a note-taker who understands the purpose of the workshop. If someone else is facilitating, that person may need to be you.

- Give the facilitator time to prepare an approach, and discuss it with you. Ninety percent of good facilitation is preparation.

- Avoid "modeling as you go." Incidentally, few things destroy the credibility of a "neutral" facilitator more effectively than their constructing a model on the whiteboard that no-one in the room could have produced, in a language no-one is comfortable using.

- Don't try to solve everything in the workshop, particularly if deep-seated differences surface or there is a question of "saving face." Make sure the problem is recognized and noted - then agree to tackle it outside the workshop.

Existing Systems and Reverse Engineering

One of the richest sources of raw material for the data modeler is existing systems, or, more specifically, existing file and database designs. Unfortunately, they are often disregarded by modelers determined to make a fresh start. Certainly, we should not incorporate earlier designs uncritically; after all, the usual reason for developing a new database is that the existing one no longer meets our requirements. But there are few things more frustrating to a user than a new application that lacks facilities provided by the old system.

Existing database designs provide both a "literal" starting point, as discussed later in this chapter, and a set of entities, relationships and attributes that we can use to ask the question "how does our new model support this?" This question is particularly useful when applied to attributes, and an excellent way of developing a first-cut attribute list for each entity. A sound knowledge of the existing system also provides common ground for interviews with users, who will frequently express their needs in terms of enhancements to the existing system.

The existing system may be manual or computerized. If you are very fortunate, the underlying data model will be properly documented. Otherwise, you should produce at least an E-R diagram, short definitions, and attribute lists by "reverse engineering," a process analogous to an architect drawing the plan of an existing building.

The job of reverse engineering combines the diagram-drawing techniques that we discussed in Chapter 3 with a degree of detective work to determine the meaning of entities, attributes, and relationships. Assistance from someone familiar with the database is invaluable. The person most able to help is more likely to be a maintenance analyst or programmer than a database administrator.

You will need to adapt your approach to the quality of available documentation, but broadly the steps are as follows:

1. Represent existing files, segments, record types, tables, or equivalents as entities. Use subtypes to handle any redefinition (multiple record formats with substantially different meanings) within files.

2. Normalize. Recognize that here you are "improving" the system, and the resulting documentation will not show up any limitations due to lack of normalization. It will, however, provide a better view of data requirements as input to the new design. If your aim is purely to document the capabilities of the existing system, skip this step.

3. Identify relationships supported by "hard links." Nonrelational database management systems usually provide specific facilities ("sets," "pointers," etc) to support relationships. Finding these is usually straightforward; determining the meaning of the relationship and hence assigning a name is sometimes less so.

4. Identify relationships supported by foreign keys. In a relational database, all relationships will be supported in this way, but even where other methods for supporting relationships are available, foreign keys are often used to supplement them. Finding these is often the greatest challenge for the reverse engineer, primarily because data item (column) naming and documentation may be inconsistent. For example, the primary key of Employee may be Employee Number, but the data item Authorized By in another file may in fact be an employee number, and thus a foreign key to Employee. Common formats are sometimes a clue, but cannot be totally relied upon.

5. List the attributes for each entity and define each entity and attribute.

The resulting model should be used in the light of outstanding requests of system enhancement, and of known limitations. The proposal for the new system is usually a good source of such information.

Function Models

If you are using a function-driven approach to systems development, as outlined briefly in Chapter 1, you will have valuable input in the form of the data used by the processes. The data may be documented explicitly (e.g., as data stores) or implicitly within the function description (e.g., "Amend product price on invoice.") Even if you have adopted a data-driven approach, in which data modeling precedes function modeling, you should plan to verify the data model against the function model when it is available, and allow time for enhancement of the data model.

In any case, you should not go too far down the track in data modeling without some sort of function model, even if detailed development is not scheduled until later. I find a one or two level data flow diagram a valuable adjunct to data modeling, and in communicating the impact of different data models on the system as a whole. In particular, the processes in a highly generic system will look quite different from those in a more traditional system, and will require additional data inputs to support "table driven" logic. A data flow diagram shows the differences far better than a data model alone (Figures 6-2 and 6-3).

(a) Data Model

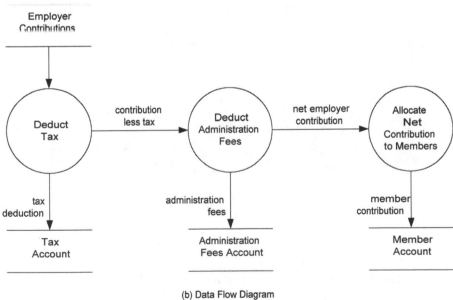

(b) Data Flow Diagram

Figure 6-2. Data Flow Diagrams Used to Supplement Data Models – Option 1

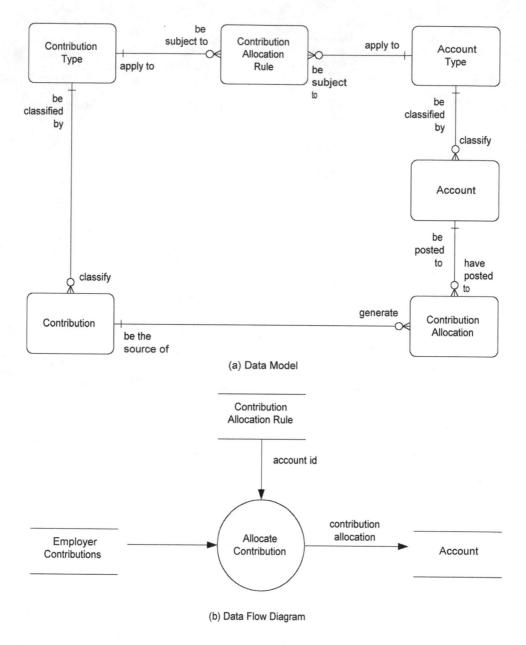

(a) Data Model

(b) Data Flow Diagram

Figure 6-3. Data Flow Diagrams Used to Supplement Data Models – Option 2

Testing the Model

Having developed one or more candidate models, it remains to verify that they are workable, and to select the most appropriate option. We can employ several different approaches, and will usually use a combination of them. The hard work is usually in checking completeness and rule enforcement, which requires some fairly rigorous testing. Communication effectiveness, stability, and elegance can be more broadly and quickly assessed. Verification often involves people unfamiliar with the language of modeling. The critical factor then becomes communication, and you should work hard at presenting the model in the most effective way. Talk in terms of tables to database specialists, business concepts to business specialists, and program logic to programmers; bring in sample data, prototypes, and data flow diagrams – use every means at your disposal to get the message through.

Comparison with the Function Model

One of the best means of verifying a data model is to ensure that it includes all the necessary data to support the function model. This is particularly effective if the function model has been developed relatively independently, as it makes available a second set of analysis results as a cross check. (This is not an argument in favor of data and function modelers working separately; if they work effectively together, the verification will take place progressively as the two models are developed).

There will be little value in checking against the function model if an extreme form of data-driven approach has been taken, and functions mechanically derived from the data model.

There are a number of formal techniques for mapping function models against data models to ensure consistency, and to provide a more sophisticated version of the approach to sequencing development than that described earlier in this chapter. They include matrices of functions mapped against data entities, entity life histories, and state transition diagrams. Martin[29] describes an approach which is representative of those supported by popular methodologies and documentation tools.

---

[29] *Information Engineering Trilogy*, Prentice Hall (1990).

Remember however, that the final database may be required to support functions as yet undefined, and hence not included in the function model. Support for the function model is therefore a necessary but not sufficient criterion for accepting a data model.

Review with the Users

Reviews with users and business specialists are an essential part of verifying a data model. But they need to be handled carefully and the results taken in the context of the users' level of understanding, which can be very difficult to assess. Several years ago, I spent some time walking through a relatively simple model with a quite sophisticated user – a recent MBA with exposure to formal systems design techniques, including data modeling. I was fully convinced that he understood the model, and it was only some years later that he confessed that his sign-off had been entirely due to his faith that I personally understood his requirements, rather than to his seeing them reflected in the data model.

This happens all too often, and many unworkable models have been duly signed off by users. I strongly counsel you to interpret the model in business terms to the user, rather than simply presenting the conventions and working through entity by entity. In particular, discuss design decisions and their rationale, instead of presenting your best solution without background.

For example: "This part of the model is based around the 'Right of Abode' concept rather than the various visas, passports, and special authorities. We've done this because we understand that new ways of authorizing immigrants to stay in the country may arise during the life of the system. Is this so? Here is how we've defined Right of Abode. Are there any ways of staying in the country that wouldn't fit this definition? We also thought of using a 'travel document' concept instead, but rejected it because an authority doesn't always tie to one document only. Did we understand that correctly?"

If the users don't find something wrong with the model, or at least prompt you to improve it in some way, you should be very suspicious about their level of understanding.

Reviews should be conducted throughout the modeling process rather than only at the end. Both the fully subtyped and the leveled model should be reviewed, as should any compromises required as physical design proceeds.

Sample Data

If sample data is available, there are few better ways of communicating and verifying a data model than to work through where each item of data would be held. The approach is particularly appropriate when the data model represents a new and unfamiliar way of organizing data: fitting some existing data to the new model will provide a bridge for understanding, and may turn up some problems or oversights.

I recall a statistical analysis system that needed to be able to cope with a range of inputs in different formats. The model was necessarily highly generalized, and largely the work of one specialist modeler. Other participants in its development were at least a little uncomfortable with it. Half an hour walking through the model with some typical inputs was far more effective in communicating and verifying the design than the many hours previously spent on argument at a more abstract level (and it showed up some areas needing more work).

Prototypes

An excellent way of testing a sophisticated model, or part of a model, is to build a simple prototype. Useful results can often be achieved in a few days, and the exercise can be particularly valuable in winning support and input from function modelers – especially if they have the job of building the prototype.

One of the most sophisticated (and successful) models in which I have been involved was to support a product management database, and associated transaction processing. The success of the project owed much to the early production of a simple PC prototype, prior to the major task of developing a system to support fifteen million accounts. A similar design that was not prototyped failed at a competitor organization, arguably because of a lack of belief in its workability.

Packaging It Up

Having verified the model, it remains to assemble the deliverables. Their exact format will vary depending on the chosen methodology and/or documentation tool. However, they should include at least the following:

1. A broad summary of requirements, covering scope, objectives, and future business directions. These should justify the overall approach taken – for example, highly generic, or customer-focused.

2. Inputs to the model – interview summaries, reverse-engineered models, function models, etc. Normally these are appended to the main documentation, and referred to as necessary in definitions.

3. A fully annotated entity-relationship diagram, including subtypes, as per Chapters 3 and 4, and possibly with many-to-many relationships left unresolved. We usually refer to this deliverable combined with the next as The Data Model.

4. Entity definitions (Chapter 3), attribute lists, and attribute definitions (Chapter 9) for every entity in the model.

5. A model suitable for direct implementation as a logical database design. If our target DBMS is a conventional relational product, the model will not include subtypes and should be fully normalized. It will also include any compromises made in collaboration with the physical database designer. We usually refer to this deliverable as The (Logical) Database Design.

6. Design notes covering decisions made in leveling the subtyped model, including choice of level of generalization, removal of entities to be implemented elsewhere, and any compromises required for implementation.

7. Cross-reference to the function model, proving that all functions are supported.

8. As necessary, higher level and local versions of the model to facilitate presentation.

9. Entity volumes. The data modeler is usually in the best position to collect this vital input to physical database design.

This is quite a lot of documentation – certainly more than a physical database designer needs to produce a default database design. Some of the additional documentation is aimed at function modelers and program designers, to ensure that they will understand the model and use it as intended. The documentation of source material provides some traceability of design decisions and allows proposals to change or compromise the model to be assessed in terms of the business requirements that they affect.

We have only recommended the permanent recording of two stages of model: the fully subtyped "no compromise" *data model* and the final *logical database design*, both of which are, of course, data models. This is to some degree a compromise, as the data model goes through many stages of transformation. However these two points in the process generally convey most of what is required for implementation and maintenance.

Maintaining the Model

The data model as initially delivered is seldom the final version. Most data models are updated and tuned as further information comes to light in detailed function modeling, programming, physical database design, and testing. Too frequently, the data modeling team has been disbanded by this time, and alterations are made indiscriminately by non-specialists.

An effective way of managing change as a system is developed is for an "owner" of the data model, preferably one of its developers, to remain involved, and to coordinate any amendments to the model and resulting logical database design. The owner can also work with program designers and programmers to ensure that the design is properly understood and used. This is particularly important for innovative and very generalized models. Many generalized database designs are undermined by programmers writing specific logic that fails to take advantage of the higher level of generalization.

An additional benefit of the data modeler being involved is that he or she becomes more aware of the model's strengths and weaknesses from the systems development perspective, and will be able to bring the experience so gained to future projects.

After the system is implemented, there will be changes needed to support system maintenance and enhancement. The maintenance process should ensure that all of the original modeling deliverables are kept up to date. Complete and reliable documentation provides a base for future changes, facilitates use of the data for other purposes, and is likely to be valuable as a reference point when the system is eventually replaced.

Summary

The development of a data model is an iterative process, involving requirements analysis, design, and evaluation of candidate solutions. It is best performed by a small team, with input from and review by a larger group of stakeholders.

Sources of requirements and ideas include system users, business specialists, system inputs and outputs, existing databases, and the function model.

The final data model should be supported by documentation to justify design decisions, in particular the implementation of subtype hierarchies. The model may be verified through presentations, walkthroughs, testing against sample data, prototypes, and mapping against the function model.

Part II
Advanced Data Modeling

Chapter 7

More About Relationships and Foreign Keys

Introduction

Relationships are one of the fundamental building blocks of entity-relationship models.

In Chapter 3, we covered the basics of relationship representation, concentrating on one-to-many and many-to-many relationships between pairs of entities. We started by translating foreign keys into lines on a diagram, and interpreting these as relationships between entities. Later, we found that relationships could be proposed and verified directly from "business rules." In Chapter 4 we looked briefly at generalizing and specializing relationships in conjunction with entity supertyping and subtyping.

In this chapter we cover some of the issues raised in the earlier chapters in more detail.

We look first at the representation of relationships using foreign keys. Although the translation from a level (no subtypes) entity-relationship model to a relational model is generally a straightforward, mechanical process, there are some situations that require more detailed guidelines or decisions on a case-by-case basis.

We introduce the concept of *transferability*, to supplement the more widely used concepts of cardinality, optionality, and degree (number of entities participating in the relationship). Knowing whether a relationship is transferable or not is vital in making decisions about primary keys (Chapter 9), one-to-one relationships, and time-dependent data (Chapter 11).

We then look at three types of relationships that appear in most data models, but that we have so far not examined in any detail: one-to-one relationships, self-referencing relationships, and relationships involving three or more entities.

We discuss generalization of relationships in greater detail and introduce the "arc" convention for identifying mutually exclusive relationships, which may signal opportunities for generalization.

Finally, we examine some common myths and misunderstandings about relationships.

Translating Relationships into Foreign Keys

The Basic Rule

In Chapter 3, we saw how to translate the links implied by primary and foreign keys in a relational model into lines representing one-to-many relationships on an E-R diagram. This is a useful technique when we have an existing database that has not been properly documented in diagrammatic form. The process of recovering the design in this all-too-frequent situation is a example of the broader discipline of "reverse engineering," and is one of the less glamorous tasks of the data modeler (Chapter 6).

Normally, however, we work from the diagram to the tables, and apply the following rule:

A one-to-many relationship is supported in a relational database by holding the primary key of the table representing the entity at the "one" end of the relationship as a foreign key in the table representing the entity at the "many" end of the relationship (Figure 7-1). Note the use of the asterisk convention to indicate that a column of a table is a foreign key.

Unfortunately, we sometimes run into trouble with this simple rule. Usually, the problems are associated with multicolumn keys.

Figure 7-1. Deriving Foreign Keys from Relationships

Overlapping Foreign Keys

Figure 7-2 is a model for an insurance company that operates in several countries. Each agent works in a particular country, and sells only to customers in that country. Note that the E-R diagram *allows* for this situation, but does not enforce the rule.

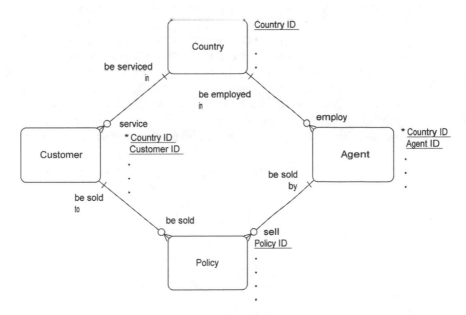

Figure 7-2. E-R Model Leading to Overlapping Foreign Keys

If we apply the rule for representing relationships by foreign keys, we find that the Country ID column appears twice in the Policy table – once to support the link to Agent, and once to support the link to Customer. We can distinguish the columns by naming one "Customer Country ID" and the other "Agent Country ID." But because of our rule that agents sell only to customers in their own country, both columns will always hold the same value. This seems a clear case of data redundancy, easily solved by combining the two columns into one. Yet there are arguments for keeping two separate columns.

The two-column approach is more flexible: If we change the rule about selling only to customers in the same country, the two-column model will easily support the new situation. But here we have the familiar trade-off between flexibility and constraints; we can equally argue that the one-column model does a better job of enforcing an important business rule, if we are convinced that the rule will apply for the life of the database.

There is a more subtle flexibility issue: What if one or both of the relationships from Policy became optional? Perhaps it is possible for a policy to be issued without involving an agent. In such cases, we would need to hold a null value for the foreign key to Agent – but this involves "nulling out" the value for Country, part of the foreign key to Customer. We would end up losing our link to Customer. I've been involved in some long arguments about this one, the most common suggestion being that we only need to set the value of Agent ID to null, and can leave Country ID untouched. But this involves an inconsistency in the way we handle foreign keys. It might not be so bad if we only had to tell *programmers* to handle the situation as a special case ("Don't set the whole of the foreign key to null in this instance"), but these days program logic is likely to be generated automatically by a CASE product that is not so flexible about handling nonstandard situations. The database management system itself may recognize foreign keys, and rely on them not overlapping in order to support referential integrity (Chapter 12).

My advice is to hold both columns, and recognize that the rule about agents and customers being from the same country will be held elsewhere (for example, in the table definition as enforced by the database management system). Alternatively, use stand-alone keys for Customer and Agent, and the problem will not arise.

Split Foreign Keys

The next structure has a similar flavor, but is a little more complex. You are likely to encounter it more often than the overlapping foreign key problem – once you know how to recognize it!

Figure 7-3 shows a model for an organization that takes orders from customers and dispatches them to the customers' branches. Note that the primary key of Branch is a combination of Customer No and Branch No, a choice that would be appropriate if we wanted to use the customers' own branch numbers rather than define new ones ourselves. In translating this model into relational tables, we need to carry two foreign keys in the Ordered Item table. The foreign key to Order is Order No, and the foreign key to Branch is Customer No + Branch No.

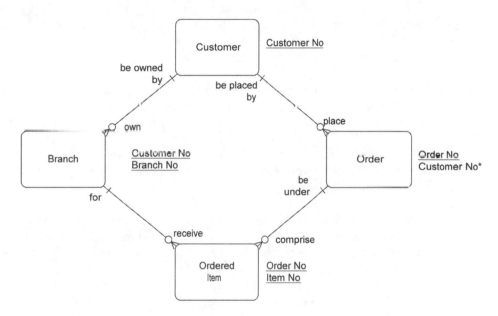

Figure 7-3. E-R Model Leading to Split Foreign Key

Our Ordered Item table, including foreign keys, is shown in Figure 7-4.

ORDERED ITEM (<u>Order No*</u>, <u>Item No</u>, Product, Customer No*, Branch No*)

Figure 7-4. Ordered Item Table

But let's assume the reasonable business rule that the customer who places the order is also the customer who receives the order. Then, since each order is placed and received by one customer, Order No is a determinant of Customer No. The Ordered Item table is therefore not fully normalized, as Order No is a determinant, but is not a candidate key of the table.

We already have a table with Order No as the key and Customer No as a nonkey item. Holding Customer No in the Ordered Item table tells us nothing new, and involves us in the usual problems of unnormalized structures. For example, if the Customer No for an order was entered incorrectly, it would need to be corrected for every Ordered Item on that order. The obvious solution seems to be to remove Customer No from the Ordered Item table. But this causes its own problems.

First, we have broken our rule for generating foreign keys from the diagram. If we were to draw a diagram from the tables, would we include a line from Ordered Item to Branch? Not according to our rules, but we started off by saying there *was* a relationship between the two. And what is Branch No doing in the Ordered Item table if not supporting a relationship to Branch?

But there is more to the problem than a diagramming nicety. Any CASE tool that generates foreign keys mechanically from relationships is going to include Customer No in the Ordered Item table. A program generator that makes the usual assumption that it can find the full primary key of Branch in the Ordered Item table will be in trouble if Customer No is excluded. Again, standard facilities for enforcing referential integrity are most unlikely to support the special situation that arises if Customer No is excluded.

Whether we include or exclude Customer No, we strike serious problems. When you encounter this situation – which you should pick up through a normalization check after generating the foreign keys – I strongly suggest you go back and select different primary keys. In this case, a stand-alone Branch No as the primary key of Branch will do the job. (The original Branch No and Customer No will become nonkey items, forming a second candidate key). You will lose the constraint that the Customer who places the order receives the order. This will need to be enforced elsewhere in the system.

Derivable Foreign Keys

Occasionally, you will model a relationship, and later discover that the foreign key values can be derived from attributes of the participating entities. The following two examples, illustrating derivable one-to-many and many-to-many relationships, are typical.

Derivable One-to-Many Relationships

In Figure 7-5, we are modeling information about diseases and their groups (or categories), as might be required in a database for medical research.

During our analysis of attributes we discover that disease groups are identified by a range of numbers (Low No through High No), and that each disease in that group is assigned a number in the range. For example, 301 through 305 might represent "Depressive Illnesses" and "Post-Natal Depression" might be allocated the number 304. Decimals can be used to avoid running out of numbers. We see exactly this sort of structure in many classification schemes, including the Dewey decimal classification used in libraries. We can use either High No or Low No as the primary key: I've arbitrarily selected Low No.

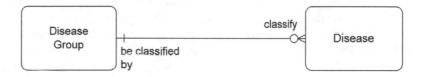

Figure 7-5. Initial E-R Model of Diseases and Groups

Applying our rule to generate foreign keys, we arrive at the tables in Figure 7-6.

> **DISEASE (<u>Disease No</u>, Disease Group Low No*, Disease Name, …)**

> **DISEASE GROUP (<u>Disease Group Low No</u>, Disease Group High No, …)**

Figure 7-6. Relational Model of Diseases and Groups

In this situation, the foreign key "Disease Group Low No" in the Disease table is derivable. We can determine which disease group a given disease belongs to by finding the disease group with the range containing its disease no.

To meet our objective of nonredundancy, we will need to remove Disease Group Low No from the Disease table. We will then also need to remove the relationship line from the diagram. Altering the diagram may seem a little unreasonable. Surely the relationship exists, regardless of the technique we use to implement it? Unfortunately, we can't adopt this view, unless we are prepared to lose the ability to move directly and mechanically from diagram to tables. In practical terms, if you describe a relationship to a CASE tool, it will generate the foreign key for you – whether you want it or not!

The alternative is to retain the relationship and the associated foreign key, and accept some redundancy as the price of consistency. As in the examples in the preceding section, carrying a derivable foreign key may be worthwhile if we are generating program logic, which is based on navigation using foreign keys. But carrying redundant data complicates update and introduces the risk of data inconsistency. In this example, we would need to ensure that if a disease moved from one group to another, the foreign key was updated. In fact this can happen only if the disease number changes (in which case we should regard it as a new disease – see Chapter 8) or if we change the boundaries of existing groups. We may well determine that the business does not require the ability to make such changes, in which case the derivable data option becomes more appealing.

The above situation also occurs commonly with dates and date ranges. For example, a bank statement might include all transactions for a given account between two dates. If the two dates were attributes of the Statement entity, the relationship between Transaction and Statement would be derivable by comparing these dates with the transaction dates. In this case, the boundaries of a future statement might well change, perhaps at the request of the customer, or because we wished to notify them that the account was overdrawn. If choosing the redundant foreign key approach, we would then need to ensure that the foreign key was updated in such cases.

Derivable Many-to-Many Relationships

A similar problem can occur with many-to-many relationships. Perhaps we have proposed Applicant and Welfare Benefit entities, and a many-to-many relationship between them (Figure 7-7).

APPLICANT (Applicant ID, Name, Date of Birth...)

WELFARE BENEFIT (Benefit ID, Minimum Eligible Age, Maximum Eligible Age...)

Figure 7-7. Derivable Many-to-Many Relationship

On further analysis, we discover that eligibility for benefits is derivable by comparing attributes of the applicant with qualifying criteria for the benefit (e.g., Date of Birth compared with Eligible Age attributes).

In such cases, we should delete the relationship, on the basis that it is derivable (and hence redundant). We don't want to generate a resolution table that contains nothing but derivable data. If you look at any model closely, you will find numerous such many-to-many "relationships," derivable from inequalities ("greater than," "less than") or more complex formulae and rules. For example:

Each Employee Absence may occur during one or more Strikes and
Each Strike may occur during one or more Employee Absences
(Derivable from comparison of dates).

Each Aircraft Type may be able to land at one or more Airfields and
Each Airfield may be able to support landing of one or more Aircraft Types
(Derivable from airport services and runway facilities and aircraft type specifications).

What do we say to the users in these cases? Having presented them with a diagram, which they have approved, we have now removed a relationship. One option is to surreptitiously amend the model on the basis that "we know better." A more formal and controllable approach that achieves the same end is to introduce another stage of modeling, to distinguish the "user model" from the "implementation model." I'm strongly opposed to either of these approaches, as they lead almost invariably to important decisions being taken without user participation, as well as further complicating modeling for little gain. I've found that the simplest and most effective approach is to explain the problem to the user. Show how the relationship is derivable from other data, and demonstrate, using sample transactions, that including the derivable relationship will add redundancy and complexity to the system.

Foreign Keys to Other Than the Primary Key

Some DBMSs (including recent versions of DB2) allow a one-to-many relationship to be implemented by holding a copy of *any* candidate key of the referenced table, not just the primary key (the candidate key must have been defined to the DBMS as unique). This prompts two questions:

1. How useful is this?

2. Does the implementation of a relationship in this way cause problems in system development?

Admittedly the vast majority of database designs cannot benefit from this option. However consider the following tables from a public transport management system (Figure 7-8):

> **SCHEDULED VEHICLE TRIP (<u>Route No</u>, <u>Trip No</u>, Direction Code, Scheduled Departure TimeOfDay)**

> **ACTUAL VEHICLE TRIP (<u>Vehicle No</u>, <u>Trip Date</u>, <u>Actual Departure TimeOfDay</u>, Route No, Direction Code, Trip No):**

> **PASSENGER TRIP (<u>Ticket No</u>, <u>Trip Date</u>, <u>Trip Start Time</u>, Route No, Direction Code)**

Figure 7-8. Tables with Candidate Keys

It can be seen that there are alternative candidate keys for Actual Vehicle Trip:

> Route No + Trip No + Trip Date, and

> Route No, Direction Code, Trip Date, Actual Departure Time Of Day

However in the system as built these were longer than the key actually chosen (by 1 and 3 bytes respectively): since a very large number of records would be stored the shortest key was chosen to minimize the storage costs of indexes, etc. There was a requirement to identify which Actual Vehicle Trip each Passenger Trip took place on: in a DBMS which constrains a foreign key to be a copy of the primary key of the other table, Vehicle No and Actual Departure Time Of Day would have had to be added to the Passenger Trip table at a cost of an extra 4 bytes in each of a very large number of rows. The ability to maintain a foreign key which refers to any candidate key of the other table meant that only Trip No needed to be added at a cost of only 1 extra byte.

Of course, exploitation of this option might be difficult if the CASE tool being used to build the application did not support it. Beyond the issue of tool support, there do not appear to be any technical problems associated with this option. However, it's always sensible to be as simple and consistent as possible: the less fancy stuff that programmers, users and DBAs have to come to grips with, the more time they can devote to using the data model properly!

Optional Relationships

In a relational database a one-to-many relationship that is optional at the "many" end (as most are) requires no special handling. However if a one-to-many relationship is optional at the "one" end, the foreign key representing that relationship must be able to indicate in some way that there is no associated row in the referenced table. The most common way of achieving this is to make the foreign key column(s) "nullable" (able to be null or empty in some rows). However this adds complexity to queries. A simple join of the two tables (an "inner join") will only return rows with nonnull foreign keys. For example, if nullable foreign keys are used, a simple join of the Agent and Policy tables illustrated in Figure 7-9 will only return those policies actually sold by an Agent. One of the major selling points of relational databases is the ease with which end-users can query the database. The novice user querying this data to obtain a figure for the total value of policies is likely to get a value significantly less than the true total. To obtain the true total it is necessary to construct an outer join or use a union query, which the novice user may not know about.

Figure 7-9. Optional Relationship

A way around this problem is to add a "Not Applicable" row to the referenced table and include a reference to that row in each foreign key that would otherwise be null. The true total can then be obtained with only a simple query. The drawback is that other processing becomes more complex as we need to allow for the "dummy" agent.

Transferability

An important property of relationships that we have not discussed so far is *transferability*. There are two reasons for not including it in the presentation of the basics:

First, it does not *directly* and mechanically affect the design of a relational database (although some facilities provided by the DBMS, such as management of "delete" operations, may need to know whether a relationship is transferable). Changing a relationship from transferable to nontransferable will not alter the set of tables and columns that result from the conversion to a relational model. Transferability is of interest primarily to function modelers and to data modelers themselves.

Second, most diagramming tools do not support a symbol to indicate transferability. However, some do provide for it to be recorded in supporting documentation, and some support the closely related concept of weak entities (Chapter 9).

The Concept of Transferability

Figure 7-10 illustrates the distinction between transferable and nontransferable relationships.

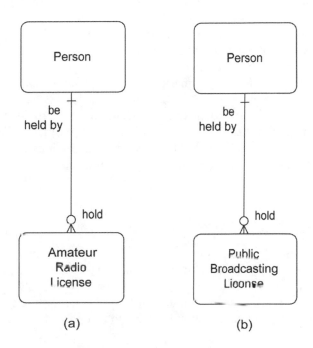

Figure 7-10. Nontransferable and Transferable Licenses

The two models appear identical in structure. However, let's impose the reasonable rule that public broadcasting licenses may be transferred from one person to another, while amateur radio licenses are nontransferable. Every time someone wants an amateur license, a new one is issued.

The Importance of Transferability

The difference in transferability has some important consequences. For example, we could choose to identify amateur licenses with a two-column key of Person ID + License No, where License No was not unique in itself. We would expect the value of the key for a particular license to be stable[30], because the Person ID associated with a license could not change. But if we used this key for public broadcasting licenses, it would not be stable, because the Person ID *would* change if the license were transferred. The role of transferability in defining primary keys is discussed in some detail in Chapter 9. Another difference is in handling historical data. If we wanted to keep an "audit trail" of changes to the data, we would need to provide for an ownership history of public broadcasting licenses, but not of amateur licenses. Later in this chapter, we will see that transferability is an important criterion when deciding whether entities participating in a one-to-one relationship should be combined.

Documenting Transferability

So transferability is an important concept in modeling, and we will refer to it elsewhere in this book, particularly in our discussions of the time dimension in Chapter 11. I've found it very useful to be able to show on E-R diagrams whether or not a relationship is transferable. Unfortunately, as previously mentioned, most documentation tools do not support a transferability symbol.

Barker[31] suggests a symbol for *non*transferability (the less common situation) and, rather than invent another, I recommend you use the adaptation shown in Figure 7-11. I have not suggested a separate symbol to indicate that a relationship is *transferable* (nor does Barker) – transferability is the default.

---

[30] The importance of stability for primary keys is discussed in Chapter 8.

[31] *CASE Method Entity Relationship Modelling*, Addison Wesley (1990).

Figure 7-11. Nontransferability Symbol

Note that transferability, unlike optionality and cardinality, is *nondirectional*. Transferring a public broadcasting license from one person to another can equally be viewed as transferring the persons from one license to another. It is usually more natural and useful to view a transfer in terms of the entity at the "many" end of the relationship being transferable. In relational model terms, this translates into a change in the value of the foreign key.

Nontransferable one-to-many relationships are usually, but not always, mandatory in the "one" direction. An example of an *optional* nontransferable relationship is shown in Figure 7-12. An insurance policy need not be sold by an agent (optionality,) but if it is sold by an agent it cannot be transferred to another (nontransferability).

Figure 7-12. Optional Nontransferable Relationship

Many-to-many relationships are usually transferable. The transferability of one-to-one relationships, as discussed later in this chapter, is critical in making decisions about whether to consolidate the participating entities into a single entity, and should therefore always be documented.

A point of definition: we regard establishment or deletion of a relationship instance without adding or deleting entity instances as a transfer. (The terms "connect" and "disconnect" are sometimes used to describe these situations). For example, if we could connect an agent to an existing policy that did not have an associated agent, or disconnect an agent from the policy, the relationship would be considered transferable. Obviously these types of transfers are only relevant to *optional* relationships.

Transferability can easily be incorporated in the business sentences we generate from relationships:

Each public broadcasting license must be owned by one person *who may change over time.*

Each amateur radio license must be owned by one person *who must not change over time.*

I generally use the nontransferability symbol only where it is relevant to a design decision, and follow the same practice in this book.

One-to-One Relationships

One-to-one relationships occur far less frequently than one-to-many and many-to-many relationships. Nevertheless, along with supertypes and subtypes, they are one of the most important tools in creative modeling, allowing us to "break up" traditional entities and reassemble them in new ways. They also present some special problems in implementation.

One-to-One Relationships and Creativity

The value of one-to-one relationships in fostering creativity is best illustrated by an example. Figure 7-13 shows a simple banking model, including provision for regular transfers of funds from one account to another.

Figure 7-13. Funds Transfer Model

There doesn't appear to be much scope for generalization or specialization here. But there is an opportunity to break Account into two parts – the "accounting part," which is basically the balance, and the "contractual part," which covers interest rates, fees, etc. – giving us the model in Figure 7-14. We now have some more material for generalization. We might choose to regard both Account Operating Contract and Funds Transfer Agreement as *agreements* between the bank and the customer (Figure 7-15) – and we're on our way to exploring a new view of data. Many banks have, in fact, implemented systems based on this new view, usually after a far longer and more painful creative process than described here!

Of course, you don't need to use one-to-one relationships to arrive at a new view. But they often provide a starting point, and can be particularly useful "after the event" in showing how a new model relates to the old. But on what basis do we decide to break an entity into two entities linked by a one-to-one relationship? Or, conversely, on what basis do we combine the entities participating in a one-to-one relationship?

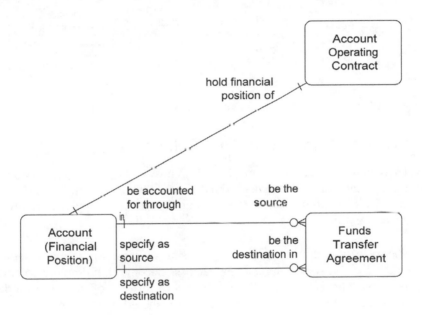

Figure 7-14. Separating Components of Account

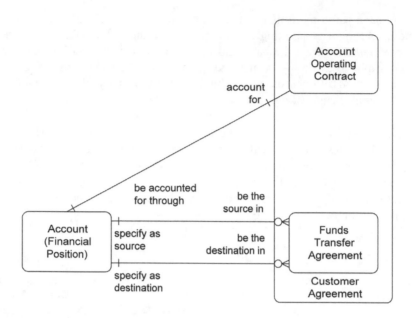

Figure 7-15. Generalizing Customer Agreements

When to Use One-to-One Relationships

There is little to stop us from taking any entity and splitting it into two or more entities, each identified by a candidate key of the original entity – provided, for the sake of nonredundancy, that each nonkey attribute appears in only one of the new entities.

The main consequence of splitting an entity in this way is that inserting and deleting full rows in the resulting database becomes a little more complicated. We now have to update two or more tables instead of one. The sacrifice in simplicity and elegance means that we should have a good reason for introducing one-to-one relationships. Once again, there are few absolute rules, but several useful guidelines.

Distinct Real World Concepts

Be very wary of combining entities that represent concepts commonly accepted as distinct, just because the relationship between them appears to be one-to-one (e.g., Person and Passport, Driver and Racing Car), particularly in the earlier stages of modeling. Closer examination may suggest supertypes in which only one of the pair participates, or even that the relationship is actually one-to-many or many-to-many. Combining the entities will hide these possibilities.

In the bank account example of Figures 7-12 through 7-14, we worked in the opposite direction, splitting a single entity into two entities that had value in their own right. The entity Telephone Exchange provides another nice example: closer examination usually shows that it can be broken into entities representing location, node, switching equipment, and the building that houses them.

In many of these cases, transferability (as discussed below) will dictate that the entities remain separate. Relationships that are optional in both directions suggest entities that are independently important. And look also at the cardinality: could we envisage a change to the business that would make the relationship one-to-many or many-to-many?

Support for Creativity

If splitting an entity or combining entities linked by a one-to-one relationship helps to develop a new and potentially useful model of the business area, then there is no need for further justification. (Of course, the professional modeler will try to look behind his or her intuition to understand the original motivation for proposing the split – e.g., are there really two concepts that the business handles differently?)

Separating Attribute Groups

In Chapter 4, we discussed the situation in which a group of attributes would be either applicable or not applicable to a particular entity instance. For example, in a Client entity, the attributes Date of Incorporation, Company Registration No, and Number of Employees might only be applicable if the client was a company rather than a person. We saw that this situation suggested a subtyping strategy – in this case, subtyping Client into Company Client and Personal Client to represent the "all applicable or none applicable" rule.

But sometimes we can better handle an attribute group by removing it to a separate entity. For example, we might have a number of attributes associated with a Client's credit rating – perhaps Rating, Source, Date Last Updated, Reason for Checking. If these were recorded for only some clients, we could model two subtypes: Client with Credit Rating and Client without Credit Rating. But this seems less satisfactory than the previous example. For a start, a given client could migrate from one entity to another where a credit rating was acquired. An alternative is to model a separate Credit Rating entity, linked to the Client entity through a one-to-one relationship (Figure 7-16). Note the optional and mandatory symbols, showing that a Client *may* have a Credit Rating.

Figure 7-16. Separate Entity for Credit Rating Attributes

Which is the better approach? The subtyping approach is based on specialization, the one-to-one relationship on disaggregation, so they are fundamentally different. But both allow us to represent the constraint that the attribute group applies to only certain instances. A few guidelines will help.

Look at the name of the attribute group. Does it suggest an entity in its own right (e.g., Credit Rating) or a set of data that applies only to certain stable subtypes (e.g., Additional Company Data?) In the first case we would prefer a one-to-one relationship, in the second, subtypes.

In Chapter 4, we introduced the guideline that real world instances should not migrate from one subtype to another – or at least that such subtypes would not remain as entities in the final (level) model. A company will not become a person, but a client may acquire a credit rating. So the "never applicable to this instance" situation suggests subtyping; the "not currently applicable to this instance" situation suggests the one-to-one approach.

Remember also that our subtyping rules restrict us to nonoverlapping subtypes. If there is more than one relevant attribute group, we will have trouble with the subtyping approach. But there is no limit to the number of one-to-one relationships that an entity can participate in. This is a good technique to bear in mind when faced with alternative useful breakdowns into subtypes based on attribute groups.

Transferable One-to-One Relationships

Transferable one-to-one relationships should always be modeled as such, and never combined into a single entity. Figure 7-17 shows a transferable one-to-one relationship between parts and bins. If we were to combine the two entities, then transferring parts from one bin to another would involve not only updating the Bin No, but all other attributes "belonging to" the bin.

Figure 7-17. Transferable One-to-One Relationship

Another way of looking at transferability is that the relationship will be many-to-many over time.

Figure 7-17 is an excellent counter-example to the popular view that one-to-one relationships that are mandatory in both directions should always be reduced to a single entity. In fact, we may want to model *three* entities. Suppose that Bin Capacity was defined as the number of parts that could be stored in a bin (and could not be calculated from the attributes of Bin and Part). Should we now hold Bin Capacity as an attribute of Part or of Bin? Updating the attribute when a part moves from one bin to another is untidy. We might want to consider modeling a separate entity with a key of Part No + Bin No as the most elegant solution to the problem.

We discuss this same example from a normalization perspective in Chapter 8.

Self-Referencing One-to-One Relationships

Self-referencing one-to-one relationships cannot be collapsed into a single entity. These are discussed later in this chapter.

Implementing One-to-One Relationships

A one-to-one relationship can be supported in a relational database by implementing both entities as tables, and using the same primary key for both. This strategy ensures that the relationship is indeed one-to-one, and is the preferred option.

But we can't use this approach for transferable relationships. If we used Part No to identify both Part and Bin in our earlier example, it would not be stable as a key of Bin (whenever a new part was moved to a bin, the key of that bin would change).

In this situation, we would identify Bin by Bin No and Part by Part No, and support the relationship with a foreign key: either Bin No in the Part table or Part No in the Bin table. Of course, what we are really supporting here is not a one-to-one relationship any more, but a one-to-many relationship. We have flexibility whether we like it or not! We will need to enforce the one-to-one rule outside the model. Some database management systems will allow you to specify that each value of the foreign key appears only once in the table, providing a simple practical solution. Since we have a choice as to the direction of the one-to-many relationship, we will need to consider other factors, such as performance and flexibility. Will we be more likely to relax the "one part per bin" or the "one bin per part" rule?

Incidentally, I once struck exactly this situation in practice. The database designer had implemented a single table, with a key of Bin No Parts that were then effectively identified by their bin no, causing real problems when parts were moved from one bin to another. In the end, they "solved" the problem by re-labeling the bins each time a part was moved!

Self-Referencing Relationships

We use the terms "self-referencing," "recursive," or "involuted" to describe a relationship that has the same entity at both ends. Such relationships are an important part of the data modeler's tool kit, and appear in most data models. Self-referencing relationships are used to represent three types of structure: hierarchies, networks, and (much less commonly) chains (Figure 7-18).

Hierarchies (One-to-Many Relationships)

Hierarchies are characterized by each instance of the entity having any number of subordinates but only one superior of the same entity type. Accordingly we use one-to-many relationships to represent them.

Examples of the types of hierarchies we need to model in practice are:

"Contains" – e.g., System may contain (component) Systems, Location may contain (smaller) Locations.

"Classifies" – e.g., Equipment Type may classify (more specific) Equipment Types, Employee Type may classify (more specific) Employee Types.

"Controls" – e.g., Organization Unit may control (subordinate) Organization Units, Network Node may control (subordinate) Network Nodes.

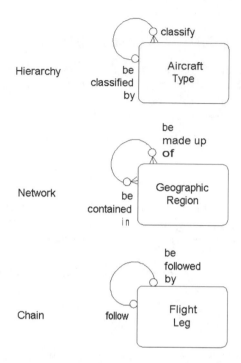

Figure 7-18. Self-Referencing Relationships

The more we generalize our entities, the more we encounter these structures. Figure 7-19 shows an organization structure at two levels of generalization. If we choose to implement the model using Branch, Department, and Section entities, we do not require any self-referencing relationships. But if we choose the higher level of generalization, the relationships between branches, departments, and sections become self-referencing relationships amongst organization units.

Implementation of one-to-many self-referencing relationships is straightforward, and was covered in Chapters 2 and 3. (Basically, we hold a foreign key such as "Superior Organization Unit.")

Programming against such structures is less straightforward, if we want to retain the full flexibility of the structure, in particular the unlimited number of levels. Some languages (e.g., COBOL, SQL) do not provide good support for recursion. Screen and report design is also more difficult, if we want to allow for a variable number of levels.

I have found data modelers to be a little cavalier in their use of self-referencing relationships, sometimes to represent quite stable two or three level hierarchies. The important thing here, as always, is to make the options clear by showing the subtypes and their explicit relationships as well as the more general entity. One way of limiting the number of levels is to use a structured primary key, as discussed in Chapter 8.

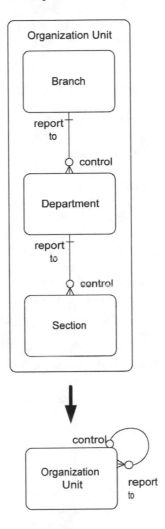

Figure 7-19. Self-Referencing Relationship Resulting from Generalization

Note that hierarchies may not be of consistent depth. For example, if not all Branches are divided into Departments and not all Departments are divided into Sections, the Organization Unit hierarchy in Figure 7-19 will be one, two or three deep in different places. If the DBMS does not provide a specialized extension for hierarchy navigation, such hierarchies can be difficult to query. In this case a query might have to be a union of three separate queries, one to handle each depth.

A neat solution to this problem is provided if each Organization Unit without a parent holds its own primary key rather than null in the foreign key representing the self-referencing relationship. It is then possible to write a simple (non-union) query that assumes the full depth (in this case three levels).

Networks (Many-to-Many Relationships)

Networks differ from hierarchies in that each entity instance may have more than one superior of the same entity type. We therefore model them using many-to-many relationships (which can be resolved as discussed in Chapter 3).

Like hierarchical structures, they are easy to draw, and not too difficult to implement, but can provide plenty of headaches for programmers and users of query languages. Again, modelers frequently fail to recognize underlying structures that could lead to a simpler system. In particular, multiple hierarchies are often generalized to networks without adequate consideration. For example, it might be possible for an employee to have more than one superior, which suggests a network structure. But further investigation might show that individual employees could report to at most three superiors – their manager as defined in the organization hierarchy, a project manager, and a technical mentor. This structure could be more accurately represented by three hierarchies (Figure 7-20) leaving us the option of direct implementation using three foreign keys, or generalization to a many-to-many relationship.

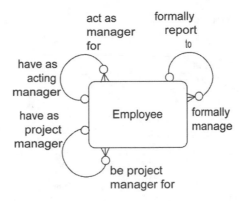

Figure 7-20. Multiple Hierarchies

Be careful in defining self-referencing many-to-many relationships to ensure that they are asymmetric: the relationship must have a different name in each direction. Figure 7-21 shows the reason. If we name the relationship "married to," we will end up recording each marriage twice. Sometimes we need to impose this asymmetry on a symmetric world, as in Figure 7-22. Here, we deliberately make the "associated with" relationship asymmetric, using the primary key as a means of determining which role each entity instance plays. The primary key is a good choice, because it should be stable (as discussed in Chapter 9). If we selected an unstable attribute as the basis of ordering the relationship, we would be faced with a complicated update problem when the value changed.

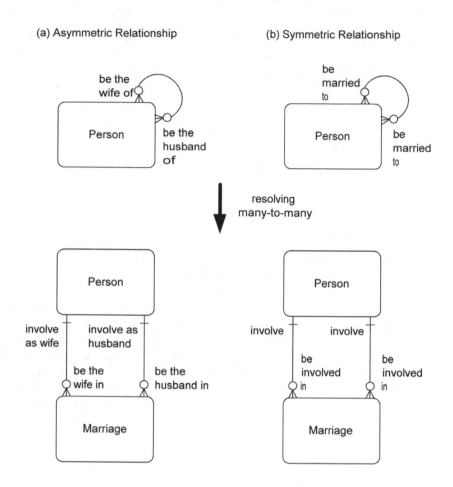

Figure 7-21. Symmetry Leading to Duplication

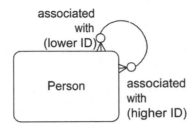

Figure 7-22. Deliberate Creation of Asymmetry

Chains (One-to-One Relationships)

Chains (sometimes called *linked lists*) occur far less frequently than hierarchies and networks. In a chain, each entity instance is associated with a maximum of one other entity of the same type in either direction. Chains are therefore modeled using one-to-one relationships. Implementation using a foreign key presents us with the same problem as for transferable one-to-one relationships: we end up implementing a one-to-*many* relationship whether we like it or not. Other mechanisms, such as unique indexes on the foreign key attribute (not always possible if the attribute can be null) will be needed to enforce the one-to one constraint.

A frequently used alternative is to group the participants in each chain and introduce a sequence number to record the order (Figure 7-23).

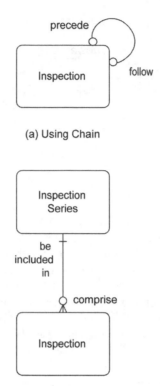

(a) Using Chain

INSPECTION (Inspection Series ID , Inspection ID , Sequence...)

(b) Using Group and Sequence Number

Figure 7-23. Chaining and Grouping

This is another example of deviating from the conventional implementation of relationships; but, unlike some of the other variations we have looked at, it is usually well supported by database management systems. But inserting a new instance in the chain will involve resequencing, an inelegant option-unless we regard the use of floating point sequence numbers (i.e., using decimals) as elegant.

Relationships Involving Three or More Entities

We saw in Chapter 3 that relationships involving three or more entities – sometimes described as "ternary" (3), "quaternary" (4), etc. – are handled by introducing a resolution entity to represent the relationship, in much the same way that many-to-many relationships between two entities can be represented with a resolution entity.

We begin to encounter problems if we start talking about the cardinality and optionality of these higher degree relationships prior to their resolution. The concepts are certainly applicable[32], but difficult to come to grips with for most data modelers, let alone business specialists asked to verify the model. Nor do we have a diagramming convention to represent the unresolved relationships. My advice is to resolve the relationships, then work with the familiar two-entity relationships that result.

Whenever you encounter what appears to be a higher degree relationship, you should check that it is not in fact made up of individual many-to-many relationships among the participating entities. The two situations are not equivalent, and choosing the wrong representation may lead to normalization problems. This is discussed in some detail in Chapter 8.

Figure 7.24 shows a number of legitimate structures, with different cardinality and optionality.

Generalization of Relationships

In Chapter 4, I referred briefly to the possibility of generalizing relationships as well as entities and attributes. Choosing the right level of generalization for relationships is important, and involves the same sorts of trade-off between enforcement of constraints and stability in the face of change.

However, our options for generalizing or specializing relationships are far more limited, because we are only interested in relationships between the same

---

[32] See, for example, Ferg, S., "Cardinality Concepts in Entity-Relationship Modeling," *Proceedings of the 10th International Conference on the Entity Relationship Approach*, San Mateo (1991).

pair of entities. Much of the time we have only one to play with! For that reason, we don't have a separate convention for "subtyping" relationships.

But as we generalize entities, we find that the number of relationships between them increases, as a result of "rolling up" from the subtypes (Figure 7-25). Much of the time, we generalize relationships of the same name almost automatically, and this very seldom causes any problems. Most of us would not bother about the intermediate stage of Figure 7-25(b) but would move directly to Figure 7-25(c). I recommend you review the level of relationship generalization at the time of leveling the model for translation into relational form.

As with entities, our decision needs to be based on commonality of use, stability, and enforcement of constraints. Are the individual relationships used in a similar way? Can we anticipate further relationships? Are the rules that are enforced by the relationships stable?

Let's look briefly at the two main types of relationship generalization.

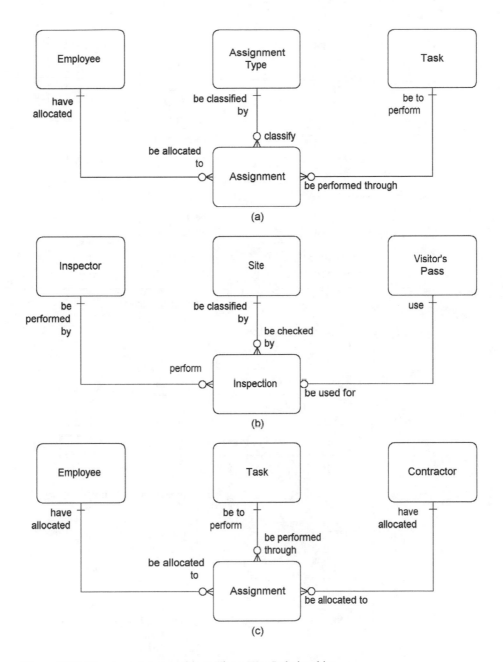

Figure 7-24. Structures Interpretable as Three-Way Relationships

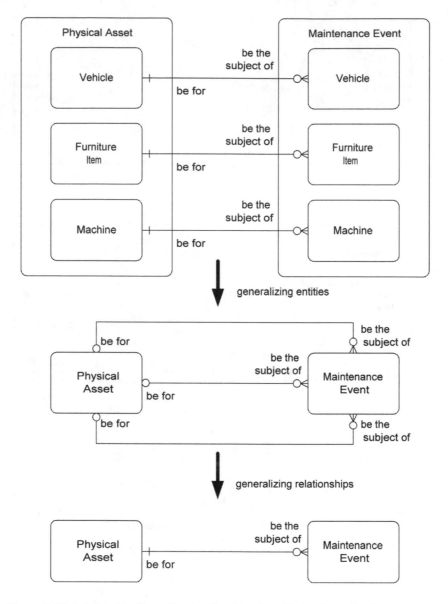

Figure 7-25. Relationship Generalization Resulting from Entity Generalization

Generalizing Multiple One-to-Many Relationships to a Single Many-to-Many Relationship

Figure 7-26 shows several one-to-many relationships between Customer and Insurance Policy. These can easily be generalized to a single many-to-many relationship.

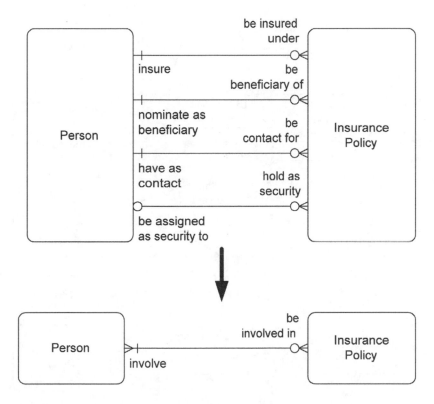

Figure 7-26. Generalization of One-to-Many Relationships

Bear in mind the option of generalizing only some of the one-to-many relationships, and leaving the remainder in place. This may be appropriate if one or two relationships are fundamental to the business, while the others are "extras." For example, we might choose to generalize the "beneficiary," "contact," and "security" relationships, but leave the "insure" relationship as it stands. This apparently untidy solution may in fact be more elegant from a programming point of view if many programs must navigate only the most fundamental relationship.

Generalizing Multiple One-to-Many Relationships to a Single One-to-Many Relationship

Generalization of multiple one-to-many relationships to form a single many-to-many relationship is appropriate if the individual one-to-many relationships are *mutually exclusive*, a more common situation than you might suspect. We can indicate this with an *exclusivity arc* (Figure 7-27).

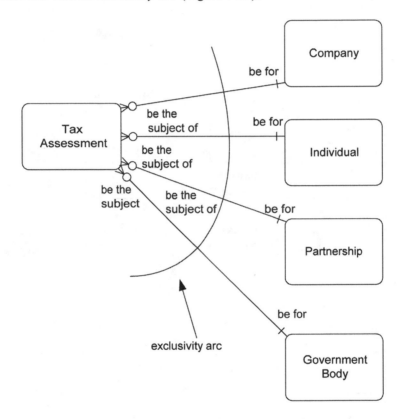

Figure 7-27. Diagramming Convention for Mutually Exclusive Relationships

In Chapter 4, I warned against introducing too many additional conventions and symbols. However, the exclusivity arc is useful enough to justify the extra complexity, and is even supported by some CASE tools[33]. As well as highlighting opportunities to generalize relationships, the exclusivity arc can suggest potential entity supertypes. In Figure 7-27, we are prompted to

---

[33] Notably Oracle Designer from Oracle Corporation.

supertype Company, Individual, Partnership, and Government Body, perhaps to Taxpayer (Figure 7-28).

I find that I use exclusivity arcs quite frequently during the modeling process, but seldom have many in the final model. In most cases, they end up disappearing when the individual relationships are replaced with a single relationship to the supertype.

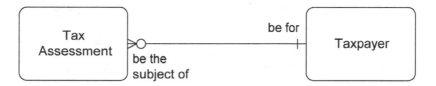

Figure 7-28. Entity Generalization Prompted by Mutually Exclusive Relationships

Myths and Folklore

As with any relatively new discipline, data modeling has acquired its own folklore of "guidelines" and "rules." Some of these can be traced to genuine attempts at encouraging good and consistent practice. Barker[34] labels a number of situations "impossible," when a more accurate description would be "possible but very uncommon." The sensible data modeler will be alerted by such situations, but will not reject a model *solely* on the basis that it violates some such edict.

Here are a few pieces of advice, including some of Barker's "impossible" relationships, which should be treated as warnings rather than prohibitions.

Entities without Relationships

"Every entity must participate in at least one relationship." It is perfectly possible, though not common, to have an entity that is not related to any other entity. A trivial case that arises occasionally is a single entity model. Other counter-examples appear in models to support management information systems, which may require data from disparate sources; for example, Economic Forecast and Competitor Profile. Entities representing rules among types may be stand-alone if the types themselves are not represented by entities (see Chapter 12).

---

[34] Barker, R., *CASE Method Entity Relationship Modelling*, Addison Wesley (1990).

Allowed Combinations of Cardinality and Optionality

Figure 7-29 shows examples of relationships with combinations of cardinality and optionality I have seen described as impossible.

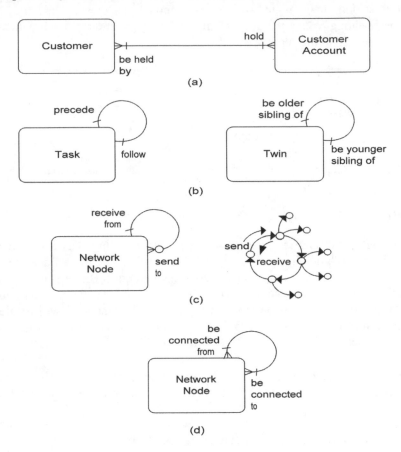

Figure 7-29. Examples of Unusual but Legitimate Relationships

The problem with relationships that are mandatory in both directions may be the "chicken and egg" question – which comes first? We can't record a customer without an account and we can't record an account without a customer. In fact, the problem is illusory, as we create both the customer and the account within one transaction. The database meets the stated constraints both at the beginning and the end of the transaction.

Remember also that self-referencing relationships need not only represent simple hierarchies, but may model loops.

Summary

The translation from relationships to foreign keys is not always straightforward. Problems may arise with overlapping foreign keys, foreign keys split across two tables, and "relationships" supported by comparison of attribute values. Selection of the best approach may involve trade-offs between consistency and rule enforcement.

Transferability is an important property of relationships, but most CASE products do not provide a means of representing it. It is important in constructing primary keys: the key of an entity at the "many" end of a transferable relationship should not include the key of the entity at the "one" end.

One-to-one relationships are useful in fostering creativity, by allowing an entity to be split into components, which may then be generalized separately. The two entities participating in a transferable one-to-one relationship should not be consolidated into a single entity.

Business relationships involving three or more entities are modeled using a resolution entity. The resulting two-entity relationships should then be checked individually for cardinality and optionality.

Much folklore surrounds relationships. Most combinations of optionality, cardinality, transferability, and recursion are possible in some context. The modeler should be alert for unusual combinations, but examine each case from first principles.

Chapter 8

Advanced Normalization

"Everything should be made as simple as possible, but not simpler."

– Albert Einstein

Introduction

In Chapter 2 we looked at normalization, a formal technique for eliminating certain problems from data models. Our focus was on situations in which the same facts were carried in more than one row of a table, causing the usual problems associated with redundancy: wasted space, more complex update logic, and the risk of inconsistency. In data structures that are not fully normalized, it can also be difficult to store certain types of data independently of other types of data. For example, we might be unable to store details of customers unless they currently held accounts with us.

The normalization techniques presented in Chapter 2 enable us to put data into third normal form (3NF). However, it is possible for a set of tables to be in 3NF and still not be *fully* normalized; they can still contain the sort of problems that we expect normalization to remove.

In this chapter, we look at three further stages of normalization: Boyce-Codd normal form (BCNF), fourth normal form (4NF), and fifth normal form (5NF).

We then discuss in more detail a number of issues that were mentioned only briefly in Chapter 2. In particular, we look further at the limitations of normalization in eliminating redundancy and allowing us to store data independently, and at some of the pitfalls of failing to follow the rules of normalization strictly.

Introduction to the Higher Normal Forms

I have left the discussion of the normal forms beyond 3NF until this chapter, not because the problems they address are unimportant, but because they occur much less frequently. Most tables in 3NF are already in BCNF, 4NF, and 5NF. The other reason for handling the higher normal forms separately is that they are a little more difficult to understand, particularly if we use only the relational notation, as in Chapter 2. Diagrams, which were not introduced until Chapter 3, make understanding much easier.

If you are a practicing data modeler, you are bound to encounter normalization problems beyond 3NF from time to time. Recognizing the patterns will save a lot of effort. And, because each higher normal form includes all the lower normal forms, you only need to be able to prove that a structure is in 5NF to be certain that it is also in 1NF through 4NF.

Common Misconceptions

Before we start on the specifics of each of the higher normal forms, it is worth clearing up a few common misconceptions.

Practitioners are frequently advised to normalize "only as far as third normal form," on the basis that further normalization offers little benefit or that it incurs serious performance costs. Let's look at these two issues in turn.

The argument that normalization beyond 3NF is not useful is only true in the sense that normalization to 3NF will remove most, and *usually* all, of the problems associated with unnormalized data. In other words, once we have put our data in 3NF, it is very often already in 5NF. But those data structures that are in 3NF but not in 5NF still exhibit serious problems, of very much the same sort we address in the earlier stages of normalization: redundancy; insertion, update, and deletion complexity; and difficulty in storing facts independently.

The performance argument is no more valid for the higher normal forms than it is for 3NF. As with the other normal forms, and good design practices in general, we may ultimately need to make compromises to achieve adequate performance, but our starting point should always be fully normalized structures. Denormalization is usually a last resort because the resulting redundancy, complexity, and incompleteness is expensive to manage.

The most common reason for not looking beyond 3NF is plain ignorance: not knowing how to proceed any further! Indeed, the general lack of understanding of the higher normal forms among practitioners has led to all sorts of data modeling advice and decisions, both good and bad, being paraded under the banner of 4NF and 5NF. Many an unsound data structure has been defended on the basis that it was required to achieve someone's spurious definition of 4NF or 5NF. And I have even seen perfectly sound design practices rejected on the basis that they lead to (incorrectly defined) 4NF or 5NF structures, which in turn are seen to be academic or detrimental to performance. If nothing else, an understanding of the higher normal forms will ensure that you are not swayed by these sorts of arguments.

Boyce-Codd Normal Form

Example of Structure in 3NF but Not in BCNF

Look at the model in Figure 8-1, representing data about an organization's branches, and how each branch services its customers.

Figure 8-2 shows the Branch-Customer Relationship table.

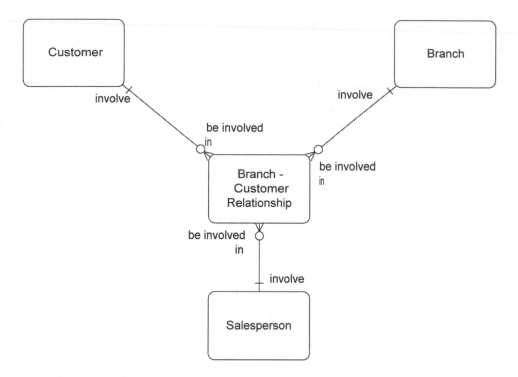

Figure 8-1. Customers, Salespersons, and Branches

BRANCH-CUSTOMER RELATIONSHIP (<u>Customer No</u>, <u>Branch No</u>, Visiting Frequency, Date Relationship Established, Salesperson No)

Figure 8-2. Branch-Customer Relationship Table

We should note three things about this table:

1. The table enforces the rule that each branch will serve a customer through only one salesperson, as there is only one Salesperson No for each combination of Customer No and Branch No. Note that this cannot be deduced from the E-R diagram alone. We need the additional information that Customer No and Branch No form the primary key of the table (hence each combination can occur only once).

2. The table is in 3NF: there are no repeating groups and every determinant of a nonkey item is a candidate key.

3. If we are told that each salesperson works for one branch only, the table still has some normalization problems. The fact that a particular salesperson belongs to a particular branch can appear in more than one row. In fact, it will appear in every row for that salesperson.

The underlying reason for the normalization problems is that we have a dependency between Salesperson No and Branch No: Salesperson No is a *determinant* of Branch No. (A reminder on the terminology: this means that for every Salesperson No, there is only one corresponding Branch No). The unusual feature here is that Branch No is part of the key. In all our examples so far, we have dealt with determinants of *nonkey* items. We now have a real problem. What we would like to do is set up a look-up table with Salesperson No as the key (Figure 8-3).

SALESPERSON (<u>Salesperson No</u>, Branch No)

Figure 8-3. Salesperson Look-up Table

But this doesn't really help. Although we can now record which branch a salesperson belongs to, regardless of whether he or she is serving any customers, we cannot take anything out of the original table. We would like to remove Branch No, but that would mean destroying the key.

The trick is to recognize that the original table has another candidate key. We could just as well have used a combination of Salesperson No and Customer No as the primary key (Figure 8-4).

CUSTOMER-SALESPERSON RELATIONSIIIP (<u>Customer No</u>, <u>Salesperson No</u>, Visiting Frequency, Date Relationship Established, Branch No)

Figure 8-4. Changing the Primary Key

The new key suggests a new name for the table. But now we are not even in 2NF. Salesperson No is a determinant of Branch No, so we need to split these off to another table (Figure 8-5).

CUSTOMER-SALESPERSON RELATIONSHIP (<u>Customer No</u>, <u>Salesperson No</u>, Visiting Frequency, Date Relationship Established)

SALESPERSON (<u>Salesperson No</u>, Branch No)

Figure 8-5. Normalized Tables

We now have our Salesperson look-up table, including the foreign key to Branch, and have eliminated the problem of repeated data. Technically, we have resolved a situation in which the tables were in 3NF but not BCNF.

Definition of BCNF

For a table to be in BCNF, we require that the following rule be satisfied:

Every determinant must be a candidate key.

In our example, Salesperson No was a determinant of Branch No, but was not a candidate key of Branch-Customer Relationship. Compare this with the definition of 3NF: "Every determinant of a *nonkey* column must be a candidate key. From the two definitions it should be clear that BCNF is stronger than 3NF in the sense that any table in BCNF will also be in 3NF.

Situations in which tables may be in 3NF but not BCNF can only occur when we have more than one candidate key – to be more precise, *overlapping* candidate keys. We can often spot them more quickly in diagrammatic form. In Figure 8-1, the Branch-Customer-Relationship box indicates a three-way relationship between Branch, Customer, and Salesperson. Approaching the problem from an Entity-Relationship perspective, we would normally draw the diagram as in Figure 8-6, recognizing the direct relationship between Salesperson and Branch. Any proposed relationship between Customer-Salesperson Relationship and Branch would then be seen as derivable from the separate relationships between Customer-Salesperson Relationship and Salesperson, and Salesperson and Branch. Taking this top-down approach, we would not have considered holding Branch No as an attribute of Customer-Salesperson Relationship, and the BCNF problem would not have arisen.

You may find it interesting to experiment with different choices of keys for the various entities in the flawed model of Figure 8-1. In each case, you will find that a normalization rule is violated or a basic business requirement not supported.

Enforcement of Rules Versus BCNF

There are some important issues about rules here, which can easily be lost in our rather technical focus on dependencies and normalization. In the original table we enforced the rule that a given customer was only served by one salesperson from each branch. Our new model no longer enforces that rule. It is now possible for a customer to be supported by several salespersons from the same branch. We have traded the enforcement of a rule for the advantages of normalization. It is almost certainly a good trade, because it is likely to be easier to enforce the rule within program logic than to live with the problems of redundant data, update complexity, and unwanted data dependencies.

But do not lose sight of the fact that changing a data structure, for whatever reason, changes the rules that it enforces. For example, in Figure 8-6, we enforce the rule that each salesperson is employed by a single branch; in the original example, the rule is only implicit in our description.

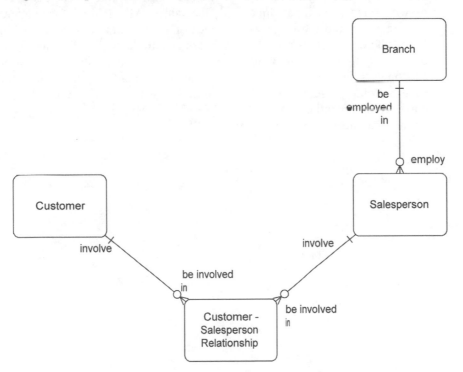

Figure 8-6. Revised E-R Model for Customer-Salesperson-Branch

A Note on Domain Key Normal Form

Finally, a slightly academic aside. You may occasionally see references to Domain Key Normal Form (DKNF), which requires that "All constraints are a consequence of domains or keys[35]." I should point out here that the word "domain" is unfortunately used in IT with at least three distinct meanings:

1. A set of business concepts, entities, and/or processes that make sense to consider together (a "business domain" or, better, a "subject area")

2. An attribute type at some (generally high) level of generality, such as a date, a Customer ID, a duration or a weight (see Chapter 10)

3. A set of values that an attribute is constrained to have.

It is the last of these meanings that applies in the definition of DKNF. The idea of a constraint being a consequence of a domain in the sense of a set of allowed values is a familiar one – if we say that the value of Gender must be drawn from a domain containing only the values "M" and "F," then Gender is constrained to those two values. The idea of a constraint being a consequence of the choice of keys is less obvious, but our example nicely illustrates it: if we choose a combination of Branch No and Customer No as the key of Branch-Customer Relationship in Figure 8-1, we are able to enforce the constraint that each customer is served by only one salesperson from each branch, but if we choose a combination of Customer No and Salesperson No as the key, we do not enforce the constraint.

---

[35] Fagin, R., "A Normal Form for Relational Databases That Is Based on Domains and Keys," *ACM Transactions on Database Systems* (September 1981).

Fourth Normal Form (4NF) and Fifth Normal Form (5NF)

Let's start our discussion of fourth and fifth normal forms with some good news. Once data structures are in BCNF, remaining normalization problems come up almost exclusively when we are dealing with "key only" tables; that is, tables in which every column is part of the key. Even then, they only apply to tables with three or more columns (and hence a three-or-more-part key). I will discuss 4NF and 5NF together, because the reason these two forms are defined separately has more to do with the timing of their discovery than anything else. We will not bother too much about a formal definition of 4NF, because the 5NF definition is simpler, and covers 4NF as well. (As mentioned earlier, any structure in 5NF is automatically in 4NF and all the lower normal forms).

Data in BCNF but Not in 4NF

Suppose we want to record data about financial market dealers, the instruments they are authorized to trade, and the locations at which they are allowed to operate. For example, Smith might be authorized to deal in stocks in New York, and in Government Bonds in London.

Let's suppose for the moment that:

> Each instrument can be traded only at a specified set of locations; and

> Each dealer is allowed to trade in a specified set of instruments.

So, if we wanted to know whether Smith could deal in Government Bonds in Sydney, we would ask:

> Can Government Bonds be traded in Sydney?

> Can Smith deal in Government Bonds?

If the answer to both questions was "yes", then we would deduce that Smith could indeed deal in Government Bonds in Sydney. Figures 8-7(a) and (b) show data models for this situation. In (b), the many-to-many relationships shown in (a) are resolved using all-key tables.

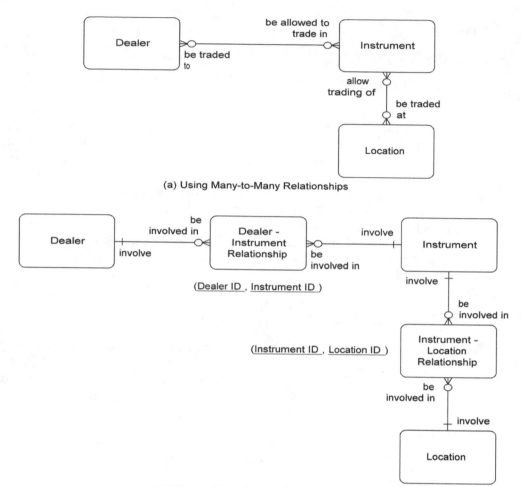

(a) Using Many-to-Many Relationships

(b) Many-to-Many Relationship Resolved

Dealer ID	Instrument ID
Smith	Ordinary Stocks
Smith	Government Bonds
Bruce	Futures
Bruce	Government Bonds

Instrument ID	Location ID
Government Bonds	New York
Government Bonds	London
Government Bonds	Sydney
Futures	Singapore
Futures	Tokyo
Options	Tokyo

Figure 8-7. Dealing Model with Sample Data

If we wanted to know all of the authorized combinations of dealer, location, and instrument, we could *derive* a list by combining (joining) the two tables to produce the single table in Figure 8-8.

Dealer	Instrument ID	Location ID
Dealer	Instrument ID	Location ID
Smith	Government Bonds	New York
Smith	Government Bonds	London
Smith	Government Bonds	Sydney
Bruce	Futures	Singapore
Bruce	Futures	Tokyo
Bruce	Government Bonds	New York
Bruce	Government Bonds	London
Bruce	Government Bonds	Sydney

Figure 8-8. Allowed Combinations of Dealer, Instrument, and Location

But what if this derived table was offered up as a solution in itself? It should be reasonably clear that it suffers from normalization-type problems of redundancy and non-independence of facts. Any authorized combination of instrument and location (e.g., the fact that Government Bonds can be traded in New York) will have to be repeated for each dealer permitted to trade in that instrument. This is the familiar normalization problem of the same fact being held in more than one row. Adding or deleting a combination will then involve updating multiple rows. A similar problem applies to combinations of dealer and instrument. Note that the derived table carries more attribute values than the two original tables. This is hardly surprising, considering that it contains duplicated data, but I have often seen derived tables offered up on the basis that they would save space.

Using the three-column table, we cannot record the fact that an instrument is allowed to be traded at a particular location unless there is at least one dealer who can trade in that instrument. Options can be traded in Tokyo, but this fact is not reflected in the derived table. Nor can we record the fact that the dealer can trade in a particular instrument unless that instrument can be traded at a minimum of one location. The derived table does not show that Smith is authorized to trade in ordinary stocks.

So our derived table appears to be unnormalized, but on checking, we find that it is in BCNF. Technically, our normalization problem is the result of a **multivalued dependency** (MVD[36]) and our table is not in 4NF (which specifies, roughly speaking, that we shouldn't have any nontrivial multivalued dependencies).

Rather than get sidetracked by more formal definitions of 4NF and multivalued dependencies, let's refer back to the E-R diagrams. In our one-table solution, we have tried to resolve two many-to-many relationships with a single table, rather than with two separate tables. The simple message is *not* to do this! Another way of looking at it is that we should record *underlying* rules rather than *derived* rules. This is a basic principle of data modeling we have encountered before when eliminating derivable attributes and relationships. It also provides a good starting point for understanding 5NF.

Fifth Normal Form (5NF)

Throughout the various stages of normalization, at least one thing has remained constant: each new stage involves splitting a table into two or more new tables. Remember: "Normalization is like marriage – you always end up with more relations."

We have taken care not to lose anything in splitting a table: we could always reconstruct the original table by *joining* (matching values in) the new tables. In essence, normalization splits each table into underlying tables from which the original table can be derived, if necessary.

The definition of 5NF picks up on this idea, and essentially tells us to keep up this splitting process until we can go no further. We only stop splitting when:

- Any further splitting would lead to tables that could not be joined to produce the original table, or

- The only splits left to us are trivial.

"Trivial" splits are defined as being splits based on candidate keys, such as those shown in Figure 8-9. A nontrivial split results in two or more tables with different keys, none of which is a candidate key of any other table.

---

[36] Instrument ID is said to *multidetermine* Location ID and Dealer ID, and conversely, these *multidetermine* Instrument No.

> EMPLOYEE (<u>Employee Number</u>, Name, Date of Birth)

can be trivially split into:

> EMPLOYEE-NAME (<u>Employee Number</u>, Name)
>
> EMPLOYEE-BIRTH (<u>Employee Number</u>, Date of Birth)

(a) Split Based on Primary Key

> DEPARTMENT (<u>Department Number</u>, Department Name, Location, Manager
>   Employee Number)

assuming Department Name is a candidate key, can be trivially split into:

> DEPARTMENT-LOCATION (<u>Department Number</u>, Department Name,
>   Location)
>
> DEPARTMENT-MANAGER (<u>Department Name</u>, Manager Employee Number)

(b) Split Based on Non-primary Candidate Key

Figure 8-9. Trivial Table Splits

The definition of 5NF differs in style from our definitions for earlier stages in normalization. Rather than picking on a certain type of anomaly to be removed, 5NF defines an end-point after which any further "normalization" would cause us to lose information. Applying the definition to the dealing authority problem, we have shown that the three-key table can be split into two without losing information; hence we perform the split.

The 5NF definition enables us to tackle a more complex version of the dealing authority problem. Suppose we introduce an additional rule: each dealer can only operate at a specified set of locations. The new model is shown in Figure 8-10 (a) and (b).

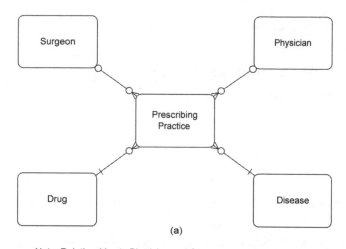

(a)

Note: Relationships to Physician and Surgeon are mutually exclusive.
Structure emerges clearly if we use the "mutually exclusive relationships" as described
in Chapter 5, or generalize Surgeon and Physician to Medical Practitioner.

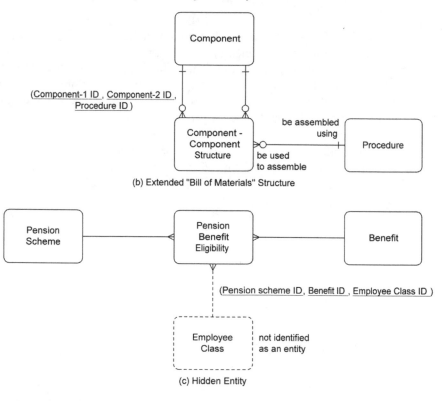

(b) Extended "Bill of Materials" Structure

(c) Hidden Entity

Figure 8-10. Dealing Model with Three Many-to-Many Relationships

Now that we have *three* separate relationships, could we resolve them all with one entity? I hope your intuitive answer based on the preceding discussion is "no." The resulting three-column table would have to be equivalent to the three separate tables, and hence could be broken down into them. Figure 8-11 shows the combined table, which still exhibits normalization problems. Changing one of the underlying rules may require multiple rows to be added or deleted, and we cannot record rules that do not currently lead to any valid combinations.

Dealer ID	Location ID	Instrument ID
Smith	Sydney	90-Day Bills
Smith	Sydney	180-Day Bills
Smith	Tokyo	90-Day Bills
Smith	Tokyo	10-Year Bonds
Philip	Sydney	180-Day Bills
Philip	Perth	180-Day Bills

is derivable from

Dealer ID	Location ID
Smith	Sydney
Smith	Tokyo
Philip	Sydney
Philip	Perth

Dealer ID	Instrument ID
Smith	90-Day Bills
Smith	180-Day Bills
Smith	10-Year Bonds
Philip	180-Day Bills

Location ID	Instrument ID
Sydney	90-Day Bills
Sydney	180-Day Bills
Tokyo	90-Day Bills
Tokyo	10-Year Bonds
Perth	180-Day Bills

Figure 8-11. Allowed Combinations Derivable from Underlying Rules

For example, deleting the rule that Smith can trade in Tokyo requires only one row to be removed from the underlying tables, but two from the derived table. As populations are increased from a few sample rows to hundreds or thousands of rows, the differences become correspondingly greater.

Technically, the three-column derived table is in 4NF, as there are no multivalued dependencies. (You may have to take my word on this!) But because we can split the table into three new tables and reconstruct it, it is not yet in 5NF. Splitting the table into three solves the problem.

In simple terms, then, the definition of 4NF effectively says that two many-to-many relationships cannot be resolved with one table. Satisfying 5NF requires that *two or more* many-to-many relationships are not resolved by a single table.

Recognizing 4NF and 5NF Situations

The first step in handling 4NF and 5NF problems is recognizing them. In a relational model, we can spot all-key tables with three or more columns; in an E-R diagram, we look for three (or more)-way resolution entities. I'm indebted to Chris Date for bringing to my attention the possibility of 4NF and 5NF being violated in situations other than those involving only "all key" tables. We will not pursue these cases here: suffice to say that:

- the examples we have seen and been able to construct involve business rules which we would not seriously contemplate enforcing in the data structure

- We have yet to encounter an example in practice.

Figure 8-12 shows some variations on the theme.

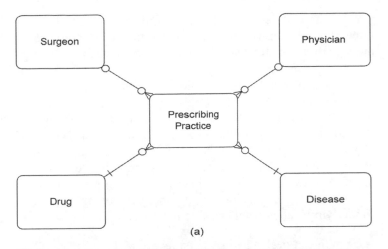

(a)

Note: Relationships to Physician and Surgeon are mutually exclusive.
Structure emerges clearly if we use the "mutually exclusive relationships" are described
in Chapter 6, or generalize Surgeon and Physician to Medical Practitioner.

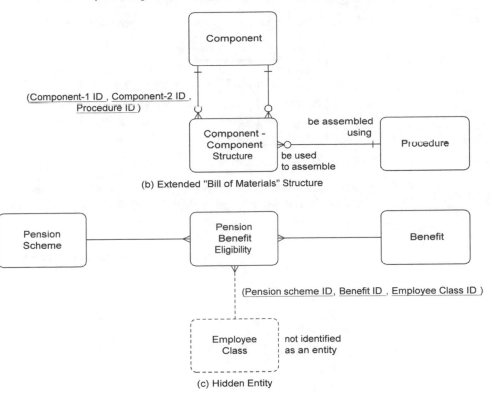

Figure 8-12. Structure Possibly Not in 4NF or 5NF

Any of these structures may exhibit 4NF or 5NF problems. Of course, some three-way relationships are perfectly legitimate. The problems arise only when they are derivable from simpler, more fundamental relationships.

If, in our dealer authority example, authorities were decided on a case-by-case basis, independent of underlying rules, then the three-way relationship entity would be valid. Figure 8-13 shows a table of values assigned in this way. You may find it an interesting exercise to try to break the table down into "underlying" tables – it can't be done because there are no underlying rules beyond "any combination may be independently deemed to be allowed." Any set of two-column tables will either fail to cover some permitted combinations, or generate combinations that are not permitted. For example, our "underlying" tables would need to record that:

1. Smith can deal in Sydney (first row of table).

2. Smith can deal in 180-day Bills (third row of table).

3. 180-day bills can be traded in Sydney (fourth row of table).

Dealer ID	Location ID	Instrument ID
Smith	Sydney	90-Day Bills
Smith	Tokyo	90-Day Bills
Smith	Tokyo	180-Day Bills
Philip	Sydney	180-Day Bills

Figure 8-13. Non-derivable Combinations

With these three facts we would derive a three-column table that recorded that Smith can deal in 180-day bills in Sydney – which, as we can see from the original table, is not true.

We have gone as far as we can in table splitting, and our tables are therefore in 5NF.

Checking for 4NF and 5NF with the Business Specialist

In determining whether all-key tables are in 4NF and 5NF, I suggest that you do not bother with the multivalued dependency concept. It's not an easy idea to grasp, and certainly not a good starting point for dialogue with a non-technical business specialist. And at the end of the day, you've only established 4NF, with 5NF still in front of you! Move straight to the 5NF definition, and look to see if there are simpler business rules underlying those represented by the multi-way relationship. Ask the following questions: On what (business) basis do we add a row to this table? On what basis do we delete rows? Do we apply any rules? Understanding the business reasons behind changes to the table is the best way of discovering whether it can be split further.

Don't expect the answers to these business questions to come easily. Often the business rules themselves are not well understood or even well defined. I've found it helpful to present business specialists with pairs of attribute values, or, equivalently, with a null value in one of the columns of a three-column table, and ask "Does this mean anything by itself?" Another useful technique is to look for possible nonkey attributes. Remember that 4NF and 5NF problems only occur with all key tables.

Further Reading on Higher Normal Forms

You will have little trouble finding texts and papers covering the higher normal forms with far more theoretical detail than presented here[37]. Most authors stick strictly with the relational notation, and don't offer a lot of context. For example, 4NF and 5NF problems usually show only one table to start with; this is technically adequate, but it can be hard coming to grips with the problem unless you imagine the attributes as foreign keys to "context" tables. If you have trouble following such examples, you are not alone! I suggest you draw an E-R diagram of the problem and add extra entities as we did in our 4NF and 5NF examples to show context.

---

[37] Kent, W., "A Simple Guide to the Five Normal Forms of Relational Database Theory," *Communications of the ACM* (February 1983) is a very readable paper at a similar level to this chapter.

Beyond 5NF – Splitting Tables Based on Candidate Keys

In defining 5NF, we indicated that the task of normalization was complete when the only ways of further splitting tables either resulted in our losing information or were based on candidate keys. 5NF is usually considered synonymous with "fully normalized."

However, as we saw in Chapter 7 in our discussion of one-to-one relationships, sometimes we *do* want to split tables based on candidate keys. We looked at an example of a manufacturing business that stored parts in bins according to the following rules:

1. Each type of part is stored in one bin only.

2. Each bin contains one type of part only.

It is interesting to reexamine this example from a normalization perspective. We might be offered the following table to represent data about parts and bins (Figure 8-14):

PART (<u>Part No</u>, Bin No, Bin Height, Bin Width, Bin Depth, Part Name, Quantity)

Figure 8-14. Parts and Bins

In checking normalization, our first reaction is likely to be that Bin No determines Bin Height, Bin Width and Bin Depth. But Bin No is a candidate key, so technically we don't have a problem. Nevertheless, most experienced data modelers would still feel uncomfortable about this structure, and with good reason. Think about the problem of moving parts from one bin to another. Suppose, for example, we want to swap the parts stored in two bins. We would expect this to involve changing only the Bin Nos for the relevant Parts. But with this structure, we will also need to update (swap) the values for Bin Height, Bin Width and Bin Depth, and of any other attributes that "belong to" bins rather than parts. If we split Bin and Part data into separate tables, we can avoid this problem, and this is indeed the best approach.

But what distinguishes the trivial Employee example in the previous section where we didn't split the original table? The difference is basically that Bin Nos and Part Nos represent different things in the real world, *and the relationship between them is transferable* i.e., a part may move from one bin to another and vice versa. Although the 5NF rule does not *require* us to split the data into separate tables, it does not prohibit us from doing so. The two resulting tables are still in 5NF.

This issue is seldom discussed in texts on normalization, and you need to be aware of it, if only to back up your intuition when a database designer argues that the two tables should be combined. In practice, if you start with an E-R diagram, you will almost certainly identify separate entities, with a one-to-one relationship between them, rather than a single entity.

Other Normalization Issues

In this section, we look more closely at some normalization issues I have mentioned only in passing so far. We start by examining some common misconceptions about what is achieved by normalization. We then look at some of the less usual situations that may arise when applying the standard rules of normalization.

Normalization and Redundancy

Normalization plays such an important role in reducing data redundancy that it is easy to forget that a model can be fully normalized and still contain redundant information. The most common situations are:

Overlapping Tables

Normalization does not address data redundancy resulting from overlapping classifications of data. If we recognize Teacher Number and Student Number as keys when normalizing data, we will build a Teacher table and a Student table. But if a teacher can also be a student, we will end up holding the values of any common attributes (such as Address) in both tables.

Derivable Data

If the value of one column can be calculated from others, normalization by itself will not eliminate the redundancy. If the underlying column values and the result are all within one row, normalization will remove the calculated value to a separate table (Figure 8-15), but we will still need to observe that the table itself is redundant and remove it.

> **ORDER ITEM** (<u>Order No</u>, <u>Item No</u>, Quantity Ordered, Quantity Delivered, Quantity Outstanding)
>
> **Quantity Outstanding = Quantity Ordered less Quantity Delivered**
>
> **Hence (Quantity Ordered, Quantity Delivered) determines Quantity Outstanding**

Normalizing:

> **ORDER ITEM** (<u>Order No</u>, <u>Item No</u>, Quantity Ordered, Quantity Delivered)
>
> **OUTSTANDING ORDER** (<u>Quantity Ordered</u>, <u>Quantity Delivered</u>, Quantity Outstanding)

Outstanding Order table contains no useful information and can be removed on this basis

Figure 8-15. Removing Derivable Data

Better to remove the derivable item at the outset rather than going through this procedure! Normalization will not help at all with values calculated from multiple rows (possibly from more than one table), such as "Total Quantity of this Item Outstanding," or Total Charge on an Invoice Header.

Another example of data derivable across multiple rows is a table used to translate contiguous numeric ranges – for example zip code ranges to States – and including columns First Number and Last Number. The value of Last Number is incremented by 1 to derive the next First Number; hence, if the Last Number column was lost, we could recreate it by subtracting 1 from the next highest First Number (Figure 8-16). (We do *not* need to have the rows sequenced to achieve this). This is, however, hardly elegant programming. And can we rely on the organization that defines the ranges to maintain the convention that they are contiguous? This therefore is a data structure holding redundant data that we should not take exception to.

Repeated data of this kind does not show up as the simple dependencies we tackle with normalization. As discussed in Chapter 2, the best approach is to remove columns representing *derivable* data (as distinct from dependent data), prior to starting normalization. But sometimes the distinction may be hard to make. And, as in the example of Figure 8-16, the sacrifice in programming simplicity and stability may not justify the reduction in redundancy. If in doubt, leave the questionable columns in, then review again after normalization is complete.

Australian Postcode Table

First Number	Last Number	State
2000	2999	New South Wales
3000	3999	Victoria
4000	4999	Queensland
5000	5999	South Australia
etc		

Figure 8-16. Data Derivable across Rows

Look-Up Tables Produced by Normalization

Each stage in normalization beyond 1NF involves the creation of "look-up" tables, insofar as some data is removed from the original table to another table where it can be "looked up" by citing the relevant value of the primary key. As well as reducing data redundancy, these tables allow us to record instances of the look-up data that do not currently appear in the unnormalized table. For example, we could record a hospital for which there were no operations or a customer who did not hold any accounts with us. We become so used to these look-up tables appearing during the normalization process that it is easy to miss the fact that normalization alone will not always generate all the look-up tables we require.

Imagine we have the table of employee information shown in Figure 8-17:

> **SKILL HELD (<u>Employee No</u>, <u>Skill Name</u>, Skill Description, Employee Name)**

Normalizing:

> **SKILL HELD (<u>Employee No</u>, <u>Skill Name</u>)**
>
> **EMPLOYEE (<u>Employee No</u>, Employee Name)**
>
> **SKILL (<u>Skill Name</u>, Skill Description)**

Figure 8-17. Normalization Producing Look-Up Table

Normalization gives us a table of all the employees and their names and another table of all the skill names and their descriptions. We have not only eliminated duplicate rows, but are now able to record a skill even though no employee has that skill. But, if we remove Skill Description from the problem, normalization will no longer give us a Skill table (which would contain the single attribute Skill Name). If we want such a list, we can certainly specify an all-key table consisting of Skill Name only. But normalization won't do it for us.

In discussing 4NF and 5NF situations, we raised the possibility of finding a nonkey attribute. If such an attribute, dependent on the full key, was added, our 4NF and 5NF problems would disappear. So why not just introduce a dummy attribute? The problem is much the same as that we encountered with employees and skills: normalization will provide an internally consistent model, but will not generate the look-up tables we require.

Suppose, for example, we found that there was a limit on the size of any deal for each combination of Dealer, Location, and Instrument. We now need the three-key table to hold the limit, even if our underlying rules are as in Figure 8-10, giving us the model in Figure 8-18. (This one can be a bit tricky to draw. Modelers often show relationships from the base entities rather than the intersection entities. I've shown it first with *all* foreign-key relationships, including redundant relationships, then with redundant relationships removed. I've also left off relationship names in the interest of minimizing clutter).

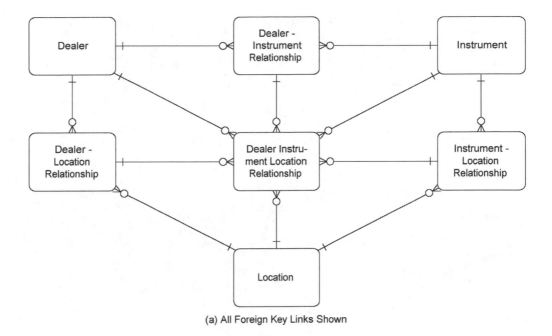

(a) All Foreign Key Links Shown

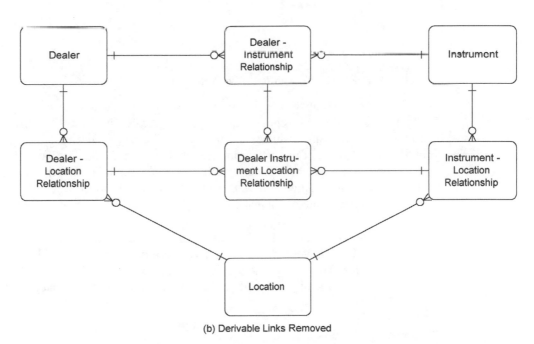

(b) Derivable Links Removed

Figure 8-18. Dealing Model including Dealer-Location-Relationship Entity

Can we now eliminate the three outside intersection entities, giving us the model in Figure 8-19?

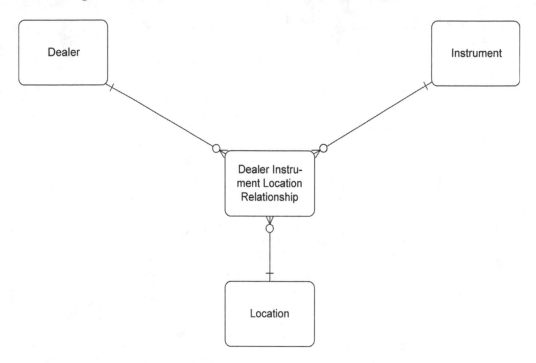

Figure 8-19. Dealing Model with Two-Way Intersection Entities Removed

At first glance, the answer may appear to be "yes." It would seem that we could find all allowable combinations of, say, dealer and location just by searching the relevant columns of the three-column Authority table. The problem is that some of the underlying (two-column) rules may not have given rise to any rows in the Authority table. For example, a dealer may be authorized to deal in New York, but may not yet be authorized to deal in any of the instruments available in that city.

In this example, if we started with just the Authority table, including Limit, no rule of normalization would lead us to the two-column intersection tables – the "look-up" tables. This is because they contain separate and additional facts to the information in the original table. But it is also the sort of thing that is easily missed.

The message here is that normalization is an adjunct to E-R modeling, not a substitute. In the two examples discussed here, we need to identify the look-up tables as entities during the E-R modeling phase.

Selecting the Primary Key after Removing Repeating Groups

In Chapter 2, we highlighted the importance of correctly identifying primary keys at each stage of the normalization process. Once the tables are in 1NF, this is usually straightforward: In progressing to BCNF, we identify determinants that become primary keys, and the new tables we create in moving beyond BCNF are "all key."

The point, therefore, at which mistakes in primary key identification are most often made is in moving from unnormalized structures to 1NF. We should already have a key for the original file (I don't use the word table here, as tables don't have repeating groups); the problem is to identify a key for the new table that represents the repeating group. The simplest approach is to look at the repeating group before removing it, and ask: What identifies one occurrence in the group, within the context of a given record in the file? Then, ask whether the context is necessary at all; in other words, do we need to add the primary key of the original file or not?

On most occasions, we *do* need to include the primary key of the original file. But this is not always so, and you will eventually get into trouble if you do so unthinkingly. Figure 8-20 shows normalization of a simple file of insurance agents and the policies they have sold.

AGENT (<u>Agent No</u>, Name, {Policy No, Customer ID, Amount Insured})

Policy No uniquely identifies Policy

Each policy is sold by only one agent

Normalizing:

AGENT (<u>Agent No</u>, Agent Name)

POLICY (<u>Policy No</u>, Customer ID, Amount Insured, Agent No*)

Figure 8-20. Repeating Group Table with Stand-Alone Key

The key of Policy is Policy No alone. Although Agent No must be included in the Policy table as a foreign key, it is not part of the primary key. Note that the result depends on the two business rules stated underneath the original model in Figure 8-20.

Surprisingly, a number of texts and papers do not recognize this possibility, or through choice of examples encourage a view that it does not occur.

Sequence of Normalization and Cross-Table Anomalies

We conclude this chapter with an example that illustrates the importance of rigorously following the rules of normalization, and of developing a sound E-R model at the outset.

Let's go back to the Customer-Salesperson example we used to illustrate BCNF earlier in this chapter (shown again in Figure 8-21):

CUSTOMER-SALESPERSON RELATIONSHIP (<u>Customer No</u>, <u>Salesperson No</u>, Visiting Frequency, Date Relationship Established)

SALESPERSON (<u>Salesperson No</u>, Branch No)

Figure 8-21. Customer-Salesperson Model

Recall that we ended up with two tables, and observed that the structure did not appear to enforce our original business rule that each branch serviced a customer through one salesperson only.

But think about the consequences of relaxing the rule. Let's assume that Date Relationship Established is the date that the branch established a relationship with the customer. Then, for a given customer, we will end up carrying that same date for each salesperson within the branch – exactly the sort of redundancy that we would expect normalization to eliminate. But both tables are fully normalized.

We can see the problem more clearly if we go back to our original single table (Figure 8-22).

CUSTOMER-SALESPERSON RELATIONSHIP (<u>Customer No</u>, <u>Salesperson No</u>, Visiting Frequency, Date Relationship Established, Branch No)

Figure 8-22. Original Customer-Branch-Salesperson Model (Not Fully Normalized)

If we now normalize, taking into account the revised rule, we see that Customer No + Branch No is a determinant of Date Relationship Established, and is no longer a candidate key. We therefore need to set up a separate table for these items, removing Date Relationship Established from the original table. Salesperson No is still a determinant of Branch No, so we set up another table for these items, removing Branch No from the original table. The result is shown in Figure 8-23.

> **CUSTOMER-SALESPERSON RELATIONSHIP (<u>Customer No</u>, <u>Salesperson No</u>, Visiting Frequency)**
>
> **CUSTOMER-BRANCH RELATIONSHIP (<u>Customer No</u>, <u>Branch No</u>, Date Relationship Established)**
>
> **SALESPERSON (<u>Salesperson No</u>, Branch No)**

Figure 8-23. Fully Normalized Customer-Branch-Salesperson Model

There are at least three lessons here:

1. If you find during normalization that assumptions you have relied on are incorrect, go back to the beginning – be very careful about "patching" the model.

2. Normalization alone is not completely reliable if you start with data already divided into more than one table. In practice, this is what we do virtually all of the time. So we need to analyze our E-R diagrams for problems as well as going through the steps of normalization.

3. Try to identify all the determinants at the start, and don't remove any part of them until all the columns they determine have first been removed. In this example, if we had removed Branch No first, we would have missed the "Branch No + Customer No determines Date Relationship Established" dependency.

Advanced Normalization in Perspective

In teaching the higher normal forms and some of the more subtle aspects of normalization, I am frequently challenged by experienced data modelers as to the value of normalization in practice. Their usual argument is that most of the problems that normalization addresses are more easily seen and resolved in the context of an E-R diagram. As we have seen in this chapter, there is a lot of truth in this.

But much of data modeling is about understanding, recognizing, and reusing patterns. The real value of the normalization to practitioners is in increasing their store of patterns, and backing it up with a deep understanding of the advantages and disadvantages of those patterns. When I see a three-way resolution entity, I automatically know to ask whether it can be derived from underlying relationships. If it is derivable, I can quote exactly the types of problems that will occur if it is not broken down into individual tables. (If I have forgotten, I need only look up a text on 4NF or 5NF, having classified the problem).

These patterns are useful enough that every professional data modeler needs to have them in his or her armory.

Summary

Tables in third normal form may not be in Boyce Codd, fourth, and fifth normal forms. Such tables will have problems with redundancy and incompleteness. The higher normal forms are frequently misunderstood by practitioners and hence ignored, or cited to support unsound modeling practices.

Boyce Codd Normal Form requires that every determinant be a candidate key. A table in 3NF will be in BCNF unless a key item is determined by a nonkey item. This will only occur if the table has multiple overlapping candidate keys. The problem is fixed by replacing the primary key with another candidate key and renormalizing.

A table in BCNF will only exhibit 4NF and 5NF problems if it has three or more columns, all of which are part of the key, and can be derived from "underlying" tables. In entity-relationship terms, 4NF and 5NF problems arise when two or more many-to-many relationships are (incorrectly) resolved using a single entity.

To use normalization as the prime modeling technique, we need to start with all data in a single table. In practice, we commence with an E-R model, which will embody numerous assumptions. Normalization will not challenge these.

Normalization by itself does not remove all redundancy from a model nor guarantee completeness.

Chapter 9

Primary Keys and Identity

"No entity without identity."

– Slogan cited by P. F. Strawson in *Contemporary British Philosophy*.

Basic Requirements and Trade-Offs

There is no area of data modeling in which mistakes are more frequently made, and with more impact, than the selection of primary keys. On the surface, the job is straightforward. For each entity, we need to select or create a set of attributes that will have a different combination of values for each entity instance.

Navigation around a relational database relies on being able to refer unambiguously to a specific row of a table by specifying the values of the primary key columns. Relationships are supported by foreign keys that need to point to one row only. Imagine the problems if we had an insurance policy referring to customer number "12345," but found two or more rows with that value in the Customer table.

So we require that a primary key be *unique*. Even more fundamentally, we require that it be *applicable* to all instances of an entity (and hence to all rows in the table). It isn't much good using Registration Number to identify vehicles if we need to keep track of unregistered vehicles. These are essential criteria.

There are further criteria that are highly desirable. We require that a primary key be *minimal*: we shouldn't add more columns beyond those necessary for uniqueness. A key should also be *stable*: it should not change value over time. The stability requirement is frequently overlooked in data modeling texts and training courses, but by observing it we can avoid the often complex program logic needed to cater to changes in key values.

A very simple way of meeting all of the requirements is to invent a new attribute for each entity, specifically to serve as its primary key, and to assign a different system-generated value to each entity instance. We refer to such an attribute as a **surrogate key**. Familiar examples are customer numbers, employee numbers, and account numbers allocated by the system.

But there might appear to be reasons for preferring a more "natural" identifier as the primary key. In the real world, we specify individual entity instances by using familiar identifiers such as names. When retrieving data from a computerized database, the natural identifier is often the most convenient starting point. Customers cannot always be expected to quote a customer number, and applicants for visas will nominate the name of their country of origin rather than our locally defined country number. In these cases the physical database designer will need to provide for efficient access to the relevant table using the natural identifier as well as the primary key. This is where indexes come in: although an index will be created automatically on the primary key to manage uniqueness and efficient joins between it and its corresponding foreign keys, additional indexes on other "natural" attributes can also be created to support efficient selection using those attributes. Despite this many contributors to database design projects confuse **primary keys** (which are purely for distinguishing instances) and **search keys** or **access keys** (which are the attributes by which selection of instances by users is most likely to occur). Do not let these arguments get in the way of adoption of the most appropriate column(s) as the primary key of the entity.

It is however true that using a natural identifier for the primary key can simplify programming logic by reducing the need to access look-up tables: if the primary key of Country is Country Name, it will have immediate meaning wherever it appears as a foreign key; but if we use a Country Number of our own invention, we will need to look up the country name in the Country table. So we have an argument for using a natural identifier as the primary key. Unfortunately, many natural identifiers fall short of meeting the requirement for applicability, uniqueness, and stability. Outside a database, these deficiencies may not cause any serious problems, because we are often working with only a subset of all of the instances (i.e., there is an implicit *context*) and can seek clarification if ambiguity arises. People's names are the obvious example: within the context of the people we know personally, names are *almost* unique, and on the odd occasion when two or more people have the same name, we resolve any ambiguity by specifying another distinguishing characteristic. But in navigating within a database, possibly containing millions of rows, we do not have the ability to seek clarification; we rely entirely on the uniqueness of primary keys.

Most arguments about primary keys come back to the choice between surrogate and natural keys. At the one extreme we have the argument that only surrogate keys should be used; at the other, a view that the natural key should always be the starting point, even if it needs to be modified or augmented to provide uniqueness. Most serious mistakes in primary key selection are the result of ill-considered decisions to use natural keys without reference to whether or not they meet the basic requirements.

Going back to these basic requirements can also help us resolve the majority of questions about primary keys that arise in practice. In this chapter, we look first at the basics of primary key selection, then draw on these to examine some specific issues that arise frequently in practice: surrogate keys, structured keys, partially null keys, and alternative candidate keys.

Applicability

We must be able to determine a value for the primary key for every entity instance. Watch for the following traps when attempting to use natural keys.

Special Cases

Often our understanding of a business area is based on a few examples that may not be adequately representative. It is worth adopting the discipline of asking the business specialists "Are there any cases in which we would not have a value for any of these (primary key) attributes?" Do we ever encounter persons without a Social Security number? Or flights without a flight number? Or sound recordings without a catalogue number? Surprisingly often, such special cases emerge. We are then faced with a choice of:

1. Setting up a mechanism to allocate key values to these cases

2. Excluding them from the entity definition altogether, or

3. Rejecting the proposed primary key, usually in favor of a surrogate key.

Selecting option 2 will lead to a change in the model at the entity level, as a new entity is added to cater to the special cases, or the overall scope of the model modified to exclude them.

Data Unavailable at Time of Entry

All components of a primary key need to be available at the time a row is first stored in the database. This can sometimes be a problem if we are building up data progressively. For example, we may propose Customer Number plus Departure Date as the primary key of Travel Itinerary. But will we always know the departure date at the time we first record information about an itinerary? Are we happy to hold off recording the travel plans until that date is available? Again, a surrogate key is often the simplest solution.

Broadening of Scope

One of the most common causes of problems with keys is a broadening of the original scope of a system, resulting in tables being used to hold data beyond that originally intended. Frequently, the primary key is not applicable to some of the instances embraced by the more general definition. For example, we may decide to market our products to individual persons, where in the past we only dealt with companies. In this case, a government-assigned Company Number will no longer be suitable as a primary key for Customer. Or our book-selling business may broaden its product range to include stationery, and International Standard Book Number will no longer be an appropriate key for Product.

One way of reducing the likelihood of being caught by scope changes is to be as precise as possible in entity naming and definition: name the original entity Company rather than Customer, or Book Title rather than Product. Then use supertyping to explore different levels of generalization, such as Customer and Product. The resulting model will prompt questions such as "Are we potentially interested in customers who are not companies?" It now comes back to the familiar task of choosing a level of generalization, and a corresponding key, that will accommodate business change. We can't expect to get it right every time, but most problems which arise in this area are a result of not having addressed the generalization issue at all, rather than coming up with the wrong answer.

Uniqueness

Uniqueness is the most commonly cited requirement of primary keys. To reiterate: *you can't build a relational database without unique primary keys.* Indeed, the term "unique primary key" is a tautology – if a combination of attributes is not unique, it does not qualify to be called a primary key. There are three ways you can be reasonably sure that a key will be unique.

The first is that it is intrinsically unique, as a result of the nature of the real world. A fingerprint or signature qualifies on this criterion, as do coordinates of a location, if sufficiently precise. Such keys occur only rarely in practice.

The second is that you, as the designer, control the allocation of key values, and can therefore ensure that no value is allocated more than once. Surrogate keys, such as computer-generated sequential Customer Numbers, are the obvious examples. Another possibility is a **tie-breaker** – a (usually sequential) number added to an "almost unique" set of attributes. A common example is a numeric suffix added to a person's or organization's name, or part of the name ("Drummond 0043.") Why use a tie-breaker when it would seem at least as easy to use a sequential number for the whole key? Performance, real or imagined, is usually the reason. The designer aims to be able to use a single index to provide access on both the primary key and a natural key (the first part of the primary key). In keeping with the "one fact per attribute" rule introduced in Chapter 2 (and discussed in detail in Chapter 10), a tie-breaker should be handled as a separate attribute, rather than simply appended to the natural key. And, as always with natural keys, you need to make sure that the stability requirement is met.

The third possibility is that someone else with the same intention as you has allocated the key values. A vehicle registration number is allocated by a state authority with the intention that it be unique in the issuing state. In these cases, the most common problem is a difference between our scope of interest and theirs. For example, we may be interested in vehicles in more than one state. We can address this problem by including in the key an attribute to identify the issuer of the number e.g., State of Registration. Again, we need to think about possible extensions to the scope of the system. Racehorse names may be unique within a country, but what happens if we want to extend our register to cover overseas events, or greyhounds?

The advantage of using someone else's scheme, particularly if it is widely accepted, is that the primary key will be useful in communicating with the world outside the system. Customers will be able to quote and verify registration numbers, and we avoid singularity problems (discussed below). But there is an element of faith in tying our primary key to another's decisions. We need to be reasonably confident that the key issuer's entity definition will remain in line with our own, and that the key also meets basic standards of soundness. Many a system has been severely disrupted by an external decision to change a numbering scheme or to reuse old numbers.

If you are not using one of these three schemes, you need to ask yourself, "How can I *guarantee* that the key will be unique?" A common mistake is to use a "statistical reduction" approach, best illustrated by the problem of choosing a primary key for persons (customers, employees, etc). The modeler starts with a desire to use Person Name as the key, prompted by its obvious real world significance as an identifier. We all know that names are not unique, but what about Name plus Date of Birth? Or Name plus Date of Birth plus Zip Code plus...? The problem is that while we can reduce the possibility of duplicates, we can never actually eliminate it, and it takes only one exception to destroy the integrity of the database. And don't forget that human beings are remarkably good at deliberately causing odd situations, including duplicates, if doing so isn't actually impossible or illegal! The fact that a primary key of this type is almost unique might prompt you to use a tie-breaker as described above: note that while this will solve the uniqueness problem it will not solve the problem that Name and Zip Code are not *stable* (they can change).

Minimality

A primary key should not include attributes beyond those required to ensure uniqueness. Having decided that Customer Number uniquely identifies a customer, we should not append Customer Name to the key. There are two reasons for this.

Firstly, whenever a primary key with an extra attribute appears as a foreign key, we will have normalization problems, as the extra attribute will be determined by the "real" key. For example, if we held both Customer Number and Customer Name in a Purchase table, we would be carrying Customer Name redundantly for each purchase made by the customer. A change of name would require a complex update procedure.

Secondly, it is possible to insert multiple rows representing the same real-world object. If, for example, Customer Name were included in the primary key of the Customer table, it would then be possible to have two different rows with the same customer number but different names which would be confusing to say the least.

Minimality problems don't often occur, and are usually a result of simple errors in modeling or documentation rather than an attempt to achieve any particular objective such as performance. They should be picked up by normalization, and there should be no argument about correcting them.

Stability

Stability is the subtlest of the design considerations for primary keys, and the one least discussed in the literature on data modeling and relational database – hence the one most often violated. The idea is that a given real world entity instance should keep the same value of the primary key for as long as it is recorded in the database. For example, a given customer should retain the same customer number for as long as he or she is a customer.

The first reason for using stable primary keys is that they are used elsewhere as foreign keys. Changing the value of a primary key is therefore not a simple process, because all of the foreign key references will also need to be updated. We will need to write program logic to cater to this, and maintain it whenever another table carrying the relevant foreign key is added to the database design. An even more serious problem arises with archived and other external data – data that is not in the database proper, but held on microfiche, tape, paper, or other backup media. What do we do with the foreign key references there? How do we find old versions of a table row whose primary key has changed?

The foreign key maintenance problem is usually the most effective method of convincing programmers and physical database designers of the need for stable primary keys. But there is an even more fundamental reason for not allowing changes to primary key values. Think about our customer example again. The customer may, over time, change his/her name, address, or even date of birth if it was misstated or entered incorrectly. To match historical data with the current picture, we require some attribute or combination of attributes that is not only unique, but does not change over time. The requirement for uniqueness points us to the primary key; to be able to conveniently match current and historical data, we require that it be stable.

Another way of looking at the issue is this: in a relational database, all of the nonkey columns hold data about real world entity instances; but the key represents the *existence* of real world entity instances. In other words, a new primary key value corresponds to a new entity instance being recorded in the database, while deletion of a primary key value corresponds to the record of an entity instance being deleted from the database. Without this discipline it is difficult to distinguish a change of key value from the deletion of one entity instance and the addition of another.

Admittedly, it is possible to build workable databases without stable primary keys, and much complicated program logic has been written to support key changes. But the *simplest* approach is to adhere rigidly to the discipline of stable primary keys. Stability can always be achieved by using surrogate keys if necessary. There is invariably a payoff in terms of simpler, more elegant databases and systems. *In all of the examples in this book, I assume that the primary keys are stable*. If you require further convincing that unstable primary keys cause complexity, I suggest you try modifying some of the time-dependent models in Chapter 11 to accommodate primary key changes.

A final illustration: in the insurance business, there are many options that we may want to add to or delete from a policy in order to provide the cover required by the client over the years. At some point, however, the business may decide that a particular change should not be accommodated under the original policy, and a replacement policy should be issued. It is important for the business to distinguish between changes and replacements to allow consistent compliance with legislation and management reporting ("How many new policies did we issue this month? What is the average cost of issuing a new policy?") The supporting information systems need to reflect the distinction, and the primary key of Policy provides the mechanism. We can change virtually every nonkey attribute of a policy, but if the key value remains the same, we interpret the table row as representing the same policy. Conversely, we can leave all other attribute values unchanged, but if the key value changes, we interpret it as a new policy being recorded with identical characteristics to the old.

Stability, then, is tied very closely to the idea of identity. In some cases, such as persons, the definition of identity is so well entrenched that we would have to be creative modelers indeed to propose alternatives (although it is worth thinking about how a database would handle the situation of a police informer being given a "new identity," or even an employee who resigns and is later reemployed). In others, such as insurance policies, products, and organization units, a variety of definitions may be workable. The data modeler needs to capture in entity definitions the essence of what distinguishes one instance from another, and define the primary key accordingly.

Structured Keys and Weak Entities

Problems with Structured Keys

A structured key is simply a key made up of more than one attribute. Because of this, structured keys are sometimes also called "concatenated keys" or "composite keys." The term also covers the situation in which several distinct attributes have been combined to form a single-column key, in contravention of the "one fact per column" rule introduced in Chapter 2. Structured keys often cause problems, but not because there is anything inherently wrong with multi-attribute keys. Rather, the problem keys usually fail to meet one or more of the basic requirements discussed above, in particular stability.

Structured keys are particularly prone to a special kind of stability problem – running out of numbers – which can ultimately require that we reallocate *all* key values. The more parts to a key, the more likely we are to exhaust all possible values for one of them. This is where the problems really start, for rather than tackling a complete redefinition of the key, we will be tempted to add new data and meaning to other parts of the key in order to keep the overall value unique. In turn, we now have to write program logic to extract the meaning of the values held in these parts.

Most experienced data modelers have a horror story to tell in this area. I recall one organization that had a team of four staff members working full time on allocating location codes, and another that had to completely redevelop a system because they ran out of insurance agent identifiers (the agent identifier consisted of a State Code, Branch Code within state, and Agent Number within state and branch; when all agent numbers for a particular branch had been allocated, new numbers were assigned by creating phantom branches and states). As a result of problems of this kind, it is often suggested that structured keys be avoided altogether. However, a structured key should involve no more risk than a single-column key, as long as we make adequate provision for growth of each component, and do not break the basic rules of column definition and key design.

Using Structured Keys to Control Transferability

Look at Figure 9-1 and note the use of the nontransferability symbol introduced in Chapter 6. Most data modelers would automatically propose a key for Stock Holding which included the primary keys of Stock and Client (e.g., Stock ID + Client ID + Effective Date). But few data modelers would suggest that the primary key of Client should include the primary key of Investment Adviser. And rightly so. The difference in the two situations is that the structured key of Stock Holding will be stable, because the Stock ID and Client ID associated with a given Stock Holding will never change (the Stock Holding cannot be transferred). On the other hand, a client may be transferred to a new Investment Adviser – hence a key that contained the primary key of Investment Adviser would not be stable.

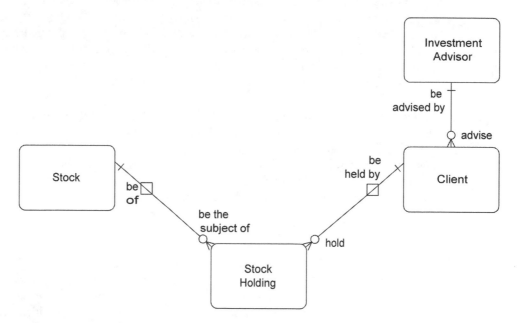

Figure 9-1. Transferability Influencing Key Choice

To summarize the rule: we only include the key of another entity in a primary key if that other entity is at the "one" end of a mandatory[38] nontransferable relationship.

We can look at this rule from another perspective. If we are rigorous in obeying the rule that primary keys be stable, then a decision to use a concatenated key is a way of *enforcing* nontransferability. In the example, we cannot record a transfer of a Stock Holding from one Client to another, because that would mean changing the value of the key, which we are not allowed to do. The most common examples of nontransferable relationships are those arising from resolving many-to-many or multi-entity real world relationships. The resulting relationships are intrinsically nontransferable, as each resolution entity instance represents a real world relationship between two (or more) specific entity instances: changing one or both of those instances would be seen as deleting the old real world relationship and establishing a new one.

Weak Entities

Chen[39] introduced the concept of a **weak entity**, an entity that relies on another for its identification. In our example, Stock Holding would be a weak entity, *if we decided to use Client ID and/or Stock ID in constructing its primary key*. An entity with a stand-alone key (i.e., a non-weak entity) is called a **regular entity**. The primary key of a weak entity is sometimes called a **weak key**. These are useful terms to have in our vocabulary for describing models and common structures (for example, the split foreign key situation covered in Chapter 7). Chen introduced special diagramming symbols to distinguish weak entities (Figure 9-2), but I find the nontransferability concept more useful at the E-R modeling stage, when we may not yet have identified or designed attributes and keys. Of course, if you stick strictly to the practice of always enforcing nontransferability by using appropriately structured keys, then nontransferability and weakness will be one and the same.

---

[38] An exception to the mandatory requirements is discussed in Chapter 8.

[39] "The Entity Relationship Model – Toward a Unified View of Data," *ACM Transactions on Database Systems* (March 1976).

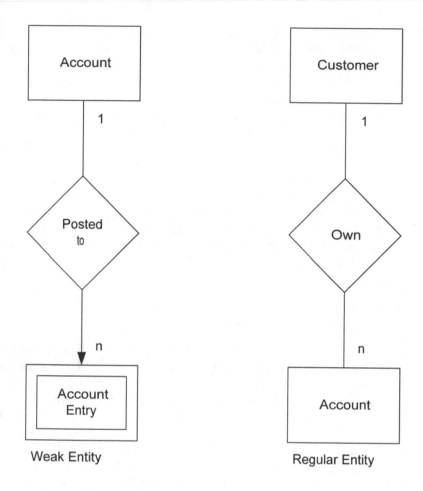

Figure 9-2. Chen's Weak Entity Convention

We can usually come close to consistently using weak keys for nontransferable entities, but will sometimes find that a nontransferable entity has an excellent stand-alone key available. We may then choose to trade enforcement of nontransferability for the convenience of using an available "natural" key. For example, it may not be possible for a visa to be transferred from one person to another; hence we could include the key of Person in the key of Visa, but we may prefer to use a well-established stand-alone Visa Number.

Programming and Structured Keys

Structured keys may simplify programming and improve performance by providing more data items in a table row without violating normalization rules. In Figure 9-3, we are able to determine which department a leave application comes from without needing to access the Employee table. But can an employee transfer from one department to another? If so, the primary key of Employee will be unstable – almost certainly an unacceptable price to pay for a little programming convenience and performance. If performance were critically affected by the decision, it would probably be better to carry Department ID redundantly as a non-primary key item in the Leave Application table.

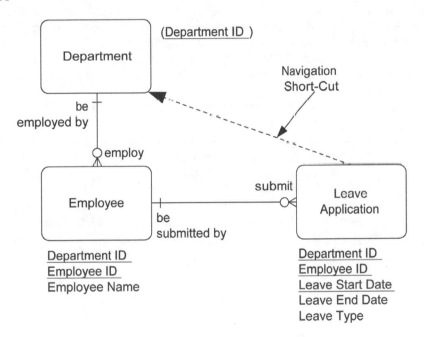

Figure 9-3. Navigation Short Cut Supported by Structured Key

Performance Issues with Structured Keys

Although performance is not our first concern as data modelers, it can be an important factor in deciding between alternatives that rate similarly against other criteria. In some cases, performance issues are paramount, and we should not leave it to the physical database designer to find models that are of similar utility to ours but perform better. Structured keys may affect performance in three principal ways:

First, they may reduce the number of tables that need to be accessed by some transactions, as in Figure 9-3, discussed above.

Second, they may reduce the number of access mechanisms that need to be supported. Take the Stock Holding example from Figure 9-1. If we proposed a stand-alone surrogate key for Stock Holding, it is likely that the physical database designer would need to construct three indexes – one for the surrogate key, and one for each of the foreign keys to Client and Stock. But if we used Client ID + Stock ID + Date, the designer could probably get by with two indexes, resulting in a saving in space and update time.

Third, as the number of attributes in a structured key increases, so does the size of table and index records. It is not unknown for a table at the bottom of a deep hierarchy to have seven or more attributes in its key. Indeed, I recall a key for insurance risk that reflected the following hierarchy: State; Branch; District; Agent; Client; Policy Class; Original Issuer; Policy; Risk – a nine part key, used throughout the organization. In this case, the key had been constructed in the days of serial files, and reflected neither a true hierarchy nor nontransferable relationships.

When we encounter large keys, we have the option of introducing a stand-alone surrogate key at any point(s) in the hierarchy, reducing the size of the primary keys from that point downwards. Doing so will prevent us from fully enforcing nontransferability and will cost us an extra access mechanism. In the record library model of Figure 9-4, we can add a surrogate key Track ID to Track, as the primary key, and use this to replace the large foreign key in Performer Role. The primary key of Performer Role would then become Track ID + Performer ID. However, the model would no longer enforce the fact that a track could not be transferred from one record to another.

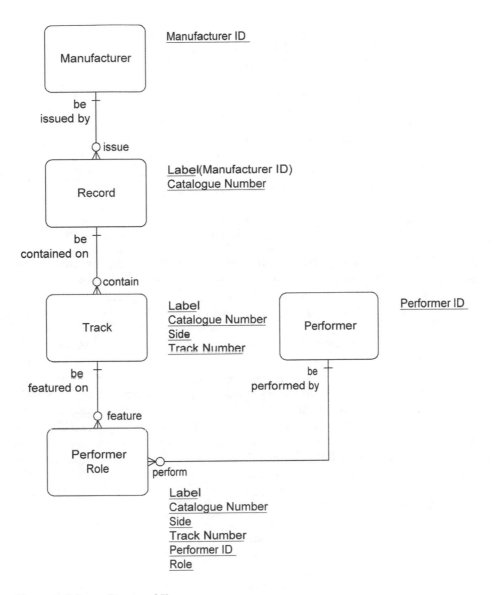

Figure 9-4. Large Structured Keys

Surrogate Keys

The requirements of applicability, uniqueness, minimality, and stability seem to have a simple answer: just create a single primary key attribute for each entity, and use the system to generate a unique value for each occurrence. For example, we could specify Branch ID as the primary key of Branch, and number the first Branch "1," the second "2," and so forth. I refer to all such attributes as **surrogate keys**, although some modelers reserve the term for keys that are not only system-generated, but are kept invisible to system users.

When to Use Surrogate Keys

The two major arguments against surrogate keys are programming complexity and performance. As discussed in the introduction to this chapter, whenever a surrogate key appears as a foreign key, we need to access a look-up table to find the corresponding natural identifier. This situation occurs often enough that programmers are frequently opponents of surrogate keys. Performance is not usually a problem if the look-up tables are small and can reside in primary storage.

The more common performance-related issue with surrogate keys is the need for additional access mechanisms such as indexes to support access on both the surrogate and natural keys. In databases handling high volumes of new data, problems may also arise with contention for "next available numbers." Some database management systems now provide sophisticated mechanisms specifically to address this problem.

A sensible general approach is to use:

- Natural identifiers when they are available always subject to the basic requirements of applicability, uniqueness, and stability

- Weak keys when the relevant entity is nontransferable

- Stand-alone surrogate keys if no suitable natural identifier is available, and the entity is transferable.

But remember when specifying surrogate keys that simply specifying "Customer ID" as the key of Customer does not solve the problem of matching real world customers with rows in a database table. However, in many cases we are able to "change the world" by making the surrogate key values available and suggesting or insisting that they be used when data is to be retrieved. This is easier to insist upon if the keys are used only within our organization, rather than externally, or if there is some incentive for using them. In general it's relatively easy to get employees and suppliers to play by our rules; customers can be more difficult!

Should Surrogate Keys Be Visible?

Theoreticians often suggest that surrogate keys be hidden from system users, and used only as a mechanism for navigation within the database. The usual arguments are:

- If the surrogate keys are visible, users may begin to attribute meaning to them ("the Contract Number is between 5000 and 6000 – hence it is managed in London.") This meaning may not be reliable.

- We may wish to change the keys, perhaps as a result of not making adequate provision for growth or to consolidate existing databases.

I have frequently seen the first problem described above, and it usually arises when specific ranges of numbers are allocated to different locations, subtypes, or organization units. In these cases we *can* place a meaning on the code, but the meaning is "issued by," which is not always equivalent to "permanently responsible for." The problem can be avoided by making it more difficult or impossible for the users to interpret the numbers, by allocating multiple small ranges, or assigning available numbers randomly to sites. At the same time, we need to make sure the real information is available where it is required so the user doesn't need to resort to interpreting the code.

The second problem described above should not often arise. Changing primary keys is a painful process even if the keys are hidden. We can insure against running out of numbers by allowing an extra digit or two. When designing the system, we should look at the likelihood of other databases being incorporated, and plan accordingly: simply adding a Source attribute to the primary key to identify the original database will usually solve the problem. If we have not made this provision, one of the simpler solutions is to assign new surrogate keys to one set of data, and to provide a secondary access mechanism based on the old key, which is held as a nonkey item.

In my experience, the disadvantages of a visible key are usually outweighed by the advantage of being able to specify simply the row we want in a table. One example of surrogate keys that is in common use throughout the world is the booking number used in airline reservation systems (sometimes called a "record locator.") If a customer provides his/her record locator, access is available quickly and unambiguously to the relevant data. If the customer doesn't have the number available, the booking can be accessed by a combination of other attributes, but this is intrinsically a more involved process.

Surrogate Keys and Subtypes

If we decide to define a surrogate key at the supertype level, that key will be applicable to all of the subtypes. An interesting question then arises if we choose to implement at the subtype level: should we allow instances belonging to different subtypes to take the same key value? For example, if we implement Criminal Case and Civil Case tables, having previously defined a supertype Legal Case, should we allocate numbers as in Figure 9-5 (a) or as in 9-5(b?) If contention for "next available number," as described earlier in this section, is not a serious problem, I recommend you choose option (b). This provides some recognition of the supertype in our relational design. A supertype table can then be constructed using the "union" operator, and easily related ("joined") to tables that hold Legal Case numbers as foreign keys (Figure 9-6).

CRIMINAL CASE   **CIVIL CASE**

Case ID	Date Scheduled	Case ID	Date Scheduled
000001	01/02/93	000001	01/02/93
000002	01/03/93	000002	01/03/93
000003	01/04/93	000003	01/05/93
000004	01/06/93	000004	01/07/93

(a) Primary Keys Allocated Independently

CRIMINAL CASE   **CIVIL CASE**

Case ID	Date Scheduled	Case ID	Date Scheduled
000001	01/02/93	000002	01/02/93
000005	01/03/93	000003	01/03/93
000006	01/04/93	000004	01/05/93
000008	01/06/93	000007	01/07/93

(b) Primary Keys Allocated from a Common Source

Figure 9-5. Allocation of Key Values to Subtypes

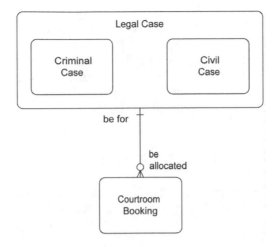

Original Tables:

CRIMINAL CASE (<u>Case ID</u>, Date Scheduled, …)

CIVIL CASE (<u>Case ID</u>, Date Scheduled, …)

COURTROOM BOOKING (<u>Courtroom ID</u>, <u>Date</u>, <u>Period</u>, Case ID*, …)

After Union of Criminal Case and Civil Case Tables:

LEGAL CASE (<u>Case ID</u>, Date Scheduled, …)

COURTROOM BOOKING (<u>Courtroom ID</u>, <u>Date</u>, <u>Period</u>, Case ID*)

Figure 9-6. Combining Subtypes

Singularity

Finally, one of the most difficult problems with surrogate keys is the possibility of allocating more than one value to the same real world object, a violation of *singularity*, which requires that each real world object have only one key value, and hence only one row in the relevant database table. This happens with natural keys as well as surrogate keys – for example, a person may have aliases – but less commonly. Merging two or more rows once the problem has been discovered can be a complicated business, especially if foreign keys also have to be consolidated.

The only real solution is good design of data capture procedures, to ensure that duplicates are picked up at data entry time. For example, a company might ask a "new" customer: "Do you already have business with us?" and back this up with a check for matching names, addresses, etc. Making the employee who captures the details responsible for fixing any duplicates has proved a useful approach to improving the quality of checking.

Null and Partially-Null Keys

There are plenty of good reasons why primary keys should never be allowed to be null (empty). One of the most obvious is the problem of interpreting foreign keys – does null mean "no corresponding row" or is it a pointer to the row with the null primary key?

But conventional wisdom also dictates that no *part* (i.e., no column) of a primary key should ever hold a null value. Some of the arguments are to do with sophisticated handling of different types of nulls, which is currently of more academic than practical relevance, since the null handling of most database management systems is very basic. In fact none, to my knowledge, allows for any column of a primary key to be null. However there are situations where not every attribute of the primary key of an entity has a legitimate value for every instance. In these situations you should be able to use "blank" (a zero-length character string) or "space" (a character string holding one space character) for those attributes in those instances.

The issue often arises when implementing a supertype whose subtypes have distinct primary keys. For example, an airline may want to implement a Service entity whose subtypes are Flight Service (identified by an Flight Number) and Accommodation Service (identified by an alphabetic Accommodation Service ID). The key for Service could be Flight Service No + Accommodation Service ID, where one value would always be logically null (physically blank or space). This is a workable, if inelegant, alternative to generalizing the two to produce a single alphanumeric attribute.

A variant of this situation is shown in Figure 9-7. The weak keys for Branch and Department are legitimate as long as branches cannot be transferred from one division to another and departments cannot be transferred from one branch to another.

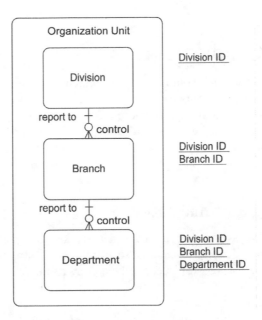

Figure 9-7. Use of a Primary Key with Logically Null Attributes

But if we decide to implement at the Organization Unit level, giving us a simple hierarchy, can we generalize the primary keys of the subtypes into a primary key for Organization Unit? The proposed key would be Division ID + Branch ID + Department ID. For divisions, Branch ID and Department ID would be logically null, and for branches Department ID would be logically null. Again we have logically null values in the primary key, and again we have a solution that is workable, which I have seen employed successfully in practice.

The choice of key in this example has some interesting implications. The foreign key, which points to the next level up the hierarchy, is contained in the primary key (e.g., Branch ID "0219" contains the key of Division "02.") This limits us to three levels of hierarchy; our choice of primary key has imposed a constraint on the number of levels and their relationships. With a surrogate key, any such limits would need to be enforced outside the data structure. This is another example of a structured key imposing constraints that we may or may not want to enforce for the life of the system.

Multiple Candidate Keys

Quite frequently we encounter tables in which there are two or more columns (or combinations of columns) that could serve as the primary key. There may be two or more natural keys or, more often, a natural and a surrogate key. We refer to each possible key as a **candidate key**. There are a few rules we need to observe, and some traps to watch out for when there is more than one candidate key.

Choosing a Primary Key

We must always nominate a single primary key for each entity. One of the most important reasons for doing so is to specify how relationships will be supported: the foreign key needs to be a copy of the primary key, not just any candidate key[40].

Selection should be based on the requirements and issues discussed earlier in this chapter. In addition to comparing applicability, stability, structure, and meaningfulness, we should ask, "Does each candidate key represent the same thing for all time?" As discussed in Chapters 6 and 7, the presence of multiple candidate keys may be a clue that an entity should be split into two entities linked by a one-to-one transferable relationship.

If after this we still genuinely have multiple candidate keys for the same entity that are equally applicable and stable, the shortest of these may result in a significant saving in storage requirements. This is because a primary key is replicated not only in foreign keys but in indexes.

Normalization Issues

We saw in Chapter 7 that multiple candidate keys can result in tables that are in third normal form but not Boyce-Codd normal form. Tables with two or more candidate keys can be also be a source of confusion in earlier stages of normalization. Some informal definitions of 3NF imply that a nonkey column is not allowed to be a determinant of another nonkey column (e.g., "Each nonkey item must depend on the key, the whole key, and *nothing but the key*.")

---

[40] Note that some DBMSs relax this requirement, as described in Chapter 6.

Look at the table in Figure 9-8:

CUSTOMER (<u>Customer No</u>, Tax File No, Name, Address, …)

Figure 9-8. Table with Two Candidate Keys

Let's assume that every customer has a Tax File No, and that no two customers have the same Tax File No. A bit of thought will show that Tax File No (a nonkey item) is a determinant of Name, Address, and indeed every other column in the table. On the basis of our informal definition of 3NF, we would conclude that the table is not in third normal form, and remove Name, Address, etc. to another table, with Tax File No copied across as the key.

We *don't* want to do this! It doesn't achieve anything useful. Remember our definition of 3NF in Chapter 2: Every determinant of a nonkey item must be a candidate key. Our table satisfies this – it's only the "rough and ready" definition of 3NF that leads us astray.

Summary

Primary keys must be applicable to all instances, unique, minimal, and stable. Stability is frequently overlooked, but stable keys lead to simpler system designs.

"Natural" keys may offer performance advantages, but are often unstable.

Structured keys consist of two or more attributes. Provided they satisfy the basic criteria of soundness, they can contribute to enforcing nontransferability, and may offer better performance. An entity that includes the key of another entity in its key is called a *weak* entity.

Surrogate keys are system-generated, meaningless keys, and can be managed to ensure uniqueness and stability. They do not guarantee singularity (one key value per real world entity instance), and may introduce a performance bottleneck. Surrogate keys may be made visible to users, but no meaning that is not constant over time for each instance should be attached to them.

Primary keys must not be allowed to take a logically null value, but individual components may be allowed to do so.

Chapter 10
Attributes

"Real Data Modelers don't do attributes."

– Anonymous (and misguided) data modeler

Introduction

Attribute definition does not always receive the attention it deserves from data modelers.

One reason is the emphasis on diagrams as the primary means of presenting a model. While they are invaluable in communicating the overall shape, they hide the detail of attributes. It is not uncommon for many of the participants in the development and review of a model to see only the diagrams, and remain unaware of the underlying attributes.

A second reason is that data models are developed progressively; in some cases the full requirements for attributes become clear only towards the end of the analysis task. By this time the specialist data modeler may have departed, leaving the supposedly straightforward and noncreative job of attribute definition to database administrators, function modelers, and even programmers. I have encountered many data modelers who believe that their job is finished when a reasonably stable framework of entities, relationships, and primary keys is in place.

On the contrary, the data modeler who remains involved in the development of a data model right through to implementation will be in a good position to ensure not only that attributes are soundly modeled as the need for them arises, but to intercept "improvements" to the model before they become entrenched.

In this chapter we look at the main issues that arise in modeling attributes.

We look at attribute identification and definition, and then discuss the different types of attributes in some detail. The classification provides a starting point for constructing attribute names. Naming of attributes is far more of an issue than naming of entities and relationships, if only because the number of attributes in a model is so much greater.

The chapter concludes with a discussion of the role of generalization in the context of attributes. As with entity modeling, we have some quite firm rules for aggregation, whereas generalization decisions often involve trade-offs among conflicting objectives As always, there is room for choice and sometimes creativity.

Attribute Definition

Proper definitions are an essential starting point for detailed modeling of attributes. In the early stages of modeling, we propose and record attributes before even the entities are fully defined, but our final model must include an unambiguous definition of each attribute. If we fail to do this, we are likely to overlook the more subtle issues discussed in this chapter, and run the risk that the resulting columns in the database will be used inappropriately by programmers or users. In fact, poor attribute definitions have the same potential to compromise data quality as poor entity definitions (see Chapter 3). Definitions need not be long: a single line is often enough if the parent entity is well defined.

An attribute definition should:

- Complete the sentence: "Assignment of a value to the <attribute name> for an instance of <object class name> is a record of ..." and should therefore refer to a single instance, e.g. "The date of birth of this Customer," "The minimum amount of a transaction that can be made by a Customer against a Product of this type"

- Answer the questions "What does it mean to assign a value to this attribute?", "What does each value that can be assigned to this attribute mean?"

It can be helpful to imagine that you are about to enter data into a data entry form or screen that will be loaded into an instance of the attribute. What information do you need to decide:

- What fact about the entity instance are you providing information about?

- What value should you enter to state that fact?

For an attribute to be completely defined, the following information is also required (although ideally your documentation tool will provide facilities for recording it in a more structured manner than writing it into the attribute definition):

- What type of attribute it is (e.g., character, numeric): attribute types are discussed in Chapter 11

- Whether it forms part of the primary key of the entity

- The constraints (business rules) to which it is subject, in particular its optionality (are null values allowed?) Business rules are discussed in Chapter 12.

- (For some types of attribute) the internal and external representations (formats) to be used: these are discussed later in this chapter.

Attribute Disaggregation – One Fact per Attribute

In Chapter 2 we introduced the basic rule for attribute disaggregation – one fact per attribute. It is almost never technically difficult to achieve this, and it generally leads to simpler programming, greater reusability of data, and easier implementation of change.

Normalization relies on the rule being observed; otherwise we may find "dependencies," that are really dependencies on only part of an attribute. (For example, Bank Name may be determined by a three-part Bank-State-Branch Number, but closer examination might show that the dependency is only on the "Bank" part of the Number).

Why, then, is the rule so often broken in practice? Violations may occur for a variety of reasons, including:

1. Failing to identify that an attribute can be decomposed into more fundamental attributes *that are of value to the business*

2. Attempting to achieve greater efficiency through data compression

3. Reflecting the fact that the compound attribute is more often used by the business than are its components

4. Relying on database management systems or programming facilities to perform "trivial" decomposition when required

5. Confusing the way data is presented with the way it is stored

6. Difficulties with handling variable length and "semi-structured" attributes (e.g., addresses)

7. Changing the definition of attributes after the database is implemented as an alternative to changing the database design

8. Complying with external standards or practices, and

9. Perpetuating past practices, which may have resulted originally from 1 through 8 above.

In my experience, most problems occur as a result of attribute definition being left to programmers or analysts with little knowledge of data modeling. In virtually all cases, a solution can be found that meets requirements without compromising the "one fact per attribute" rule. Compliance with external standards or user wishes is likely to require little more than a translation table or some simple data formatting and unpacking between screen and database. However, as in most areas of data modeling, rigid adherence to the rule will occasionally compromise other objectives. For example, dividing a date attribute into components of Year, Month, and Day may make it difficult to use standard date manipulation routines. When conflicts arise, we need to go back to first principles and look at the total impact of each option.

The most common types of violation are:

Simple Aggregation

An example of simple aggregation is an attribute Quantity Ordered that includes both the numeric quantity and the unit of measure (e.g., "12 cases"). Quite obviously, this aggregation of two different facts restricts our ability to compare quantities and perform arithmetic without having to "unpack" the data. Of course, if the business was only interested in Quantity Ordered as, for example, text to print on a label, we would have a good argument for treating it as a single attribute. A good test as to whether an attribute is fully decomposed is to ask:

- Does the attribute correspond to a single business fact? (The answer should be "Yes.")

- Can the attribute be further decomposed into attributes that themselves correspond to meaningful business facts? (The answer should be "No.")

- Are there business processes that update only part of the attribute? (Answer should be "No.") We should also look at processes that read the attribute (e.g., for display or printing). However, if the reason for using only part of the attribute is merely to provide an abbreviation of the same fact as represented by the whole, there is little point in decomposing the attribute to reflect this.

- Are there dependencies (potentially affecting normalization) that apply to only part of the attribute? (Answer should be "No.")

Let's look at a more complex example in this light. A Person Name attribute might be a concatenation of salutation (Prof.), family name (Deng), given names (Chan, Wei), and honors (MD BS, FRANZCP). Will the business want to treat given names individually (in which case we will regard them as forming a repeating group and normalize them out to separate entities?) Or will it be sufficient to separate "First Given Name" from "Other Given Names?" Should we separate the different qualifications represented by the honors? It depends on whether the business is genuinely interested in individual qualifications, or simply wants to address letters correctly. To answer these questions, we need to consider the needs of all potential users of the database, and employ some judgment as to likely future requirements.

Experienced data modelers are inclined to err on the side of disaggregation, even if familiar attributes are broken up in the process. The situation has parallels with normalization, in which familiar concepts (Invoice) are broken into less obvious components (Invoice Header, Invoice Line) to achieve a technically better structure. But most of us would not split First Given Name into Initial and Remainder of Name, even if there was a need to deal with the initials separately. We can verify this decision by using the questions suggested earlier:

- "Does First Given Name correspond to a single business fact?" (Most people would agree that it does. This provides a strong argument that we are already at a "one fact per attribute" level).

- "Can First Given Name be meaningfully decomposed?" (Initial has some real world significance, but only as an abbreviation for another fact. Rest of Name is unlikely to have any value to the business in itself).

- "Are there business processes that change the initial or the rest of the name independently?" (We would not expect this to be so; a change of name is a common business transaction, but we are unlikely to provide for "change of initial" or "change of rest of name" as distinct processes).

- "Are there likely to be any other attributes determined by (i.e., dependent on) Initial or Rest of Name?" (Probably no).

On this basis, we would accept First Given Name as a "single fact" attribute.

Complex Codes

We encountered a complex code in Chapter 2 with the Hospital Type attribute, which carried two pieces of information (whether the hospital was public or private, and whether it offered teaching services or not). Codes of this kind are not as easy to spot as simple aggregations, but they lead to more awkward programming and stability problems.

The problems arise when we want to deal with one of the underlying facts in isolation. Values may end up being included in program logic ("If Hospital Code equals 'T' or 'P' then …" making change more difficult.

One apparent justification for complex codes is their value in enforcing data integrity. Only certain combinations of the component facts may be allowable, and we can easily enforce this by only defining codes for those combinations. For example, private hospitals may not be allowed to have teaching facilities, so we simply do not define a code for "Private & Teaching." This is a legitimate approach, but the data model should then specify a separate table (see Chapter 10) to translate the codes into their components, in order to avoid the sort of programming mentioned earlier.

The constraint on allowed combinations can also be enforced by holding the attributes individually, and maintaining a look-up table of allowed combinations. Enforcement now requires that programmers follow the discipline of checking the look-up table. Note also that such a look-up table will not be produced by mechanical normalization (see Chapter 8).

Meaningful Ranges

A special case of the complex codes situation results from assigning meaning not only to the value of the attribute, but to the (usually numeric) range in which it falls.

For example, we may specify an attribute Status Code for an immigration application, then decide that values 10 through 50 are reserved for applications requiring special exemptions. What we actually have here is a hierarchy; with status codes subordinate to special exemption categories. In this example the hierarchy is two levels deep, but if we were to allocate meaning to subranges, subsubranges, and so on, the hierarchy would grow accordingly. The obvious, and correct, approach is to model the hierarchy explicitly.

Sometimes, ranges are allocated as a means of ensuring uniqueness of a primary key. This is a legitimate approach, often used when data is captured by independent, perhaps geographically scattered systems for later consolidation ("Policy Numbers 800,000 to 850,000 are reserved for the Northern Territory branch.") The important thing is not to attach meaning to the ranges when using the data. This problem has been discussed further in Chapter 9.

Variants of the "meaningful range" problem occur from time to time, and should be treated in the same way. An example is a "meaningful length;" in one database I worked with, a four-character job number identified a permanent job while a five-character job number indicated a job of fixed duration.

Inappropriate Generalization

Every COBOL programmer can cite cases where data items have been inappropriately redefined, often to save a few bytes of space, or to avoid reorganizing a file to make room for a new item. The same occurs under other file management and database management systems, often even less elegantly. (COBOL at least provides an explicit facility for redefinition; relational databases allow only one name for each column of a table – although different names can be used for columns in views based on that table).

The result is usually a data item that has no meaning in isolation but can only be interpreted by reference to other data items: for example, an attribute of Client, which means "Gender" for personal clients and "Industry Category" for company clients. Such a generalized item is unlikely to be used anywhere in the system without some program logic to determine which of its two meanings is appropriate.

Again, we complicate programming, in exchange for a notional space saving, and enforcement of the constraint that the attributes are mutually exclusive. These are seldom-adequate compensation. In fact, data compression at the physical level may allow most of the "wasted" space to be retrieved in any case. On the other hand, few would argue with the value of generalizing, say, Assembly Price and Component Price if we had already decided to generalize the entities Assembly and Component to Product.

But not all attribute generalization decisions are so straightforward. In the next section, we look at the factors that contribute to making the most appropriate choice.

Is a Foreign Key an Attribute?

In some methodologies foreign key columns are not included in attribute lists supporting Entity-Relationship Diagrams, since they duplicate the information provided by the relationship lines in the diagram. If you decide to adhere to this principle, be consistent: in other words show either all foreign key columns or none at all.

Remember that the primary keys of some entities include foreign keys, as in Figure 10-1. If you are not including foreign key columns in your attribute lists, you have no way of indicating in the attribute list for Order Line that its primary key includes Order No. In this case you must mark the relationship between Order and Order Line to indicate that the foreign key implementing the relationship is part of the primary key of the entity at the "many" end of the relationship. Not all diagramming tools support such marking, so if you are using a tool that doesn't, you should, for consistency, list *all* attributes including foreign key columns.

ORDER (Order No, Customer No, Order Date, …)

ORDER LINE (Order No, Line No, Product Code, Order Quantity, …)

Figure 10-1. A Primary Key that Includes a Foreign Key

If you decide to include foreign key columns in your attribute lists, they should be marked as such (e.g., "Order No: foreign key to Order.") If a foreign key consists of more than one column the marking should read "part of foreign key to …" (e.g., "Order No: part of foreign key to Order Line.")

Types of Attributes

Along with the name and definition, many modelers include for each attribute a datatype available in the intended DBMS, such as "integer", "character(4)" or "date". While this is useful information *if* the DBMS is already known *and* the modeler has reviewed the available datatypes, it should not be regarded as a substitute for information about how the attribute is to be used. Consider the attributes Order No and Order Quantity in Figure 10-1. A modeler may well decide to define them both as integers. This however overlooks some fundamental differences in the way those attributes will be used:

- Order Quantity can participate in arithmetic operations, such as Order Quantity × Unit Price or sum (Order Quantity), whereas it does not make sense to include Order No in any arithmetic expressions.

- Inferences can legitimately be drawn from the fact that one Order Quantity is greater than another, thus the expressions Order Quantity > 2, Order Quantity < 10 and max (Order Quantity) make sense, as do attributes such as Minimum Order Quantity or Maximum Order Quantity. On the other hand, Order No > 2, Order No < 10, max (Order No), Minimum Order No and Maximum Order No do not make sense, since there is no guarantee that Order Nos are generated in sequence. Despite this I often see database designs that include a table in which there is a pair of references to some other table labeled Minimum and Maximum. This is a lazy and inconsistent way of handling a many-to-many relationship that falls down as soon as there is a requirement to refer to a nonconsecutive set of records in the other table.

- Although the current set of Order Nos may be solely numeric there may be a future requirement for non-numeric characters in Order Nos. The use of integer for Order No effectively prevents the business taking up that option, but without an explicit statement to that effect.

Attributes should therefore be initially classified according to the following taxonomy, and only then should a DBMS datatype be selected. The attribute documentation should then include both the classification and datatype. At the highest level attributes can be divided into the following types:

- An **Identifier** exists purely to identify entity instances and does not imply any properties of those instances (e.g., Order No, Product Code, Line No).

- A **Category** can only hold one of a defined set of values (e.g., Product Type, Customer Credit Rating, Payment Method, Delivery Status).

- A **Quantity** is an attribute on which some arithmetic can be performed (e.g. addition, subtraction), and on which comparisons other than '=' and '≠' can be performed (e.g., Order Quantity, Order Date, Unit Price, Discount Rate).

- A **Text** can hold any string of characters that the user may choose to enter (e.g., Customer Name, Product Name, Delivery Instructions).

This broad classification of attributes corresponds approximately to that advocated by Tasker[41].

The Attribute Taxonomy in Detail

Identifiers

Identifiers may be system-generated, administrator-defined or externally-defined. Examples of **system-generated identifiers** are Customer Numbers, Order Numbers and the like, that are generated automatically without user intervention whenever a new instance of the relevant entity is created. These are often generated in sequence although there is no particular requirement to do so. Again, these are often but not exclusively numeric: an example of a nonnumeric system-generated identifier is the booking reference "number" assigned to an airline reservation. In the early days of relational databases, the generation of such an identifier required a separate table in which to hold the latest value used; nowadays DBMSs support such identifiers directly without the need for such a table. Note that system-generated identifiers may or may not be visible to users.

---

[41] Tasker, D., *Fourth Generation Data – A Guide to Data Analysis for New and Old Systems*, Prentice Hall, Australia (1989).

Administrator-defined identifiers are really only suitable for relatively low-volume entities but are ideal for these. Examples are Department Codes, Product Codes and Room, Staff and Class Codes in a school administration system. These can be numeric or alphanumeric. The system should provide a means for an administrative user of the system to create new identifiers at system start-up and as new ones are required.

Externally-defined identifiers are those over which neither the system nor its users has any say, since they have been defined by an external party, often a national or international standards authority. Examples include Country Codes, Currency Codes, State Codes, Zip Codes etc. Of course, an externally-defined identifier in one system is a user-defined (or possibly system-generated) identifier in another (for example, Zip Code is externally-defined in most systems but may be user-defined in a Postal Authority system!) Again these can be numeric or alphanumeric. Ideally these are loaded into a system in bulk from a dataset provided by the defining authority.

A particular kind of identifier attribute is the **tie-breaker** which is often used in a entity that has been created to hold a repeating group removed from another entity (see Chapter 2). These are used when none of the "natural" attributes in the repeating group appears suitable for the purpose, or in place of a longer attribute. Line No in Order Line in Figure 10-1 is a tie-breaker. These are almost always system-generated and almost always numeric to allow for a simple means of generating new unique values.

It should be clear that identifiers are used in primary keys (and therefore in foreign keys) although keys may include other types of attribute. For example, a date attribute may be included in the primary key of an entity holding a version or snapshot of something about which history needs to be maintained: e.g., a Product Version entity could have a primary key consisting of Product Code and Date Effective attributes.

Names are a form of identifier but may not be unique, and in most cases a name is treated as a text attribute, in that there are no controls over what is entered (e.g., in an Employee Name or Customer Name attribute). There are some exceptions to this situation. For example, you could identify the departments of an organization by their names alone rather than using a Department Code or Department No, although there are good reasons for choosing one of the latter, as described in Chapter 11. Another situation in which names are used as identifiers is where a Locality entity is used to validate Place Name/Zip Code combinations in address data: the primary key of such an entity includes both Zip Code and Place Name.

Categories

Categories are typically administrator-defined but some may be externally-defined. Externally (on screens and reports) these are represented using character strings (e.g., "Cash", "Check", "Credit Card", "Charge Card", "Debit Card") but may be represented internally using shorter codes or integer values. The internal representations may even be used externally if users are familiar with them and their meanings.

A particular kind of category attribute is the **flag** which holds a Yes or No answer to a suitably-worded question about the entity instance, in which case the question should appear as a legend on screens and reports alongside the answer (which is usually represented both internally and externally as either "Y" or "N"). Many flags also need to be able to hold "Not applicable" and/or "Unknown", which can be represented by a dash and a question mark respectively.

Quantities

Quantities come in a variety of forms:

- A **Count** enumerates a set of discrete instances (e.g., Vehicle Count, Employee Count), it answers a question of the form *"How many ...?"*. It represents a dimensionless (unitless) magnitude.

- A **Dimension** answers a question of the form *"How long ...?"*, *"How high ...?"*, *"How wide ...?"*, *"How heavy ...?"*, etc. (e.g., Room Width, Unit Weight). It requires a unit (e.g. feet, miles, millimeters).

- An **Currency Amount** answers a question of the form *"How much ...?"* and specifies an amount of money (e.g., Unit Price, Payment Amount, Outstanding Balance). It requires a currency unit.

- A **Factor** is (conceptually) the result of dividing one magnitude by another (e.g., Interest Rate, Discount Rate, Hourly Rate, Blood Alcohol Concentration). It requires a unit (e.g., $/hour, m/second) unless both magnitudes are of the same dimension, in which case it is a unitless ratio (or percentage).

- A **Specific Time Point** answers a question of the form *"When ...?"* in relation to a single event (e.g., Transaction Timestamp, Order Date, Arrival Year).

- A **Recurrent Time Point** answers a question of the form *"When ...?"* in relation to a recurrent event (e.g. Departure TimeOfDay, Scheduled DayOfWeek, Mortgage Repayment DayOfMonth, Annual Renewal DayOfYear).

- An **Interval** (or **Duration**) answers a question of the form *"For how long ...?"* (e.g. Lesson Duration, Mortgage Repayment Period). It requires a unit (seconds, minutes, hours, days, weeks, months, years).

- A **Position** answers a question of the form *"Where ...?"* and may be a point, a line segment or a 2-, 3- (or higher-) dimensional figure.

Where a quantity requires units, there are two options:

1. Ensure that all instances of the attribute are expressed in the same units.

2. Create an additional attribute in which to hold the units in which the quantity is expressed and provide conversion routines.

Obviously the first option is by far the simpler but there may be a legal requirement to use the second option, such as in a system handling amounts in different currencies.

For many quantities it is important to establish and document what accuracy is required by the business. For example, most currency amounts are required correct to the nearest cent (or local currency equivalent) but some (e.g., stock prices) may require fractions of cents whereas others may always be rounded to the nearest dollar. It should also be established whether the rounding is merely for purposes of display or whether arithmetic is to be performed on the rounded amount (e.g. in an Australian Income Tax return, Earnings and Deductions are rounded to the nearest dollar before computations using those amounts).

Time Points can have different accuracies and scope depending on requirements:

- A **Timestamp** (or **DateTime**) specifies the date and time on which something happened.

- A **Date** specifies the date on which something happened but not the time.

- A **Month** specifies the month and year in which something happened.

- A **Year** specifies the year in which something happened (e.g., the year of arrival of an immigrant).

- A **Time of Day** specifies the time but not the date (e.g., in a timetable).

- A **Day of Week** specifies only the day within a week (e.g., in a timetable).

- A **Day of Month** specifies only the day within a month (e.g., a mortgage repayment date).

- A **Day of Year** specifies only the day within a year (e.g., an annual renewal date).

- A **Month of Year** specifies only the month within a year.

For quantities other than Currency Amounts and Points in Time we also need to define whether exact arithmetic is required or whether floating-point arithmetic can be used.

Attribute Datatype and Length Requirements

Identifiers

An *Identifier* should use the char or varchar datatype (which is better depends on particular properties of these datatypes in the DBMS being used: consult the documentation for that DBMS), unless it is known that nonnumeric values will never be required, in which case the integer datatype can be used. Even if only numeric values are used at present, this may not always be the case. For example, Australian postcodes, like US Zip codes, are numeric; while nonnumeric codes may never be introduced in those countries, an Australian or US-based company may want to allow for expansion into countries like Canada where nonnumeric codes are used. This is flexibility at (usually) no cost.

The length should be chosen to accommodate the maximum number of instances of the entity required over the life of the system: as reuse of identifiers is not advisable we're not talking about the maximum number of instances at any one time! The numbers of instances that can be accommodated by various lengths of (var)char and integer column are shown in Figure 10-2, in which it is assumed that only letters and digits are used in a (var)char column. Of course, with an administrator-defined or externally-defined identifier there may already be a standard for the length of the identifier, in which case that should be followed.

Categories

If a *Category* attribute is represented internally using the same character strings as are used externally, the char or varchar datatype should be used with a length sufficient to accommodate the longest character string.

If (as is more usually the case) it is represented internally using a shorter code, the char or varchar datatype should again be used; now, however, the length depends on the number of values that may be required over the life of the system, according to Figure 10-2.

Datatype	Length	Number accommodated
(var)char	1	36
	2	1,296
	3	46,656
	4	1,679,616
	5	60,466,176
	6	2,176,782,336
	7	78,364,164,096
	8	2.82×10^{12}
integer	1	127
	2	32,767
	4	2,147,483,647

Figure 10-2. Identifier Capacities

If integer values are to be used internally, the integer datatype should be used. Once again Figure 10-2 indicates how many values can be accommodated by each length of integer column.

Flags should be held in char(1) columns unless Boolean arithmetic is to be performed on them, in which case use integer1 and represent Yes by 1 and No by 0 (zero). However these should still be represented in forms and reports using Y and N. Subsequent sections in this chapter discuss conversion between external and internal representations.

Quantities

- *Counts* should use the integer datatype. The length should be sufficient to accommodate the maximum value (i.e., if more than 32767 use integer4, otherwise if more than 127 use integer2).

- *Dimensions*, *Factors* and *Intervals* should generally use the decimal datatype if available in the DBMS, unless exact arithmetic is not required, in which case the float datatype can be used. The decimal datatype requires the number of digits after the decimal point to be specified. If the decimal datatype is not available, the integer datatype must be used: a decision must then be taken as to where the decimal point is understood to occur (this will of course be the same for all instances of the attribute) and data entry and display functionality programmed accordingly. For example, if there are two digits after the decimal point, any value entered by the user into the attribute must be multiplied by 100 and all values of the attribute must be displayed with a decimal point before the second to last digit. This is discussed further in this chapter.

- *Currency Amounts* should use the currency datatype if available in the DBMS. If this is not available, the decimal datatype should be used with the appropriate number of digits after the decimal point (normally 2) specified. If there is a requirement to record fractions of a cent and the DBMS currency datatype does not accommodate more than 2 digits after the decimal point, again the decimal datatype should be used. If the decimal datatype is not available, the integer datatype should be used in the same way as described for dimensions and factors.

- *Timestamps* should use whichever datatype is defined in the DBMS to record date and time together (this is often called simply "date.")

- If there is a specific datatype in the DBMS to hold just a date without a time, this should be used for *Dates*. If not, the datatype defined in the DBMS to record date and time together can be used: the time should be standardized to 00:00 for each date recorded. This however can cause problems with comparisons. If an expiry date is recorded and an event occurs with a timestamp during the last day of the validity period, the comparison Event Timestamp <= Expiry Date will return False even though the event is valid. To overcome this, Expiry Dates using date/time datatypes must be recorded as being at 00:00 on the day after the actual date (but displayed correctly!) This is discussed further in this chapter.

- *Months* should probably use the datatype suitable for dates and standardize the day to the 1st of the month.

- *Years* should use the integer2 datatype.

- *Times of Day* can use the datatype defined in the DBMS to record date and time together: the date should be standardized to some particular day throughout the system, such as 1/1/2000.

- *Days of Week* should use the integer1 datatype and a standard sequential encoding starting at 0 or 1 representing Sunday or Monday. The ideal external representation is the first 2 letters of the day name. Conversion between external and internal representations is discussed in 10.5.3.

- *Days of Month* should also use the integer1 datatype but the internal and external representations can be the same.

- *Days of Year* should probably use the datatype suitable for dates: the year should be standardized to some particular year throughout the system, such as 2000.

- *Months of Year* should use the integer1 datatype and a standard sequential encoding starting at 1 representing January. The external representation should be either be the integer value or the first 3 letters of the month name. Conversion between external and internal representations is discussed in 10.5.3.

- If there is a specific datatype in the DBMS to hold position data, that should be used for *Positions*. If not, the most common "contingency plan" is to use a coordinate system (e.g. a point is represented by two decimal columns holding the x and y coordinates, a line segment by the x and y coordinates of each end, a polygon by the x and y coordinates of each vertex, etc).

Texts

Texts must use the char or varchar datatype (which is better depends on particular properties of these datatypes in the DBMS being used: consult the documentation for that DBMS). The length should be sufficient to accommodate the longest character string that the business may require to record. The DBMS may impose an upper limit on the length of a (var)char column, but may also provide a means of storing character strings of unlimited length: again consult the documentation for that DBMS).

A particular type of text attribute is the *Comment* in which the business may require the ability to enter as much or as little text as each instance demands. If the DBMS does not provide a means of storing character strings of unlimited length, use the maximum length available in a standard varchar column. Do not under any circumstances define the comment as char(80) or thereabouts and provide for the comment to be spread over multiple rows. This makes editing of a comment well-nigh impossible since there is no word-wrap between rows as in a word processor.

Conversion between External and Internal Representations

We have seen that a number of attribute types may have different external and internal representations. In a relational DBMS SQL views can be used to manage the conversion from internal to external representation as in the following example:

```
create PRODUCT_VIEW (Product Code, Unit Price, Obsolete Flag) as
    select Product Code, Unit Price/100.00, case Obsolete Flag when 1 then 'Y' else
    'N' end
```

This particular example uses an arithmetic expression to convert an amount stored as an integer to dollars and cents and a case statement to convert a flag stored as 0 or 1 to N or Y respectively. Functions may also be used in views, particularly for date manipulation. None of these conversions will work in reverse however, so such a view is not updateable (e.g., one cannot enter Y into Obsolete Flag and have it recorded as 1. Such logic must therefore be written into the data entry screen(s) for the entity in question: ideally there would only be one for each entity.

Attribute Names

Objectives of Standardizing Attribute Names

Many organizations have put in place detailed standards for attribute naming, typically comprising lists of component words with definitions, standard abbreviations, and rules for stringing them together. Needless to say, there has been much "reinvention of the wheel." Names and abbreviations tend to be organization-specific, so most of the common effort has been in deciding sequence, connectors, and the minutiae of punctuation. IBM's "OF" language, originally proposed in the early 1970s, has been particularly influential. Attribute names constructed using the OF language consist of a single "class word" drawn from a short standard list (Date, Name, Flag, etc) and one or more organization-defined "modifiers," separated by connectors (primarily "of" and "which is" – hence the name). Examples of names constructed using the OF language are "Date of Birth," "Name of Person," and "Amount which is Discount of Product which is Retail." Some of these names are more natural and familiar than others!

The objectives of an attribute-naming standard are usually to:

- Reduce ambiguity in interpreting the meaning of attributes (the name serving as a short form of documentation)

- Reduce the possibility of "synonyms" – two or more attributes with the same meaning but different names, and

- Reduce the possibility of "homonyms" – two or more attributes with the same name but different meanings.

Some Guidelines for Attribute Naming

The naming standard you adopt may be influenced by the facilities provided by your documentation tool or data dictionary, and by established practices within your organization or industry, ideally the result of a well-thought-out and consistent approach. If you're starting with a blank slate, here are some basic guidelines and options:

1. Build a list of standard class words to be used for each attribute type, along the following lines:

    Identifiers: Number (or No), Code, Identifier (or Id), TieBreaker

    Categories: Type, Method, Status, Reason, etc.

    Counts: Count (*never* Number as in "Number of ..."[42])

    Dimensions: Length, Width, Height, Weight, etc.

    Amounts: Amount, Price, Balance, etc.

    Factors: Rate, Concentration, Ratio, Percentage, etc.

    Specific Time Points: Timestamp, DateTime, Date, Month, Year

    Recurrent Time Points: TimeOfDay, DayOfWeek, DayOfMonth, DayOfYear, MonthOfYear

    Intervals: Duration, Period

    Positions: Point, LineSegment, Polygon, etc.

    Texts: Name, Description, Comment, Instructions.

While it is desirable not to use different words for the same thing, it is more important to use terminology with which the business is comfortable. Thus, for example, Price is included as well as Amount since Unit Price Amount does not read as comfortably as Unit Price.

---

[42] To avoid confusion with identifier attributes with names ending in "Number."

2. Select suitable qualifiers or modifiers to precede class words in attribute names (e.g. Registration in Registration Number and Purchase in Purchase Date). There may be value in building a standard list of modifiers, but the list should include all terms in common use in the business unless these are particularly ambiguous.

3. Sequence the qualifiers in each attribute name using the "reverse" variation of the IBM OF language. The traditional way of achieving this is to string together the words using "which is" and "of" as connectors, to produce an OF language name, then to reverse the order and eliminate the connectors. For example an attribute to represent the average annual dividend amount for a stock could be (using the OF language):

   Amount of Dividend which is Average which is Annual of Stock

   Reversing gives:

   Stock Average Annual Dividend Amount.

This is pretty painful, but with a little practice you can move directly to the reverse OF language name, which usually sounds reasonable, at least to an information systems professional!

4. Determine a policy for inclusion of the name of the entity in attribute names. This continues to be a matter of debate, probably because there is no overwhelming reason for choosing one option over another. Workable variants include:

   • Using the "home" entity name as the first word or words of each attribute name. The "home" entity of a foreign key is the entity in which it appears as a primary key; the "home" entity of an attribute inherited or rolled up from a supertype or a subtype is that supertype or subtype respectively. So attributes of Vehicle might include *Vehicle* Registration Number, *Asset* Purchase Date (inherited), *Truck* Capacity (rolled up), and Responsible *Organization Unit* Code (foreign key);

   • Using home entity names only in primary and foreign keys;

   • Using home entity names only in foreign keys.

5. In addition to using the home entity name, prefix foreign keys according to the name of the relationship they implement: e.g., *Issuing* Branch No, *Responsible* Branch No. This is not always easy, and it is reasonable to bend the rule if the relationship is obvious and the name clumsy, or an alternative role name is available: e.g., *Advanced* Customer No, meaning the key of the customer to whom a loan was advanced, could be better named Borrower (Customer) No.

6. Avoid abbreviations in attribute names, unless they are widely understood in your organization (by business people!) or you are truly constrained by your documentation tool or data dictionary. It's very likely that the DBMS will impose length and punctuation constraints. These apply to *columns*, not to attributes!

7. Look hard at any proposal to use "aliases" i.e., synonyms to assist access. This is really a data dictionary management issue rather than a modeling one, but take note that alias facilities are often established but relatively seldom used.

8. Establish a simple translation from attribute names to column names. Here is where abbreviations come in.

In the pursuit of consistency and purity, don't lose sight of one of the fundamental objectives of modeling: communication. Sometimes we must sacrifice rigid adherence to standards for familiarity and better-quality feedback from non-technical participants in the modeling process. Conversely, it is sometimes valuable to introduce a new term to replace a familiar, but ambiguous term.

A final word on attribute names. If building your own data dictionary, do not use Attribute Name as the primary key for the table containing details of Attributes. Names and even naming standards will change from time to time, and we need to be able to distinguish a change in attribute name from the creation of a new attribute. A simple meaningless identifier will do the job – it need not be visible to anyone. Most documentation tools and data dictionaries support this; a few do not.

Attribute Generalization

Options and Trade-Offs

In Chapter 4, we looked at entity generalization (and its converse, specialization), and the use of supertypes and subtypes to represent the results. Recall that higher levels of generalization meant fewer entities, fewer rules within the data structure, and greater resilience to change. On the other hand, specialization provided a more detailed picture of data and enforcement of more business rules, but less stability in the face of changes to these rules.

The best design was necessarily a trade-off among these different features. Making the best choice started with being aware of the different possibilities (by showing them as subtypes and supertypes on the model), rather than merely recording the first or most obvious option.

Much the same trade-offs apply to attribute definition. In some cases, the decision is largely predetermined by decisions taken at the entity level – we generalize two or more entities, and then review their attributes to look for opportunities for generalization. In other cases, the discovery that attributes belonging to different entities are used in the same way may prompt us to consider generalizing their parent entities.

Alternatively, close examination of the attributes of a single entity may suggest that the entity could usefully be subtyped. One or more attributes may have a distinct meaning for a specific subset of entity instances (e.g., Ranking, Last Review Date, and Special Agreement Number apply only to those Suppliers who have *Preferred Supplier* status). Often a set of attributes will be null under certain conditions. We need to look at the conditions, and decide whether they provide a basis for entity subtyping.

Generalizing attributes *within* an entity can also affect the overall shape of the model. For example, we might generalize Standard Price, Trade Price, and Preferred Customer Price to Price. The generalized attributes will then become a repeating group, requiring us to separate them out in order to preserve first normal form (as discussed in Chapter 2).

Finally, at the attribute level, *consistency* of format, coding, naming, etc., is an important consideration, particularly when we are dealing with a large number of attributes. The starting point for consistency is generalization: Without recognizing that several attributes are in some sense similar, we cannot recognize the need to handle them consistently. In turn, consistent naming practices may highlight opportunities for generalization.

Some examples will illustrate these ideas.

Attribute Generalization Resulting from Entity Generalization

Figure 10-3 shows a simple example of entity generalization/specialization. The generalization of Company and Person to Client may have been suggested by their common attributes; equally it may have resulted from our knowledge that the two are handled similarly. Alternatively, we may have worked top-down, starting with the Client entity and looking for subtypes. The subtyping may have been prompted by noting that some of the attributes of Client were applicable only to people, and others only to companies

> **CLIENT (<u>Client ID</u>, Name, Title, Address, Responsible Salesperson, Date of Birth, Gross Income, Annual Turnover, Date of Incorporation, Occupation, Industry Code)**

Figure 10-3. Allocating Attributes among Subtypes

Our initial task is to allocate attributes among the three entities. We have three options for each attribute:

1. Allocate the attribute to one of the subtypes only. We do this if the attribute can apply only to that subtype. For example, we may allocate Date of Birth to Person only.

2. Allocate the attribute to the supertype only. We do this if the attribute can apply to all of the subtypes, and has essentially the same meaning wherever it is used. For example, Address might be allocated to Client.

3. Allocate the attribute to more than one of the subtypes, indicating in the documentation that the attributes are related. We do this if the attribute has a different meaning in each case, but not so different that we cannot see any value in generalization. For example, we might allocate Name to both subtypes, on the basis that some processes will handle the names of both persons and companies in the same way (e.g., "display client details") while others will be specific to company or person names (e.g., "print envelope for person, including title").

If we are thorough about this, handling of attributes when we level the model (by selecting the final level of generalization for each entity) will be reasonably straightforward. If we follow the largely intuitive "inheritance" and "roll up" rules in Chapter 4, the only issue in leveling the model will be what to do in situation (3) if we implement at the supertype level. We will then have to decide whether to specify a single generalized attribute, or retain the distinct attributes as rolled up from the subtypes.

A good guide is to look closely at the reasons for selecting the higher level of generalization for the entity. Are we anticipating further, as yet unidentified, subtypes? If so, will they require a corresponding attribute? Have we decided that the subtypes are subject to common processes? How do these processes use the attribute in question? In practice, I tend to carry through the entity generalization to the attribute more often than not.

I also find frequently that I haven't been as thorough as I should have been in spotting possible attribute generalizations. Once the entity level has been decided upon, it's worth reviewing all of the attributes "rolled up" from subtype entities to ensure that opportunities for generalization have not been overlooked.

Attribute Generalization within Entities

Opportunities for attribute generalization can arise quite independently of entity generalization. The following (rather long) example illustrates the key possibilities and issues.

The Financial Performance table in Figure 10-4 represents data about budgeted and annual expenditure on a quarterly basis.

FINANCIAL PERFORMANCE
    (Department No.,
    Year,
    Approved By,
    Budget First Quarter Material,
    Budget Second Quarter Material,
    Budget Third Quarter Material,
    Budget Last Quarter Material,
    Actual First Quarter Material,
    Actual Second Quarter Material,
    Actual Third Quarter Material,
    Actual Total Material,
    Budget First Quarter Labor,
    Budget Second Quarter Labor,
    Budget Third Quarter Labor,
    Budget Last Quarter Labor,
    Actual First Quarter Labor,
    Actual Second Quarter Labor,
    Actual Third Quarter Labor,
    Actual Total Labor,
    Budget Other,
    Actual Other,
    Discretionary Spending Limit)

Figure 10-4. Financial Performance Table prior to Attribute Generalization

There are such obvious opportunities for attribute generalization here (most data modelers can't wait to get started on a structure like this) that it's worth pointing out that the structure as it stands is a legitimate option, useable without further generalization. In particular, it is in at least first normal form. Technically, there are no repeating groups in the structure, despite the temptation to view, for example, the four material budget items as a repeating group. Doing this requires that we bring to bear our knowledge of the problem domain, and recognize the items as representing *at some level of generalization*, the "same thing."

Having conceded that the structure is at least workable, we can be a bit more critical, and note some problems with resilience to change. Suppose we were to make a business decision to move to monthly rather than quarterly reporting, or to include some other budget category besides "labor," "material," and "other" – perhaps "external subcontracts." Changing the table structures and corresponding programs would be a major task, particularly if the possible generalizations had not been recognized even at the program level; in other words, if we had written separate program logic to handle each quarter, or to handle labor figures in contrast to material figures. Perhaps this seems an unlikely scenario; on the contrary, I have seen very similar structures on many occasions in practice.

Let's start our generalization with the four material budget attributes. We make two decisions here.

First, we confirm that there is value in treating all four in a similar way; that there are business processes that handle first, second, third, and last quarter budgets in much the same way. If this is so, we make the generalization to Material Quarterly Budget Amount, noting that the new attribute occurs four times. We flag this as a repeating group to be normalized out. Because sequence within the group is important, we need to add a new attribute Quarter Number. Another way of looking at this is that we have removed some information from the data structure (the words first, second, third, and last) and need to provide a new place to store that information; hence the additional attribute.

Second, we relax the upper limit of four. We know that normalization is going to remove the constraint in any case, so we might as well recognize the situation explicitly and consider its consequences. In this example, the effect is that we are no longer constrained to quarterly budgets, so we need to change the names of the attributes accordingly – "Material Budget Amount" and "Period Number."

We can now remove the repeating group, creating a new table Material Budget Item (Figure 10-5).

> **MATERIAL BUDGET ITEM (<u>Department No</u>, <u>Year</u>, <u>Period Number</u>, Material Budget Amount)**

Figure 10-5. Material Budget Table

The example thus far has illustrated the main results of attribute generalization within an entity:

- The increased flexibility obtainable through sensible generalization.

- The need to add data items to hold information taken out of the data structure by generalization.

- The creation of new entities to normalize out the repeating groups resulting from generalization.

Continuing with the financial results example, we could apply the same process to labor and other budget items, and to material, labor, and other actual items, producing a total of seven tables as in Figure 10-6.

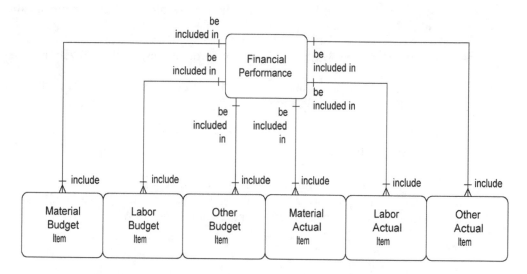

FINANCIAL PERFORMANCE (<u>Department No</u>, <u>Year</u>, Approved By, Discretionary Spending Limit)

MATERIAL BUDGET ITEM (<u>Department No</u>, <u>Year</u>, <u>Period Number</u>, Material Budget Amount)

LABOR BUDGET ITEM (<u>Department No</u>, <u>Year</u>, <u>Period Number</u>, Labor Budget Amount)

OTHER BUDGET ITEM (<u>Department No</u>, <u>Year</u>, <u>Period Number</u>, Other Budget Amount)

MATERIAL ACTUAL ITEM (<u>Department No</u>, <u>Year</u>, <u>Period Number</u>, Material Actual Amount)

LABOR ACTUAL ITEM (<u>Department No</u>, <u>Year</u>, <u>Period Number</u>, Labor Actual Amount)

OTHER ACTUAL ITEM (<u>Department No</u>, <u>Year</u>, <u>Period Number</u>, Other Actual Amount)

Figure 10-6. Budget and Actual Data Separated

In doing this, we would notice that there was no attribute named Actual Fourth Quarter Material. Instead we have Actual Total Material. This does break any data modeling rules, since one value could be derived from the others. But if we choose to generalize, we will have to replace the "total" attribute with a "fourth quarter" attribute to make generalization possible. Even if we decide not to model the more generalized structure, we are likely to change the attribute anyway, for the sake of consistency. It is important to recognize that this "common sense" move to consistency *relies on our having seen the possibility of generalization in the first place*. To achieve consistency, we need to recognize first that the attributes have something in common.

There is a flavor of creative data modeling here too. We deliberately choose a particular attribute representation in order to provide an opportunity for generalization.

Inconsistencies that become visible as a result of trying to generalize may suggest useful questions to be asked of the user. Why, for instance, are "other" budgets and expenditures recorded on an annual basis rather than quarterly? Do we want to bring them into line with labor and materials? Alternatively, do we need to provide for labor and materials also being reported at different intervals?

We can take generalization further, bringing together labor, material, and other budgets, and doing likewise for actuals. We gain the flexibility to introduce new types of financial reporting, but will need to add Budget Item Type and Actual Item Type attributes to replace the information lost from the data structure (Figure 10-7). Note that we can do this either by supertyping the entities in Figure 10-6, or generalizing the attributes in the original model of Figure 10-4.

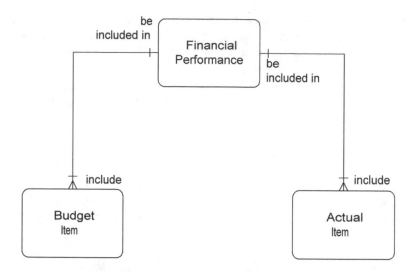

FINANCIAL PERFORMANCE (<u>Department No</u>, <u>Year</u>, Approved By,
   Discretionary Spending Limit)

BUDGET ITEM (<u>Department No</u>, <u>Year</u>, <u>Period Number</u>, <u>Budget Type</u>, Budget
   Amount)

ACTUAL ITEM (<u>Department No</u>, <u>Year, Period Number</u>, <u>Budget Type</u>, Actual
   Amount)

Figure 10-7. Generalization of Labor, Material, and Other Data

Finally, we could consider generalizing budget and actual data. After all, they
are represented by identical structures. When I present this example on training
courses, there is often strong support for doing this, as in Figure 10-8, perhaps
because we have been doing so well with generalization to that point!

BUDGET/ACTUAL ITEM (<u>Department No</u>, <u>Year</u>, <u>Period Number</u>, <u>Budget Type</u>,
   <u>Budget/Actual Flag</u>, Budget/Actual Amount)

Figure 10-8. Generalization of Budget and Actual Amounts

But we need to ask: does the business have processes that treat budget and
actual items in much the same way? Is there the possibility of a new category
(in addition to "budget" and "actual") arising that can take advantage of
existing processes? Chances are that the answer to both is no, and we may
achieve only unnecessary obscurity by generalizing any further. The data
model may look elegant, but the program logic needed to unravel the different
data will not.

But before we abandon the idea completely, we could consider the option shown in Figure 10-9, which is different from the previous generalizations in that it *joins* Budget Item and Actual Item. This seems to make more sense.

BUDGET ITEM (<u>Department No</u>, <u>Year, Period Number</u>, <u>Budget Item Type</u>, Budget Amount, Actual Amount)

Figure 10-9. Joining Budget Item and Actual Item

To summarize: we need to look always at how the business treats the data, using commonality of shape only as a prompt, not as a final arbiter.

Limits to Attribute Generalization

In the preceding example, we reached the point of limited further gains from generalization while we still had a number of distinct attributes. But there are situations in which a higher level of attribute generalization is justified. Figure 10-10 shows an example of a very high level of attribute generalization, in which all attributes are generalized to a single "Parameter Value" attribute, and subsequently removed as a repeating group. I've called the new entity Parameter Value rather than Attribute – an entity named Attribute is not going to do much for communication with the uninitiated!

Figure 10-10. Highly Generalized Attributes

This is the attribute level equivalent of the Thing entity (Chapter 4). It has application when structures are genuinely unstable and unpredictable. In this example, every time we purchased a new type of equipment, we might want to record new attributes: perhaps bandwidth, range, tensile strength, or mean time between failures. Rather than add new attributes to Equipment Item, we simply record new values for Parameter Type Code.

Commercial software packages may employ high levels of generalization to support "user-defined attributes." I have seen the technique used very successfully in product databases, allowing new products with unanticipated attributes to be defined very quickly without altering the database structure. But I have also seen it used far too often as a substitute for rigorous analysis. You need to keep in mind the following:

- Some of the entity's attributes may be stable and handled in a distinct way. Model them separately, and don't include them in the generic repeating group.

- Consider subtyping Parameter Value based on data type, e.g., Numeric Parameter Value, Text Parameter Value.

- You will need to add attributes to replace the information removed from the data structure. This includes anything you would normally specify for an attribute, including name, format, editing rules, and optionality. These become attributes initially of the Parameter Value entity, then, through normalization, of a Parameter Type entity (Figure 10-11). Parameter Types can be related to Equipment Types (not shown) to specify which parameter types are applicable to each type of equipment (see Chapter 11 for examples of this technique).

- The technique is only useful if the different parameter types can utilize common program code. If not, you may as well make the change to the system in the conventional fashion by modifying the database and writing the necessary code. Good candidates for the parameter approach are attributes that are simply entered and displayed, rather than those which drive or are involved in more complex logic.

- Programs will need to be suitably parameter-driven, to the extent that you may need to support run-time decisions on screen and report formatting. You will need to look hard at how well your tool set supports the approach. Many program generators cannot effectively handle challenges of this kind. Even human programmers will need guidance from someone very familiar with the data model if they are to exploit it properly.

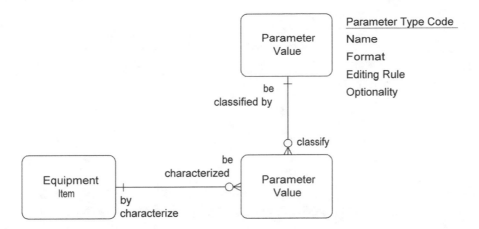

Figure 10-11. Highly Generalized Attributes with Look-Up Table

Summary

Proper definitions are an essential starting point for detailed modeling of attributes and can make a significant contribution to the quality of the data in the eventual system.

Each attribute should represent one fact type only. The most common types of violations are simple aggregations, complex codes, meaningful ranges, and inappropriate generalization.

Be consistent in including foreign key columns in attribute lists or excluding them.

Analyze how attributes will be used and classify them according to the taxonomy provided in this chapter before deciding on a DBMS datatype and length. Choose the length of each attribute according to the business's capacity requirements.

Name attributes according to whatever standard is in place or develop a standard according to the guidelines provided in this chapter.

There is value in exploring different levels of generalization for attributes. Attributes can be allocated to different levels of the entity subtype hierarchy, and will influence the choice of level for implementation. Attributes belonging to the same entity may also be generalized, possibly resulting in repeating groups, which will be separated by normalization.

Chapter 11

Time-Dependent Data

"Les vrais paradis sont les paradis qu'on a perdus"
- Proust

The Problem

Few areas of data modeling are the subject of as much confusion as the handling of time-related and time-dependent data.

Perhaps we're modeling data for an insurance company. It's certainly important for us to know the current status of a client's insurance policy – how much is insured and what items are covered. But in order to handle claims for events that happened some time ago, we need to be able to determine the status at any given date in the past.

Or, we may want to support planning of a railway network, and be able to represent how the network will look at various times in the future.

Underlying these questions is the concept of effective dates, past or future, and how we handle them in a data model.

A closely related issue is the maintenance of "audit trails:" a history of changes to the databases, and of the transactions that caused them. What cash flows contributed to the current balance? Why was a customer's credit rating downgraded?

The difficulties that even experienced data modelers encounter in these areas are often the result of trying to find a simple recipe for "adding the time dimension" to a model. There are two fundamental problems with this approach: first, the initial model usually includes time-dependent data already, and second, we seldom need to maintain a full history and set of past positions for *everything* in the database.

In this chapter we look at some basic principles and structures for handling time-related data. You should be able to solve most problems you encounter in practice by selectively employing combinations of these. We look at some techniques specific to data warehouses in chapter 13. Once again, the choice of the best approach in a given situation is not always straightforward, and, as in all our modeling, we need to actively explore and compare alternatives.

Audit Trails and Snapshots

Let's start with a very simple example – a single entity. Our client is an investor, and the entity Share (stock) Holding represents their holdings of each share type (Figure 11-1). As it stands, the model enables us to record the *current* quantity and price of each type of share. But we may also need to hold data about past holdings and prices, to support queries such as "How many shares in company *xyz* did we hold on July 1, 1992?" or "by how much has the total value of our investments changed in the past month?"

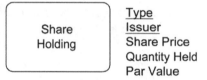

Figure 11-1. Model of Current Share Holdings

There are essentially two ways of achieving this:

1. Record details of each *change* to a share holding – the "audit trail" approach; or

2. Include an "effective date" attribute in the Share Holding entity, and record new instances either periodically or each time there is a change – the "snapshot" approach.

If you are familiar with accounting, you can think of these as "profit and loss" and "balance sheet" approaches, respectively. Balance sheets are snapshots of a business's position at particular times, while profit and loss statements summarize changes to that position.

The Basic Audit Trail Approach

We'll start with the audit trail approach. Let's make the reasonable assumption that we want to keep track not only of changes, but also of the events that cause them. This suggests the three-entity model of Figure 11-2. Note that Share Holding represents current share holdings.

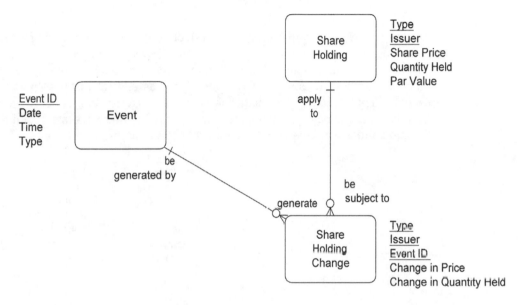

Figure 11-2. Basic Audit Trail Approach

This is the basic audit trail solution, and often quite workable as it stands. But there are a number of variations we can make to it.

Event is a very generic entity that may be usefully subtyped to reflect different sets of attributes and associated processes. In this example we might model separate entities for purchase, sale, rights issue, bonus issue, revaluation, etc.

There is often value in grouping events into higher-level events, or, conversely, breaking them down into component events. For example, we might group a number of different share purchases into the aggregate event "company takeover," or break them down into individual parcels. We can model this with a variable or fixed-depth hierarchy – e.g., a recursive relationship on Event, or separate entities for Aggregate Event, Basic Event, and Component Event, suitably defined and/or subtyped.

In some circumstances, we may not require the Event entity at all. Attributes of the Share Holding Change entity (typically Date and Time, or External Reference Number) can sometimes provide all the data we need about the source of the change. One common situation in which this is likely to be so is when values are recorded at predetermined intervals. For example, we might record share prices on a daily basis, rather than each time there was a movement.

Another possibility is that each event affects only one share holding – i.e., generates only one share holding change. We can very often propose workable definitions of Event to make this so. For example, we could choose to regard a bundled purchase of shares of different types as several distinct "purchase events." This reduces the relationship between Event and Share Holding Change to a mandatory, nontransferable one-to-one, and suggests combining the two entities (see chapter 6). Figure 11-3 shows the result.

Figure 11-3. Event Defined as Generating Only One Change

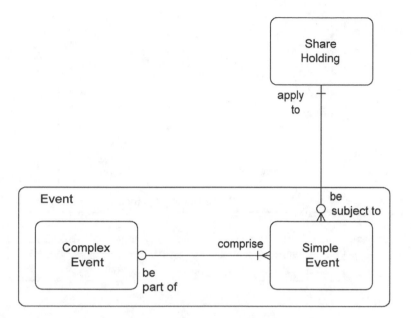

Figure 11-4. Separating Complex and Simple Events

Even if some types of event do cause more than one change, we can extend the model to accommodate them as in Figure 11-4.

Returning to the model in Figure 11-2, Share Holding Change can also be subtyped to distinguish price changes from quantity changes (Figure 11-5).

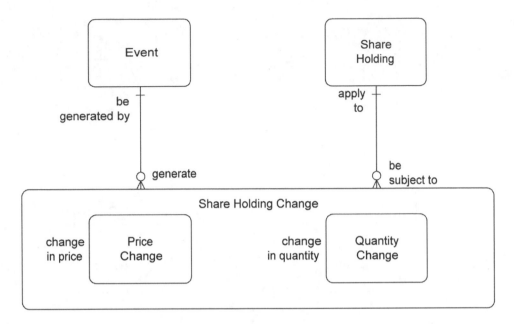

Figure 11-5. Subtyping to Reflect Different Types of Changes

With only two attributes, our choices are straightforward, but as the number of attributes increases, so does the variety of subtyping options. It can be helpful to look at the different types of events (whether formal subtypes or not) and the combination of attributes that each affects. This will often suggest subtypes based on groups of attributes that are affected by particular types of events. For example, "Share Acquisition" might be suggested by the Event Subtypes "Share Purchase," "Bonus Issue," "Rights Issue," and "Transfer In." But you do need to look closely at the stability of these groups of attributes. If they reflect well-established business events, there may be no problem, but if they are based around, for example, our current breakup of a dialogue, we may find ourselves changing the database structure simply because we want to update an attribute at a different point in the dialogue.

The Share Holding entity not only contains the current values of all attributes, but also is the only place in which any static attributes (other than the primary key) need to be held. For example, the Par Value of the share never changes, and therefore should not appear in Share Holding Change.

Instead of defining Share Holding as representing current share holdings, we could have used it to represent *initial* share holdings (Figure 11-6).

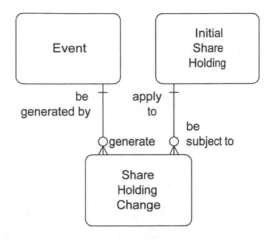

Figure 11-6. Model Based on Changes to Initial Share Holding

In one way this is more elegant, as updates will need only to create rows in the Event and Share Holding Change tables – they will not need to update the Initial Share Holding. On the other hand, inquiries on the current position require that it be built up by applying all changes to the initial holding. Note also that the collection of all the instances of Initial Share Holding will not represent our "opening position;" rather, they represent the opening position plus the initial quantities and values of each share acquired since.

One very important assumption in the model of Figure 11-6 is that Events and Share Holding Changes cannot themselves be updated (or, at least, that we are not interested in keeping any history of such changes). Imagine for a moment that we *could* update the attributes of Share Holding Change. Then we would need to extend the model to include "Share Holding Change Change" to keep track of these changes, and so on until we reached a "nonupdatable" entity – one in which each instance, once recorded, never changed. So an interesting feature of the audit trail approach to modeling time-dependent data is that it relies on defining some data that is invariant.

In our example, it's difficult to envision any business event that would cause the values of Share Holding Change attributes to change. But there is always the possibility that we record some data in error (perhaps we have miss-keyed a price change). We then have essentially three options:

1. Correct the data without keeping a history of the change. This is a simple solution, but it will cause reconciliation problems if reports have been issued or decisions made based on the incorrect data.

2. Maintain a separate history of "changes to changes." This complicates the model, but does separate business changes from error corrections.

3. Allow for a "reversal" or "correction" event, which will create another Share Holding Change row. This is the approach used in accounting. This is often the cleanest solution to the problems of 1, above, and to situations where the correction event can cause more complex changes to the database (e.g., reversal of commission and government tax).

All of these approaches may be used, depending on the circumstances. The important thing is to plan explicitly for changes resulting from error corrections as well as those caused by the more usual business events.

Handling Nonnumeric Data

You may have noticed that I conveniently chose numeric attributes (Number of Shares and Share Price) as the time-dependent data in the example. It makes sense to talk about the change (increase or decrease) to a numeric attribute. But how do we handle changes to the value of nonnumeric attributes – for example "Share Holding Custodian?" One approach is to hold the value prior to the change, rather than the amount of change. The value *after* the change will then be held either in the next instance of Share Holding Change or in the Current Share Holding.

Holding the prior value is also an option when dealing with numeric data. We could just as well have held "Previous Price" as "Change in Price." One will be derivable from the other, and selecting the best option usually comes down to which is more commonly required by the business processes, and perhaps maintaining a consistency of approach – elegance again!

The Basic Snapshot Approach

The idea of holding prior values rather than changes provides a nice lead-in to the "snapshot" approach.

One of the options available to us is to consistently hold prior values rather than changes, to the extent that "no change" is represented by the prior value being the same as the new value. If we take this approach, then Share Holding Changes start to look very like Current Share Holdings as they stood prior to updating. The only difference in the attributes is the inclusion of the event identifier or effective date, and the exclusion of data that is not time-dependent, such as Par Value.

Share Holding Change is now badly named, as we are representing past positions, rather than changes. "Historical Share Holding" is more appropriate (Figure 11-7). This change of name reflects a change in the flavor of the model. Queries of the form "what was the position at a particular date" are now supported in a very simple way (just find the relevant Historical Share Holding), while queries about changes are still supported, but require some calculation to assemble the data. If typical updates to share holdings involve changes to only a small number of attributes, this snapshot approach will be less tidy than an audit trail with subtypes: we will end up carrying a lot of data just to indicate "no change."

Figure 11-7. Basic Snapshot Approach

Note that the event associated with a particular historical share holding is the event that ended that set of attribute values – not the event that set them up. The relationship name "update" (in contrast to "create") reflects this. Another option is to link events to the historical share holding they *create*. In this case, we will also need to link Current Share Holding to Event (Figure 11-8).

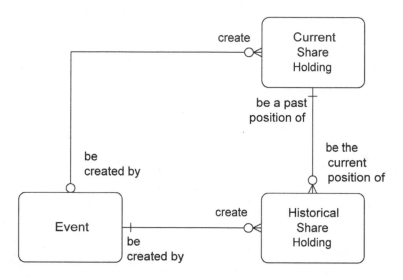

Figure 11-8. Linking Events to the Positions Which They Create

This gives us yet another option, with some advantages in elegance if the business is more interested (as it often is) in the event that *led* to a particular position.

Note that the two relationships to Event are now optional. This is because the initial share holding (which may be an instance of either Current Share Holding or Historical Share Holding) may represent an opening position, not created by any event we have recorded. Of course, we have the option of defining an "initialize" or "transfer in" event to set up the original holdings, in which case the two relationships would become mandatory.

The model as it now stands has at least two weaknesses. The first is the inelegance of having two separate relationships to Current Share Holding and Historical Share Holding. The second is more serious. Each time we create a new current share holding, we will need to create a historical share holding that is a copy of the previous current share holding. This is very close to breaking our rule of not transferring instances from one entity to another (chapter 4).

We can overcome both problems by generalizing the two relationships, along with the two entities. We do this by first splitting out the time-dependent portion of Current Share Holding, using a one-to-one relationship, according to the technique described in chapter 6. The result is shown in Figure 11-9.

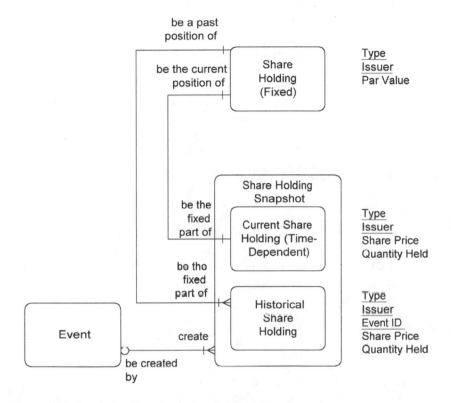

Figure 11-9. Separating Time-Dependent and Static Data

Historical Share Holding will have basically the same attributes as this extracted part of Current Share Holding, and there may well be important processes (e.g., portfolio valuation plotted over time) that treat the two in much the same way.

The Share Holding (Fixed) entity represents attributes that are not time-dependent, or for which we require only one value (perhaps the current value, perhaps the original value). If there are no such attributes besides the key, we will not require this entity at all. Nor will we require it if we take the "sledge hammer" approach of assuming at the outset that *all* data is time-dependent, and that we need to record all historical values.

We've now come quite some distance from our original audit trail approach. The path we took is a nice example of the use of creative modeling techniques. Along the way we've seen a number of ways of handling historical data, even for the simplest one-entity model. The one-entity example is quite general, and can easily be adapted to handle future positions (for example, the results of a planned share purchase) as well as (or instead of) past positions.

We often arrive at models like those discussed here without ever explicitly considering the time dimension. For example, a simple model of bank accounts and transactions is an example of the audit trail approach, and a "Staff Appraisal" entity, which represents multiple appraisals of the same person over time, is an example of the snapshot approach.

Sequences and Versions

In our examples so far, we have used the term "time-dependent" in a very literal way, to mean that events, snapshots, and changes have an attribute of Date or Date and Time. We can equally apply these rules to sequences that are not explicitly or visibly tied to dates and times. For example, we may wish to keep track of software according to "Version No," or to record the effect of events that can be placed in sequence without specifying absolute times – perhaps the stages in a human-computer dialogue.

Handling Deletions

Sometimes instances of an entity become obsolete in the real world. Consider the case of the Soviet Union. If we have a table of countries and there are references to that table in, for example, our employee table (country of birth), our customer table (country in which the business is registered) or our product table (country of manufacture) we cannot simply delete the record for the Soviet Union from our country table unless there are no records in any other table that refer to the Soviet Union. In fact we cannot rely on there being no such records so we must design for the situation in which a country is no longer current but there are records that continue to refer to it (after all there may be employees who were born in what was then the Soviet Union).

Often these noncurrent entity instances will still have relevance in the context of relationships with other entities. For example, the country "East Germany" may no longer exist, and hence be flagged as noncurrent; nevertheless it will still have meaning as a place of birth for a visa applicant.

A simple solution in this case is to include a flag in the Country table that can be set to mark a country as no longer current (or obsolete). This enables us to include logic which, say, prevents the Soviet Union being recorded as either the country of registration of a new customer or the country of manufacture of a new product (unless we were dealing in antiques!) We would still wish to be able to record the Soviet Union as the country of birth of a new employee.

It is possible for an entity instance to be deleted and then reinstated (see, for example, the Employee/Equipment Item example in this chapter). In these cases, we can simply keep a history of the currency attribute in the same way that we would for any other attribute.

Archiving

In modeling time-dependent data, you need to take into account any archiving requirements, and the associated deletion of data from the database.

Snapshot approaches are generally amenable to having old data removed; it is even possible to retain selected "snapshots" from among the archived data. For example, we might remove daily snapshots from before a particular date, but retain the snapshots from the first day of each month, to provide a coarse history.

Audit trail approaches can be less easy to work with. If data is to be removed, it will need to be summarized into an aggregate "change" or "event," or a "starting point snapshot." Similarly, if a coarse history is required, it will be necessary to summarize intermediate events.

Modeling Time-Dependent Relationships

One-to-Many Relationships

We have now had a fairly good look at the simplest of models, the one-entity model. If we can extend this to a model of two entities linked by a relationship, we have covered the basic building blocks of a data model, and should be able to cope with any situation that arises. In fact, handling relationships requires no new techniques at all if we think of them as being represented by foreign keys: a change to a relationship is just a change to a (foreign key) data item.

So let's develop the share holding example further to include an entity representing the company that issued the shares (Figure 11-10).

We can use any of the preceding approaches to represent a history of changes to Company and Share Holding. Figure 11-11 shows the result of applying a version of the snapshot approach. The Event, Share Holding Snapshot, and Company Snapshot entities are a result of using the techniques for single-entity models. The new problem is what to do with the relationship between Company and Share Holding. In this case, we note that the "issued by" relationship is *nontransferable*, and hence is part of the *fixed* data about share holdings. (The foreign key – Issuer – will not change value for a given Share Holding).

We already hold the Company ID on Share Holding (Fixed), and the relationship is therefore between Share Holding (Fixed) and Company (Fixed), as shown.

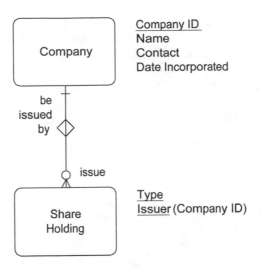

Figure 11-10. Companies and Shares – Current Position

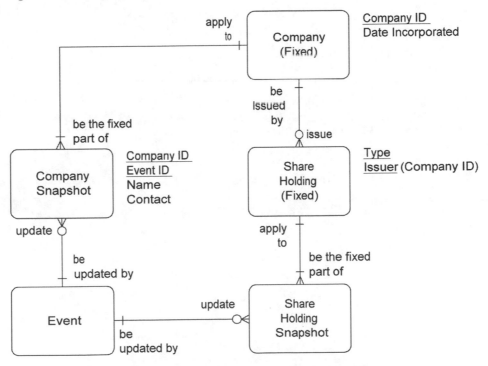

Figure 11-11. Basic Snapshot Approach Applied to Nontransferable Relationship

But what if the relationship were transferable? In Figure 11-12 we include the entity Location, and the rule that shareholdings can be transferred from one location to another. Each shareholding *snapshot* is now related to a single instance of Location. A new shareholding snapshot is created whenever a share holding is moved from one location to another. From a relational model perspective, the foreign key to Location is now time-dependent, and therefore needs to be an attribute of the Shareholding Snapshot (Figure 11-13).

Figure 11-12. Location and Shareholding – Current Data

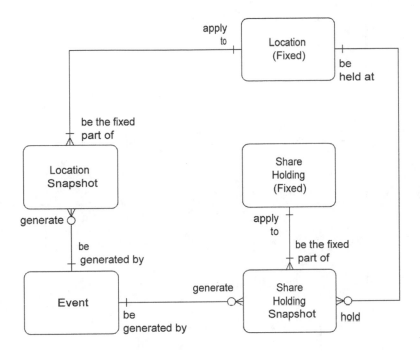

Figure 11-13. Basic Snapshot Approach Applied to Transferable Relationship

The effects on the original relationship under the two options (transferable and non transferable) are summarized in Figure 11-14. Note the use of the nontransferability symbol introduced in chapter 7.

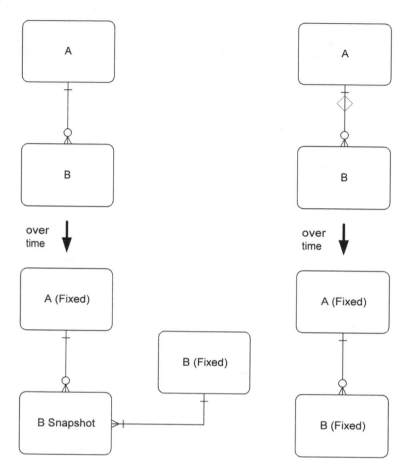

Figure 11-14. Adding History to Transferable and Nontransferable Relationships

You might find it interesting to compare this result with the often-quoted guideline that "when you include the time dimension, one-to-many relationships become many-to-many." If you think of the Shareholding Snapshot entity as a resolution entity, you will see that this guideline only applies to *transferable* relationships.

This makes sense. If a relationship is nontransferable, it will not change over time; hence there is no need to record its history.

Many-to-Many Relationships

Many-to-many relationships present no special problems, as we can start by resolving them into two one-to-many nontransferable relationships, plus a resolution entity.

Figure 11-15 shows a worked example using the snapshot approach (I've left out the individual histories of the Employee and Equipment Item entities).

In the simplest case, when the resolution entity does not contain any attributes other than the key, we need only keep track of the periods for which the entity applies (i.e., for which the relationship exists). We can use either of the structures in Figure 11-16. Option 1 is based on an audit trail of changes, option 2 on periods of currency.

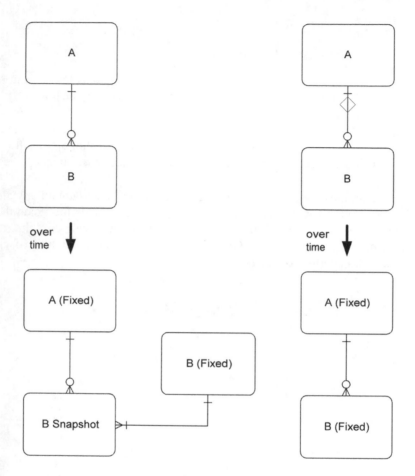

Figure 11-15. History of Many-to-Many Relationships

Option 1:

> RESPONSIBILITY (<u>**Employee ID**</u>, <u>**Equipment ID**</u>, <u>**Date Effective**</u>, **Currency Indicator**)

Option 2:

> RESPONSIBILITY (<u>**Employee ID**</u>, <u>**Equipment ID**</u>, <u>**Date Effective From**</u>, **Date Effective To**)

Figure 11-16. Alternatives for Handling History of Simple Resolution Entity

Self-Referencing Relationships

Handling self-referencing relationships is no different in principle from handling relationships between two entities, but it's easy to get confused. Figure 11-17 shows solutions to the most common situations.

Date Entities

Occasionally, we need to set up an entity called Date or something similar, to record such data as whether a given date is a public holiday. (Incidentally, I've often seen this entity named "Calendar" – a violation of our "one instance" rule covered in chapter 3).

There is no problem with the entity as such, but a difficulty does arise when we note that the primary key is Date, and that this attribute appears in entities throughout the data model, where, technically, it is a foreign key to the Date entity According to our diagramming rules we should draw relationships between the Date entity and all the entities in which the foreign key appears, a tedious and messy exercise.

My advice is to break the rules, and not to worry about drawing the relationships. The rules that the relationships enforce (i.e., ensuring that only valid dates appear) are normally handled by standard date-checking routines; our explicit relationships add virtually nothing except unnecessary complexity. The situation is different if the dates are a special subset – for example, public holidays. In this case, you should name the entity appropriately ("Public Holiday!") and show any relationships that are constrained to that subset (e.g., Public Holiday Bonus *paid for work on* Public Holiday).

Changes to the Data Structure

Our discussion so far has related to keeping track of changes to data *content* over time. From time to time, we need to change a data model, and hence the database *structure*, to reflect a new requirement or changes to the business.

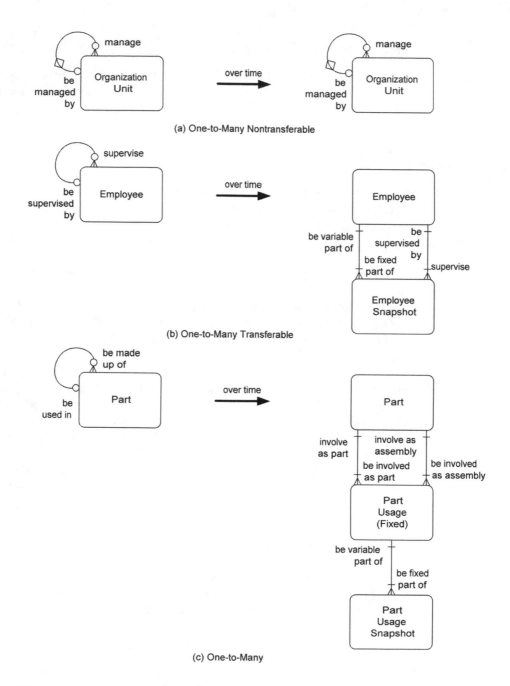

Figure 11-17. History of Self-Referencing Relationships

Handling this falls outside the realm of data modeling, and is a serious challenge for the database administrator. The problem is not only to implement the changes to the database, and the (often-considerable) consequent changes to programs. The database administrator also needs to ensure the ongoing usefulness of archived data, which remains in the old format. Usually, this means archiving copies of the original programs, and of any data conversion programs.

Putting it into Practice

In this chapter, we've worked through a number of options for incorporating time and history in data models. In practice, I suggest that you don't worry too much about these issues in your initial modeling. On the other hand, you should not consciously try to exclude the time dimension. You will find that you automatically include much time-related data, through the use of familiar structures such as account entries, transactions, and events.

You should then review the model to ensure that time-related needs are met. The best approach often does not become clear until attributes are well defined, and functional analysis has identified the different event types and their effects on the data.

Keep in mind that every transaction that changes or deletes data without leaving a record of the previous position is destroying data the organization has paid to capture. It's important to satisfy yourself and the user that such data is no longer of potential value to the organization before deciding that it will be deleted without trace.

Summary

There are numerous options for modeling historical and future (planned or anticipated) data. The most appropriate technique will vary from case to case, even within the same model.

The two basic approaches are the "audit trail," which records a history of changes, and the "snapshot," which records a series of past or future positions. Other variations arise from different levels of generalization and aggregation for events and changes, and the choice of whether to treat current positions separately or as special cases of historical or future positions.

Transferable relationships that are one-to-many with the time factor excluded become many-to-many over time. Nontransferable relationships remain one-to-many.

Chapter 12

Modeling Business Rules

"Let's just go through it again slowly, point by point, 'cos I'm thick."

- Saul Enderby in Smiley's People by John Le Carre.

Introduction

Information systems contain and enforce *rules* about the businesses they support. (Some writers prefer the word *constraints* – I use the two interchangeably). For example, a human resource management system might incorporate the following rules (among others):

"Each employee can belong to at most one union at one time."

"A minimum of 4% of each employee's salary up to $80,000 must be credited to the company pension fund."

"If salary deductions result in an employee's net pay being negative, include details in an exception report."

"At most two employees can share a job position at any time."

"Only employees of Grade 4 and above can receive entertainment allowances."

"For each grade of employee, a standard set of base benefits applies."

"Each employee must have a unique employee number."

"An employee's employment status must be either Permanent or Casual."

"Employee number 4787 has annual salary $82,000."

What is a rule? Systems contain information in various forms (data structure, data content, program logic, procedure manuals) that may be:

- Assertions that something has happened (e.g., a particular customer has placed an order for a particular product)

- Information about how the system[43] is to behave in particular situations (e.g., if the user attempts to raise an order without any products specified, reject it).

The latter are rules. Thus it is fair to say that all of the statements listed above are rules since each describes in some way in which the system is to behave. Even the last, which is quite specific, affects the outcome of a process in the payroll system.

In this chapter we begin with a broad look at business rules, then focus on the types of rules that are of concern to the data modeler. We look at what rules can be captured in E-R and relational models, and discuss the problem of documenting those which cannot.

We then look at where and how rules should be implemented within an application focusing on options available within DBMSs.

But before we get into the detail of rules, an important caveat: as discussed in chapter 1, a new database is usually developed for the purpose of supporting a new way of doing business. Some of the recent writing on business rules has overlooked the fact that our job is to model what will be, not what was. And we should be proactive in suggesting new possibilities and new rules to the business.

---

[43] I am using the term 'system' in its broadest sense to mean not only the database and programs that operate upon it but the people who interact with it.

Types of Business Rules

If we accept that a business rule is information about how the system is to behave in a particular situation, we can see that there are a number of different types of business rule.

Data Rules

Firstly, there are rules that constrain the data the system can handle and how they relate to each other. These fall into the following categories:

- **structural** or **cardinality rules** which determine how many of a particular data item can be recorded in the database in association with some other data item

- **data validation rules** (strictly speaking data update rules), which determine what data may be recorded in the database and what changes may be made to that data

- **data derivation rules**, which specify the methods by which items of derived data (on screens and in reports) are calculated

- **referential integrity rules** require that both entity instances involved in each relationship instance must exist.

Examples of cardinality rules include *"Each employee can belong to at most one union at any time"* and *"At most two employees can share a job position at any time."* Some 'laws of physics' fall under this heading, such as *"Each employee can only be in one place at the one time:"* while hardly a *business* rule, it is presumably a requirement of the system that we cannot enter data that indicates that an employee was in two different places at the same time.

Strictly speaking, we should distinguish between rules about real-world objects and rules about the data that represents those objects. In most cases, the distinction is academic, but, as we see in sections in this chapter, there are sometimes requirements to record information about real-world objects that have broken the rules.

Examples of data validation rules include *"Each employee must have a unique employee number," "An employee's employment status must be either Permanent or Casual"* and *"Only employees of Grade 4 and above can receive entertainment allowances."* It is likely to be a requirement of the system that any attempt to record two employees with the same employee number, an employee with an employment status other than Permanent or Casual, or an entertainment allowance for an employee of Grade 3 will be rejected.

An example of a data derivation rule is *"An employee's gross monthly salary is the sum of 1/12 of their annual salary plus 52/12 of the total of each of the nontaxable weekly allowances for each week for which that allowance applies less the total of each of the before-tax deductions for each week for which that deduction applies."*

In a relational database there is an implicit referential integrity rule for each foreign key, which states that each instance of that foreign key must match one of the primary keys in the referenced table (e.g., we cannot have an Order without an associated Customer). There is no need to explicitly document these rules if the relevant relationships or foreign keys are fully documented, although there may occasionally be a requirement to relax such rules. Referential integrity is discussed further later in this chapter.

The rule *"Only employees of Grade 4 and above can receive entertainment allowances"* includes two items ("Grade 4" and allowance type "entertainment") that could be recorded in any of a number of places, including the database. So we also need to consider **data that supports data rules**: most often data validation rules like this one but possibly cardinality (e.g., "What is the maximum number of unions an employee can belong to at one time?") or data derivation rules (e.g., "is allowance x nontaxable – and hence included in the calculation of an employee's gross monthly salary?") We discuss the options for recording this data later in this chapter.

Process Rules

A system will also be constrained by **process rules**, such as *"A minimum of 4% of each employee's salary up to $80,000 must be credited to the company pension fund."* and *"If salary deductions result in an employee's net pay being negative, include details in an exception report."* These determine what processing the system is to do in particular circumstances.

The first of these rules includes two numbers (4% and $80,000) which may or may not be recorded as data in the database itself. We also discuss recording **data that supports process rules** later in this chapter.

Another example of a process rule that requires some data somewhere is *"For each grade of employee, a standard set of base benefits applies."* What are the base benefits for each grade of employee?

"Employee number 4787 has annual salary $82,000" is, as already indicated, a process rule. It is reasonable to expect that the data to support this process rule is going to be held in the database.

What Rules are Relevant to the Data Modeler?

The data modeler should be concerned with both data and process rules and the data that supports them with one exception: other than in making a decision where and how the data supporting a process rule is to be recorded, it is not in the data modeler's brief to either model or decide on the implementation of any process rules. Therefore references to "business rules" in the rest of this chapter include only the various data rule types listed above, whereas references to "data that supports rules" covers both data that supports process rules and data that supports data rules.

Discovery and Verification of Business Rules

While the business people consulted will volunteer many of the business rules that a system must support, it is important to ensure that all bases have been covered. Once we have a draft data model, the following activities should be undertaken to check in a systematic way that the rules that it embodies correctly reflect the business requirements.

Cardinality Rules

We can assemble a candidate set of cardinality rules by constructing business sentences from each relationship as described in chapter 3. We should also check the cardinality of each *attribute* (how many values it can have for one instance of the entity). This should be part of the process of normalization, as described in chapter 2. However if you have worked top-down to develop an Entity-Relationship model, you need to check that each attribute can only have one value for each instance of the entity in which it has been placed. For example, if there is a Nickname attribute in the Employee entity and the business needs to record all nicknames for those employees that have more than one, the data model needs to be modified, either by creating a separate entity for nicknames (related to the Employee entity) or allowing the Nickname attribute in the Employee entity to hold more than one nickname (in which case its description must be changed). To establish attribute cardinalities, we can ask questions in the following form for each attribute:

"Can an employee have more than one nickname?"

"If so, is it necessary to record more than one in the database?"

Data Validation Rules

Data validation rules can be discovered by asking, for each entity:

"What restrictions are there on adding an instance of this entity?"

"What restrictions are there on the values that may be entered in each attribute of a new instance of this entity?"

"What restrictions are there on the values that may be entered in each attribute when changing an existing instance of this entity?" (The answer to this question is often the same as the answer to the previous question but on occasion they may differ).

"What restrictions are there on removing an instance of this entity?"

Data Derivation Rules

Data derivation rules are best discovered by analyzing each screen and report that has been specified and list each value that appears that does not correspond directly to an attribute in the data model. For each value, it is necessary to establish with the business exactly how that value is to be derived from the data that is in the database. In the case of a data warehouse (chapter 13), or any other database in which we decide to hold summary data, we will need to ask similar questions – and document the answers.

Documentation of Business Rules

Documentation in an Entity-Relationship Diagram

Only a few types of business rule can be documented in an entity-relationship diagram:

1. The referential integrity rules implicit in each relationship (further discussed in this chapter)

2. The cardinalities of each relationship (as discussed in chapter 3): these are (of course) cardinality rules

3. Whether each relationship is mandatory or optional (as also discussed in chapter 3): these are data validation rules, since they determine restrictions on the addition, changing and/or removal of entity instances

4. Various limitations on which entity instances can be associated with each other (by specifying that a relationship is with a subtype of an entity rather than the entity itself; this is discussed further in this chapter): these are also data validation rules

5. The fact that that attribute is restricted to a discrete set of values can be documented by adding an entity to represent the relevant set of categories and a relationship from that entity to one containing a category attribute (the familiar "look-up table" structure – discussed in this chapter): another data validation rule.

Further business rules can be documented in the attribute lists supporting an entity-relationship diagram:

1. The uniqueness of each primary key (data validation)

2. The cardinality of each attribute (cardinality)

3. The optionality (nullability) of each attribute (data validation)

4. The datatype of each attribute (e.g., if the attribute is given a numeric datatype, this specifies a data validation rule that nonnumerics cannot be entered; if a date datatype, that the value entered must be a valid date).

If the transferability notation (see chapter 6) is available, an additional type of business rule can be documented:

5. The transferability of each relationship (data validation).

Documentation in a Relational Model

All but the last of the rule types listed above can be documented in a relational model (i.e., tables with columns rather than an E-R diagram with attributes) with the following provisos:

1. Marking a column as a foreign key (or part of a foreign key) implies referential integrity on that foreign key (discussed in this chapter).

2. Marking a column as a foreign key (or part of a foreign key) also implies that there is a one-to-many relationship; there is no way of marking the foreign key that has been included to support a one-to-one relationship.

3. Only the optionality at the "one" end of a relationship can be documented, by marking the foreign key column(s) as optional ("nullable").

4. Limitations on which entity instances can be associated with each other can be documented if each set of entity instances that behaves similarly is recorded as a separate table.

5. The fact that a column is restricted to a discrete set of values is documented by adding a table to represent the relevant set of categories and marking the original column as a foreign key to the new table.

6. The uniqueness of one column or set of columns in a table can be documented by marking it or them as the primary key.

7. Inclusion of a column in a table documents that that column can only have one value for each row in the table.

8. Columns can be marked as optional (nullable).

9. The datatype of each column can be documented.

Documenting Other Rules

Unfortunately there are many other types of rule, including all data derivation rules and the following types of data validation rule, which are not readily represented in an E-R or relational model:

- nondiscrete constraints on attribute values (e.g., *"The Unit Price of a Product must be positive"*)

- attribute constraints dependent on values of other attributes in the same instance (e.g., *"The End Date must be later than the Start Date"*)

- most attribute constraints that are dependent on values of attributes in different instances (e.g., *"The amount of this allowance for this employee cannot exceed the maximum for this employee grade"*): exceptions that *can* be modeled in an entity-relationship diagram or relational model are uniqueness of an attribute or set of attributes, referential integrity, and those involving allowable combinations of values of different attributes

- cardinality/optionality constraints such as *"There can be no more than four subjects recorded for a teacher"* or *"There must be at least two subjects recorded for each teacher"* (actually the first of these could be documented using a repeating group with four items but, for reasons discussed in chapter 2, this is not advisable)

- restrictions on updatability (other than transferability) such as *"No existing transaction can be updated,"* *"This date can only be altered to a date later than previously recorded"* and *"This attribute can only be updated by the Finance Manager."*

Entity-relationship diagrams and relational models do not provide any means of documenting these other rule types, yet such rules tell us important information about the data, its meaning, and how it is to be correctly used. They logically belong with the data model, so some supplementary documentation technique is required. Some other modeling approaches recognize this need. The "object role" or "fact-based" approach[44] provides a well-developed and much richer language for modeling constraints, and the resulting models can be converted to relational database designs fairly mechanically. We can also choose to take advantage of one or more of the

---

[44] See, for example, Nijssen, G.M. and Halpin, T.A., *Conceptual Schema and Relational Database Design – A Fact Based Approach*, Prentice Hall (1989).

techniques available to specify *process* logic: decision tables, decision trees, data flow diagrams, function decompositions, pseudo-code, etc. These are particularly relevant for rules we would like to hold as data, in order to facilitate change, but which would more naturally be represented within program logic. The important thing is that, whichever techniques are adopted, they be readily understandable by all participants in the system development process. It is also important that rules not be ignored as "too hard". The rules are an integral part of the system being developed and it is essential to be able to refer back to an agreed specification.

Plain language is still one of the most convenient and best understood ways to specify rules. One problem with plain language is that it provides plenty of scope for ambiguity. To address this deficiency, Ross[45] has developed a very sophisticated diagrammatic notation for documenting rules of all types: while he has developed a very thorough taxonomy of rules and a wide range of symbols to represent them, the complexity of the diagrams produced using this technique may make them inaccessible to business people. However Ross's technique may be most useful in documenting rules for the benefit of those building a system and in gaining an appreciation of the types of rules we need to look for. The great advantage of textual description of rules is that the rules remain understandable to all participants in the system development process. While Ross's technique does enforce rigor compared with the freedom offered by text to make ambiguous statements, careful choice of the wording of rules can add rigor without loss of understanding.

Data validation rules that cannot be represented directly in the data model proper should be documented in text form against the relevant entities and attributes, as illustrated in Figure 12-1. Data derivation rules should be documented separately because they relate to data items that have not been defined as attributes in the data model.

---

[45] Ross, R. G., *The Business Rule Book: Classifying, Defining & Modeling Rules*, Business Rule Solutions (1997).

Entity / Data Item	PK	Constraints
Student Absence		No date/time overlaps between records for the same Student
be for Student	P	Mandatory; Student must already exist
Start Date	P	Mandatory; must be valid date; must be within reasonable range
End Date		If entered: must be valid date; must be not be before Start Date; must be within reasonable range
First Timetable Period No	P	Mandatory; integer; must be between 1 and maximum timetable period no inclusive
Last Timetable Period No		If entered: integer; must be between 1 and maximum timetable period no inclusive; must not be less than First Timetable Period No
be classified by Student Absence Reason		Mandatory; Student Absence Reason must already exist
Notification Date		If entered: must be valid date; must be within reasonable range
Absence Approved Flag		If entered: must be Yes or No
Student Absence Reason		
Absence Reason Code	P	Mandatory; must be unique
Description		Mandatory; must be unique

Figure 12-1. Some Data Validation Rules

Where there is any doubt about the accuracy of a rule recorded against the model, obtain and list examples. These serve not only to clarify and test the accuracy of our specified requirements and verify that the rules are real and important, but provide "bullets" to fire at proposed solutions. On occasions, I have seen requirements dropped or significantly modified after the search for examples failed to turn up any, or confirmed that the few cases from which the rules had been inferred were in fact the only cases!

Use of Subtypes to Document Rules

Subtypes can be used to document limitations on which entity instances can be associated with each other, as outlined in chapter 4. Figure 12-2 illustrates the simplest use of subtypes to document a rule. The initial model relates workers and annual leave applications, but we are advised that only certain types of workers – employees – can submit annual leave applications. A straightforward subtyping captures the rule.

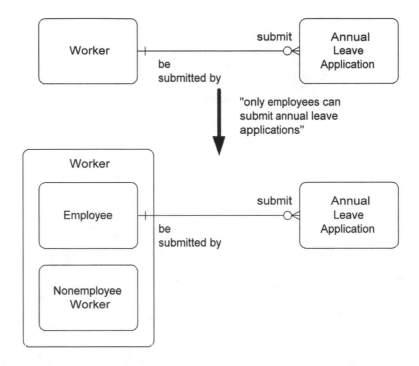

Figure 12-2. Using Subtypes to Model Rules

"Nonemployee Worker" is not an elegant classification or name, and we should be prompted to ask what other sorts of workers the user is interested in. Perhaps we might be able to change the entity name to "Contractor."

Note that, as described in chapter 4, we have a variety of options for implementing a supertype/subtype structure: inclusion of subtypes in the model does not necessarily imply that each will be implemented in a separate table. We may well decide not to, perhaps because we can envision other worker types in the future, or a relaxation of the rule as to who can submit leave applications. We would then implement the rule either within program logic, or through a table listing the types of workers able to submit annual leave applications.

This simple example provides a template for solving more complex problems. For example, we might want to add the rule that *"Only noncitizens require work permits."* This could be achieved by using the partitioning convention introduced in chapter 4 to show alternative subtypings (Figure 12-3).

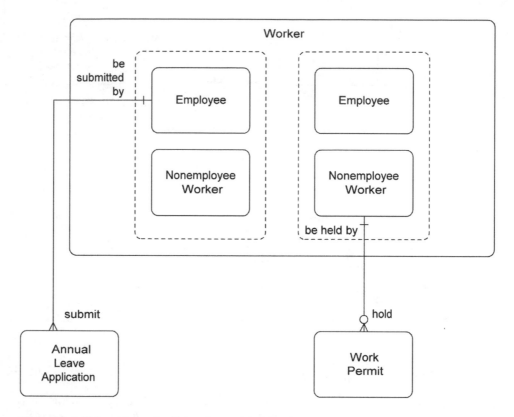

Figure 12-3. Using Alternative Subtypings to Model Rules

Note that the relationship from Noncitizen to Work Permit is *optional*, even though the original rule could have been interpreted as requiring it to be mandatory. We would have checked this by asking the user: "Could we ever want to record details of a noncitizen who did not have a work permit – perhaps prior to their obtaining one?" With more than one subtyping, the term "Worker Type" becomes ambiguous. It is always best to use more descriptive terms if available – perhaps Employment Status and Citizenship Status. A useful convention is to reserve the term "type" for stable (intrinsic) types, in the sense that an instance is not allowed to change types.

Suppose we wanted to model the organizational structure of a company so as to enforce the rule that an employee could be assigned only to a lowest level organizational unit. This kind of structure also occurs in hierarchical charts of accounts, in which transactions can be posted only to the lowest level.

Figure 12-4 shows the use of subtypes to capture the rule. Note that the structure itself defines a Lowest Level Organization Unit as an Organizational Unit that cannot control other Organizational Units (since it lacks the "control" relationship). Once again, we might not implement the subtypes, perhaps because a given lowest level organizational unit could later control other organization units, thus changing its entity classification. (chapter 4 discusses why we want to avoid instances changing from one entity to another).

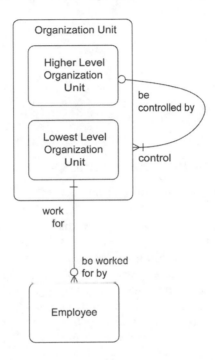

Figure 12-4. Using Unstable Subtypes to Capture Rules

Wherever subtyping allows you to capture a business rule easily in the data model, I recommend that you do so, *even if you have little intention of actually implementing the subtypes as separate tables in the final database design.* Even if you plan to have a single table in the database holding many different types of real-world objects, documenting those real-world objects as a single entity is likely to make the model incomprehensible to users. Do not omit important rules that can be readily documented using subtypes, simply because those subtypes are potentially volatile. This is an abdication of the data modeler's responsibility for doing detailed and rigorous analysis and the function modelers will not thank you for having to ask the same questions again!

Implementation of Business Rules

Deciding how and where each rule is to be implemented is one of the most important aspects of information system design. Depending on the type of rule, one or more of the following techniques can be used to implement a rule in a database:

- the structure of the database (its tables and columns)

- various properties of columns (datatype, nullability, uniqueness, referential integrity)

- program logic (stored procedures, screen event handling, application code)

- data values held in the database.

Implementing Particular Rules

Some rules by their nature suggest one of the above techniques in particular. For example, the rule *"Each employee can belong to at most one union at one time"* is most obviously supported by data structure (a foreign key in the Employee table representing a one-to-many relationship between the Union and Employee entities). Similarly the rule *"If salary deductions result in an employee's net pay being negative, include details in an exception report"* is clearly a candidate for implementation in program logic. Other rules suggest alternative treatments: for example, the values 4% and $80,000 supporting the rule *"A minimum of 4% of each employee's salary up to $80,000 must be credited to the company pension fund"* could be held as data in the database or constants in program logic.

Choosing from Alternatives

Where there are alternatives, the selection of an implementation technique should start with the following questions:

1. How readily does this implementation method support the rule?

2. How volatile is the rule (how likely is it to change during the lifetime of the system?)

3. How flexible is this implementation method (how easily does it lend itself to changing a rule?)

For example, changing the database structure after a system has been built is a very complex task whereas changing a data value is very easy. Changes to program logic involve more work than changing a data value but less than changing the database structure (which will involve program logic changes in at least one, and possibly many, programs). Changes to column properties can generally be made quite quickly but not as quickly as changing a data value.

Note that rules implemented primarily using one technique may also affect the design of other components of the system. For example, if we implement a rule in data structure, that rule will also be reflected in program structure; if we implement a rule using data values, we will need to design the data structure to support the necessary data, and the programs to allow their processing logic to be driven by the data values.

This is an area in which it is crucial that data modelers and function modelers (analysts) work together. Many a data model has been rejected or inappropriately compromised because it placed demands upon function modelers that they didn't understand or were unprepared to tackle.

If a rule is volatile then we may need to consider a more flexible implementation method than the most obvious one. For example, if the rule *"Each employee can belong to at most one union at one time"* is volatile, rather than use an inflexible data structure to implement it, the alternative of a separate Employee Union Membership table (which would allow an unlimited number of memberships per employee) should be adopted. The current rule can then be enforced by adding a unique index to the Employee No column in that table. Removal of that index is quick and easy, but we would then have no limit on the number of unions a particular employee could belong to. If a limit other than 1 were required, it would be necessary to enforce that limit using program logic e.g., a stored procedure triggered by insertion to or update of the Employee Union Membership table.

Here once again there are alternatives. The maximum number of union memberships per employee could be included as a constant in that piece of program logic or held as a value in the database somewhere, to be referred to by that piece of program logic. However, given the very localized effect of stored procedures, and the resultant ease of testing changes to them, there would be no great advantage in holding the limit in a table.

One other advantage of stored procedures is that, if properly associated with triggers, they always execute whenever a particular data operation takes place and therefore are the preferred location for rule enforcement logic. Since the logic is now only in one place rather than scattered among all the various programs that might access the data, the maintenance effort in making changes to that logic is much less than with traditional programming.

Let's look at the implementation options for some of the other rules listed at the start of this chapter:

1. *"At most two employees can share a job position at any time"* can be implemented in the data structure by including two foreign keys in the Job Position table to the Employee table. This could be modeled as such with two relationships between the Job Position and Employee entities. If this rule was volatile and there were the possibility of more than two employees in a job position, a separate Employee Job Position table would be required. Program logic would then be necessary to impose any limit on the number of employees that could share a job position.

2. *"Only employees of Grade 4 and above can receive entertainment allowances"* can be implemented using a stored procedure triggered by insertion to or update of the Employee Allowance table (in which each individual employee's allowances are recorded). This and the inevitable other rules restricting allowances to particular grades could be enforced by explicit logic in that procedure or held in an Employee Grade Allowance table in which legitimate combinations of employee grades and allowance types could be held (or possibly a single record for each allowance type with the range of legitimate employee grades). Note that the recording of this data in a table in the database does not remove the need for a stored procedure; it merely changes the logic in that procedure.

3. *"For each grade of employee, a standard set of base benefits applies"* can be implemented using a stored procedure triggered by insertion to the Employee table or update of the Grade column in that table. Again the base benefits for each grade could be explicitly itemized in that procedure or held in held in an Employee Grade table in which the benefits for each employee grade are listed. Note once again that the recording of this data in a table in the database does not remove the need for a stored procedure; it merely changes the logic in that procedure.

4. *"Each employee must have a unique employee number"* can be implemented by addition of a unique index on Employee No in the Employee table: this would of course be the inevitable result of declaring Employee No to be the primary key of the Employee table, but additional unique indexes can be added to a table for any other columns or combinations of columns that are unique.

5. *"An employee's employment status must be either Permanent or Casual"* is an example of restricting an attribute to a discrete set of values: implementation options for this type of rule are discussed in this chapter.

A detailed example of alternative implementations of the same rules is provided in this chapter.

Assessment of Rule Volatility

Clearly we need to assess the volatility (or, conversely, stability) of each rule before deciding how to implement it. Given a choice of "flexible" or "inflexible," we can expect system users to opt for the former and, consequently, to err on the side of volatility when asked to assess the stability of a rule. But the net result can be a system that is far more sophisticated and complicated than it need be.

It is important, therefore, to gather reliable evidence as to how often and in what way we can expect rules to change. Figure 12-5 provides an illustration of the way in which the volatility of rules can vary.

Type of Rule	Example	Volatility
Laws of physics	A person can only be in one place at the one time	Zero
International or national standards for the industry or business area	Each customer has only one Social Security Number	Low
Generally accepted practice	An invoice is raised against the customer who ordered the goods delivered	Low
Documented procedure within the company	Reorder points for a product are centrally determined rather than being set by warehouses	Medium
The way it's done at the moment	We never raise orders against requisitions from multiple departments	High

Figure 12-5. Volatility of Rules

History is always a good starting point. We can prompt the user: "This rule hasn't changed in ten years; is there anything that would make it more likely to change in the future?" Volume is also an indication. If we have a large set of rules, of the same type or in the same domain, we can anticipate that the set will change.

When you find that a rule is volatile, at least to the extent that it is likely to change over the life of the system, it is important to identify the components that are the cause of its volatility. One useful technique is to look for a more general "higher level" rule that *will* be stable.

For example, the rule *"5% of each contribution must be posted to the Statutory Reserve Account"* may be volatile. But what about *"A percentage of each contribution must be posted to the Statutory Reserve Account?"* But perhaps even this is a volatile instance of a more general rule: *"Each contribution is divided among a set of accounts, in accordance with a standard set of percentages."* And will the division always be based on percentages? Perhaps we can envision in the future deducting, say, $10 from each contribution regardless of size to cover administration costs.

This sort of exploration and clarification is absolutely essential if we are to avoid going to great trouble to accommodate a change of one kind to a rule, only to be caught by a change of a different kind.

It is important that volatile rules can be readily changed. On the other hand, stable rules form the framework on which we design the system, by defining the boundaries of what it must be able to handle. Without some stable rules, system design would be unmanageably complex – every system would need to be able to accommodate any conceivable possibility or change. We want to implement these stable rules in such a way that they cannot be easily bypassed or inadvertently changed.

In some cases, these two factors conflict. The most common situation involves rules that would most easily be enforced by program logic, but which need to be readily updateable by users. Increased pressure on businesses to respond quickly to market or regulatory changes has meant that rules which were once considered stable are no longer so. One solution is to hold the rules as data. If such rules are central to the system, we often refer to the resulting system as being "table-driven." Note however that no rule can be implemented by data values in the database alone. Where the data supporting a rule is held in the database, program logic must be written to use that data. While the cost of changing the rule during the life of the system is reduced by opting for the "table-driven" approach, the sophistication and initial cost of a table-driven system is often significantly greater, due to the complexity of that program logic.

A different sort of problem arises when we want to represent a rule within the data structure, but cannot find a simple way of achieving it. Rules that "almost" follow the pattern of those we are used to specifying in data models can be particularly frustrating. We can readily enforce the rule that only one person can hold a particular job position, but what if the limit is two? Or five? A minimum of two? How do we handle more subtle (but equally reasonable) constraints, such as *"the customer who receives the invoice must be the same as the customer who placed the order?"*

There is room for choice and creativity in deciding how each rule will be implemented. We now look at an example in detail, than at some commonly encountered issues.

Implementation Options: a Detailed Example

Figure 12-6 shows part of a model to support transaction processing for a medical benefits fund. Very similar structures occur in many systems that support a range of products against which specific sets of transactions are allowed. Note the use of the exclusivity arc introduced in chapter 7 to represent, for example, that each dental services claim must be lodged by either a Class A member or a Class B member.

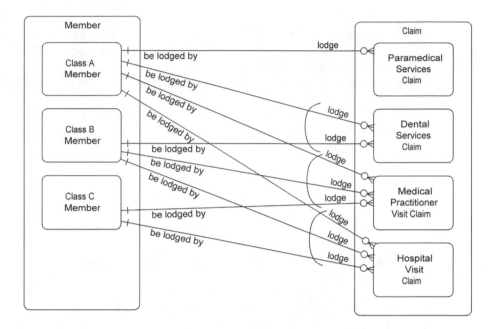

Figure 12-6. Members and Medical Insurance Claims

Let's consider just one rule that the model represents: *"Only a Class A member can lodge a claim for paramedical services."*

Rules in Data Structure

If we implement the model at the lowest level of subtyping, the rule restricting paramedical services claims to Class A members will be implemented in the data structure. The Paramedical Services Claim table will hold a foreign key supporting the relationship to the Class A Member table. Program logic will take account of this structure in, for example, the steps taken to process a paramedical claim, the layout of statements to be sent to Class B members (no provision for paramedical claims), and in ensuring that only Class A members are associated with paramedical claims, through input vetting and error messages. If we are confident that the rule will not change, then this is a sound design, and the program logic can hardly be criticized for inflexibility.

Suppose now that our assumption about the rule being stable is incorrect, and we need to change the rule to allow Class B members to claim for paramedical services. We now need to change the database design to include a foreign key for Class B members in Paramedical Claim. We will also need to change the corresponding program logic.

In general, changes to rules contained within the data structure require the participation of data modelers and database administrators, analysts, programmers, and, of course, the users. Facing this, we may well be tempted by "quick and dirty" approaches – perhaps we could transfer all Class B members to Class A, distinguishing them by a flag in a spare column. Many a system bears the scars of continued "programming around" the data structure rather than incurring the cost of changes.

Rules in Programs

From chapter 4, we know broadly what to do with unstable rules in data structure: we generalize them out. If we implement the model at the level of Member, the rules about what sort of claims can be made by each type of member will no longer be held in data structure.

Instead, the model holds rules:

"Each Paramedical Claim must be lodged by one Member"

"Each Dental Claim must be lodged by one Member", etc.

But we do need to hold the original rules somewhere. Probably the simplest option is to move them to program logic. The logic will look a little different from that associated with the more specific model, and we will essentially be checking the claims against the new attribute Member Type.

Enforcement of the rules now requires some discipline at the programming level. It is technically possible for a program that associates any sort of claim with any sort of member to be written. Good practice suggests a common module for checking, but good practice isn't always enforced!

Now, if we want to change a rule, only the programs that check the constraints will need to be modified. We will not need to involve the data modeler and database administrator at all. The amount of programming work will depend on how well the original programmers succeeded in localizing the checking logic. It may include developing a program to run periodic checks on the data to ensure that the rule has not been violated by a rogue program.

Rules in Data

Holding the rules in program logic may still not provide sufficient responsiveness to business change. In many organizations, the amount of time required to develop a new program version, fully test it, and migrate it into production may be several weeks or months.

The solution is to hold the rules in the data. In our example, this would mean holding a list of the valid member types for each type of claim. An Allowed Claim Type for Member Type table as in Figure 12-7 will provide the essential data.

ALLOWED CLAIM TYPE FOR MEMBER TYPE (<u>Claim Type Code</u>, <u>Member Type Code</u>)

Figure 12-7. Table of Allowed Claim Types for Each Member Type

But our programs will now need to be a deal more sophisticated. If we implement the database at the generalized Member and Claim level (Figure 12-8), the program will need to refer to the Allowed Claim Type for Member Type table to decide which subsets of the main tables to work with in each situation.

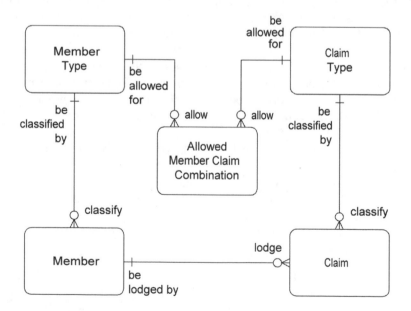

Figure 12-8. Model at Claim Type and Member Type Level

If we implement at the subtype level, the program will need to decide at run time which *tables* to access, by referring to the Allowed Claim Type for Member Type table. For example, we may want to print details of all claims made by a member. The program will need to determine what types of claim can be made by a member of that type, and then access the appropriate claim tables. This will involve translating Claim Type Codes and Member Type Codes into table names, which we can handle either with look-up tables or by translation in the program. The latter approach means that we will have to change the program if we add further tables; the former raises the possibility of a system in which we could add new tables without changing any program logic. Again, we would need to be satisfied that this sophisticated approach was better overall than simply implementing the model at the supertype level. Many programming languages (in particular SQL) do not comfortably support run-time decisions about which table to access.

The payoff for the "rules in data" or "table-driven" approach comes when we want to change the rules. We can leave both database administrators and programmers out of the process, and handle the change with conventional transactions. Because such changes may have a significant business impact, they are typically restricted to a small subset of users, or a system administrator. Without proper control, there is a temptation for individual users to find "novel" ways of using the system, which may invalidate assumptions made by the system builders. The consequences may include unreliable or uninterpretable outputs, and unexpected system behavior.

For some systems and types of change, the administrator needs to be an information systems professional who is able to assess any systems changes that may be required beyond the changes to data values (not to mention taking due credit for the quick turnaround on the "systems maintenance" requests). In our example, the tables would allow a new type of claim to be added by changing data values, but this might need to be supplemented by changes to program logic to handle new processing specific to claims of that type.

Implementing Mandatory Relationships

As already discussed, a one-to-many relationship is implemented in a relational database by declaring a column (or set of columns) in the table at the "many" end to be a foreign key and specifying which table is referenced. If the relationship is mandatory at the "one" end, this is implemented by declaring the foreign key column(s) to be nonnullable; conversely if the relationship is optional at the "one" end, this is implemented by declaring the foreign key column(s) to be nullable. However if the relationship is mandatory at the "many" end, additional logic must be employed.

Relationships that are mandatory at the "many" end are more common than some modelers realize. For example, in Figure 12-9, the relationship between Order and Order Line is mandatory at the "many" end since an order without anything ordered does not make sense. The relationship between Product and Product Size is mandatory at the "many" end for a rather less obvious reason. In fact, intuition may tell us that in the real world not every product is available in multiple sizes. If we model this relationship as optional at the "many" end then we would have to create two relationships from Order Line, one to Product Size – to manage products that are available in multiple sizes – and one to Product – to manage products that are not. This will make the system more complex than necessary. Instead we establish that a Product Size record is created for each product, even one that is only available in one size.

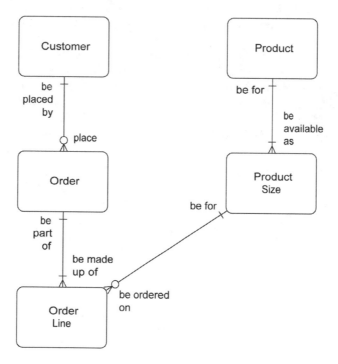

Figure 12-9. An Order Entry Model

To enforce these constraints it is necessary to employ program logic that does not allow an Order to be created without at least one Order Line, nor a Product to be created without at least one Product Size. In addition (and this is sometimes forgotten) it is necessary to prohibit the deletion of either the last remaining Order Line for an Order or the last remaining Product Size for a Product.

Referential Integrity

What It Means

The business requirements for referential integrity are straightforward: if a column supports a relationship (i.e., is a foreign key column), the record referred to:

• must exist at all times that the reference does

• must be the one that was intended at the time the reference was created or last updated.

How It Is Achieved in a Database

These requirements are met in a database are as follows:

Reference Creation: If a column is designed to hold data references, the only values that may be written into that column are primary key values of existing records in the referenced table. For example, if there is a foreign key column in the student table designed to hold references to families, only the primary key of an existing family record can be written into that column.

Key Update: If the primary key of a record is changed, all references to that record must also be changed in the same update process (this is known as **Update Cascade**). For example, if the primary key of a family record is changed, any student record with a reference to that family record must have that reference updated at the same time. Alternatively the primary key of any table may be made nonchangeable (**No Update**) in which case no provision needs to be made for Update Cascade on that table.

Key Delete: If an attempt is made to delete a record and there are references to that record, one of three policies must be followed, depending on the type of data:

1. the deletion is prohibited (**Delete Restrict**)

2. all references to the deleted record are replaced by nulls (**Delete Set Null**)

3. all records with references to the deleted record are themselves deleted (**Delete Cascade**).

Alternatively, we can prohibit deletion of data from any table irrespective of whether there are references (**No Delete**), in which case no provision needs to be made for any of the listed policies on that table.

Modeling Referential Integrity

Most data modelers will simply create a relationship (in an Entity-Relationship model) or (in a relational model) indicate which columns in each table are foreign keys. It is then up to the process modeler or designer, or sometimes even the programmer or DBA to decide which update and delete options are appropriate for each relationship/foreign key. However, since the choice should be up to the business and it is modelers rather than programmers or DBAs who are consulting with the business, it should be either the data modeler or the process modeler who determines the required option in each case. My own view is that even though updating and deleting of records are processes, the implications of these processes for the integrity of data are such that the data modeler has an obligation to consider them.

Restricting an Attribute to a Discrete Set of Values

Use of Codes

Having decided that we require a category attribute such as Account Status, we need to determine the set of possible values and how we will represent them. For example, allowed statuses might be "Active," "Closed," and "Suspended." Should we use these words as they stand, or introduce a coding scheme, such as "A," "C", and "S" or "1," "2," and "3" to represent "Active," "Closed," and "Suspended?"

Most practitioners would introduce a coding scheme automatically, in line with conventional practice since the early days of data processing. They would also need to provide somewhere in the system (using the word "system" in its broadest sense to include manual files, processes, and human knowledge) a translation mechanism to code and decode the fully descriptive terms.

Given the long tradition of coding, it's worth looking at what it actually achieves:

First, and most obviously, we save space. "A" is more concise than "Active." The analyst responsible for dialogue design may well make the coding scheme visible to the user, as one means of saving keystrokes and reducing errors.

We also improve flexibility, in terms of our ability to add new codes in a consistent fashion. We don't have the problem of finding that a new value of Account Status is a longer word than we have allowed for.

Probably the most important benefit of using codes is the ability to change the text description of a code while retaining its meaning. Perhaps we wish to rename the "Suspended" status "Under Review." This sort of thing happens as organizational terminology changes, sometimes to conform to industry standards and practices. The coding approach provides us with a level of insulation, so that we distinguish a change in the meaning of a code (update the translation table) from a change in actual status of an account (update the Account table).

To achieve this distinction, we need to be sure that the code can remain stable if the full description changes. Use of initial letters, or indeed anything derived from the description itself, will interfere with this objective. How many times have you seen coding schemes that only partially follow some rule, because changes or later additions have been impossible to accommodate?

The issues of code definition are much the same as those of primary key definition, discussed in chapter 8. This is hardly surprising, as a code is the primary key of a computerized or external look-up table.

Simple Look-Up Tables

As soon as we introduce a coding scheme for data, we need to provide for a method of coding and decoding. In some cases, we may make this a human responsibility, relying on users of the computerized system to memorize or look up the codes themselves. Another option is to build the translation rules into programs. The third option is to include a table for this purpose as part of the database design. Such tables are commonly referred to as "look-up tables" by analogy with manual records in which we "look up" the meanings of codes. The advantage of the latter two options is that the system can ensure that only valid codes are entered.

In fact, even if we opt for full text descriptions in the category attribute rather than codes, a table of allowed values can be used to ensure that only valid descriptions are entered. In either case referential integrity (discussed in this chapter) should be established between the category attribute and the table of allowed values.

In practice, I make a point of considering an entity for each category attribute in the initial data model. It's not as daunting a task as it may sound, and it forces me to think about how the translation mechanism will be handled in each case. However, in presenting a model, I frequently omit these "category entities" in order to reduce the complexity of the diagram.

There are certain circumstances in which the look-up table approach should be strongly favored:

- If the number of different allowed values is large enough to make human memory, manual look-up, and programming approaches cumbersome. At 20 values, you are well into this territory.

- If the set of allowed values is subject to change. This tends to go hand in hand with large numbers of values. Changing a data value is simpler than updating program logic, or keeping people and manual documents up to date.

- If we want to hold further data about allowed values that is to be used by the system at run-time (as distinct from documentary data for the benefit of programmers, etc). For example, we may need to hold a more complete description of the meaning of each code value for inclusion in reports, or maintain "Applicable From" and "Applicable To" dates.

- If the category entity has relationships with other entities in the model, besides the obvious relationship to the entity holding the category attribute that it controls

Conversely, the look-up table approach is less attractive if we need to "hard code" actual values into program logic. Adding new values will then necessitate changes to the logic, so the advantage of being able to add values without affecting programs is lost.

Generalization of Look-Up Tables

The entities that specify look-up tables tend to follow a standard format: Code, Full Name, and possibly Description. This suggests the possibility of generalization, and I have frequently seen models that specify a single supertype look-up table (which, incidentally, should not be named "Look-Up Table," but something like "Code" in keeping with our rule of naming entities according to the meaning of a single instance).

Again, we need to go back to basics, and ask whether the various code types are subject to common processes. The answer is usually "Yes" as far as their update is concerned, but the inquiry pattern is likely to be less consistent. A consolidated look-up table offers the possibility of a generic code update module, and easy addition of new code types, not inconsiderable benefits when you have seen the alternative of individual program modules for each code type. Views can provide the subtype level pictures required for enquiry.

Be ready for an argument with the physical database designer if you recommend implementation at the supertype level. The generalized table will definitely make referential integrity management more complex, and may well cause an access bottleneck. As always, you will want to see evidence of the real impact on system design and performance, and will need to negotiate trade-offs accordingly. Programmers may also object to the less obvious programming required if full advantage is to be taken of the generalized design. On the other hand, I have seen generalization of all look-up tables proposed by database administrators as a general rule.

And, as usual, recognizing the generalization is valuable even if the supertype isn't implemented directly. You may still be able to write or clone generic programs to handle update more consistently and at reduced development cost.

Rules Involving Multiple Attributes

Occasionally, we encounter a rule that involves two or even more attributes, usually but not always from the same entity. If the rule simply states that only certain combinations of attribute values are permissible, we can set up a table of the allowed combinations. If the attributes are from the same entity, we can use the referential integrity features of the database management system to ensure that only valid combinations of values are recorded. However if they are from different entities enforcement of the rule requires the use of program logic e.g., a stored procedure.

Indeed we can and should include an entity in the data model representing the table of allowed combinations, and, if the controlled attributes are from the same entity, include a relationship between that entity and the "Allowed Combination" entity.

Some DBMSs provide direct support for describing constraints across multiple attributes as part of the database definition. Since such constraints are frequently volatile, be sure to establish how easily such constraints can be altered.

Multiattribute constraints are not confined to category attributes – they may involve range checks (*"If Product Type is 'Vehicle,' Price must be greater than $10,000"*) or even cross-entity constraints (*"Only a Customer with a credit rating of 'A' can have an Account with an overdraft limit of over $1,000"*). These too can be readily implemented using tables specifying the allowed combinations of category values and maxima or minima, but require program logic to ensure that only allowed combinations are recorded. Once again the DBMS may allow such constraints to be specified in the database definition.

As always, the best approach is to document the constraints as you model and defer the decision as to exactly how they are to be enforced until you finalize the logical database design.

Recording Data that Supports Rules

Data that supports rules often provides challenges to the modeler. For example, rules specifying allowed combinations of three or more categories (e.g. Product Type, Customer Type, Contract Type) may require analysis as to whether they are in 4th or 5th normal form (see chapter 7).

Another challenge is presented by the fact that many rules have exceptions. Subtypes can be valuable in handling rules with exceptions. Figure 12-10 is a table recording the dates on which post office branches are closed. (A bit of creativity may already have been applied here – the user is just as likely to have specified a requirement to record when the post offices were *open*).

POST OFFICE CLOSURE (Branch No, Date, Reason)

Branch No	Date	Reason
18	12/21/93	Maintenance
63	12/23/93	Local Holiday
1	12/25/93	Christmas Day
2	12/25/93	Christmas Day
3	12/25/93	Christmas Day
4	12/25/93	Christmas Day
5	12/25/93	Christmas Day
6	12/25/93	Christmas Day

Figure 12-10. Post Office Closures Model

Look at the table closely. There is a definite impression of repetition for national holidays, such as Christmas Day, but the table is in fact fully normalized. We might see what appears to be a dependency of Reason on Date, but this only applies to some rows of the table.

The restriction "only some rows" provides the clue to tackling the problem. We use subtypes to separate the two types of row, as in Figure 12-11.

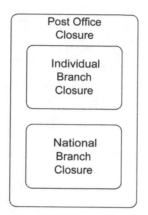

INDIVIDUAL BRANCH CLOSURE (<u>Branch No</u>, <u>Date</u>, Reason)

NATIONAL BRANCH CLOSURE (<u>Branch No</u>, <u>Date</u>, Reason)

Branch No	Date	Reason
18	12/21/93	Maintenance
63	12/23/93	Local Holiday

Branch No	Date	Reason
1	12/25/93	Christmas
2	12/25/93	Christmas
3	12/25/93	Christmas
4	12/25/93	Christmas
5	12/25/93	Christmas
6	12/25/93	Christmas

Figure 12-11. Subtyping Post Office Closure

The National Branch Closure table is not fully normalized, as Reason depends only on Date; normalizing gives us the three tables of Figure 12-12.

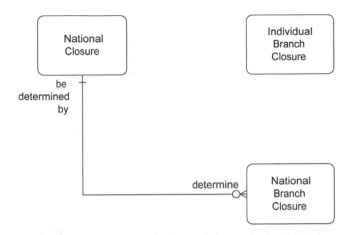

INDIVIDUAL BRANCH CLOSURE (<u>Branch No</u>, <u>Date</u>, Reason)

NATIONAL BRANCH CLOSURE (<u>Branch No</u>, <u>Date</u>)

NATIONAL CLOSURE (<u>Date</u>, Reason)

Branch No	Date	Reason
18	12/21/93	Maintenance
63	12/23/93	Local Holiday

Branch No	Date
1	12/25/93
2	12/25/93
3	12/25/93
4	12/25/93
5	12/25/93
6	12/25/93

Date	Reason
12/25/93	Christmas

Figure 12-12. Post Office Closures – Normalized After Subtyping

We now need to ask whether the National Branch Closure table holds any information of value to us. It is fully derivable from a table of branches (which we probably have elsewhere), and the National Closure data. Accordingly, we can delete it. We now have the two-table solution of Figure 12-13.

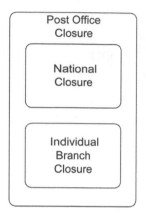

INDIVIDUAL BRANCH CLOSURE (<u>Branch No</u>, <u>Date</u>, Reason)

NATIONAL CLOSURE (<u>Date</u>, Reason)

Branch	Date	Reason
18	12/21/93	Maintenance
63	12/23/93	Local Holiday

Date	Reason
12/25/93	Christmas

Figure 12-13. Final Post Office Closure Model

In solving the problem of capturing an underlying rule, we have produced a far more elegant data structure. Recording a new national holiday, for example, now requires only the addition of one row. In effect we found an unnormalized structure hidden within a more general structure, with all the redundancy and update anomalies that we expect from unnormalized data.

Recording Information about Breaking the Rules

It is a fact of life that in the real world the existence of rules does not preclude them being broken. Each rule discovered should be subject to the following questions:

"Is it possible for instances to occur which break this rule?"

"If so, is it necessary to record such instances in the database?"

If the answers to both questions are "Yes" implementation of the rule should be in such a way as to allow nonconforming instances to be recorded. In particular if the rule is or includes a referential integrity rule, DBMS referential integrity enforcement cannot be used.

The following is an example of the kind of situation that can arise if this requirement is overlooked. A local government system for managing planning applications did not allow for recording of land usage that broke the planning regulations. As a result data entry personnel would record land details using alternative usage codes that they knew would be accepted. In turn the report requested by the town clerk that is designed to show how many properties did not conform to planning regulations regularly showed 100% conformity!

Enforcement of Rules through Primary Key Selection

The structures available to us in data modeling were not designed as a comprehensive "tool kit" for representing rules. To some extent, the types of rules we are able to model are a byproduct of database management system design, in which other objectives were at the fore. Most of these are well understood (cardinality, optionality, etc)., but others arise from quite subtle issues of key selection.

In chapter 7, we looked at an apparently simple customer orders model, reproduced with different primary keys in Figure 12-14.

By using a combination of Customer No and Order No as the key for Order, and Customer and Branch No as the key for Branch, as shown, we are able to enforce the important constraint that the customer who placed the order also received the order (because the Customer No in the Ordered Item table is part of the foreign key to both Order and Branch). But this is hardly obvious from the diagram, or even from fairly close perusal of the attribute lists, unless you are a fairly experienced and observant modeler. Don't expect the database administrator, user, or even your successor to see it.

I counsel you not to rely on these subtleties of key construction to enforce constraints. Clever they may be, but they can easily be overridden by other issues of key selection, or forgotten as time passes. It is better to handle such constraints with a check within a common program module, and strongly enforce use of that module.

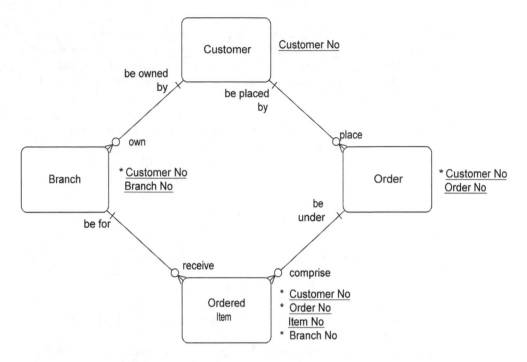

Figure 12-14. Constraint Enforced by Choice of Keys

Summary

A data model captures a variety of business rules in its structure, definitions and supporting documentation. The data that will be held in the resulting database will also serve to enforce business rules.

A conventional information system may implement rules as data, data structure, or program logic. Rules held in data structure are difficult to circumvent or change. Rules held in data values are more readily changed, but may demand more sophisticated programming.

Subtleties of key construction should not generally be used to enforce rules.

Chapter 13

Modeling for Data Warehouses and Data Marts

"But to live outside the law you must be honest."

– Bob Dylan, Absolutely Sweet Marie

Introduction

Data warehouses and data marts emerged in the 1990s as a practical solution to the problem of drawing together data to support management and (sometimes) external reporting requirements. The basic architecture of a data warehouse and associated data marts is shown in Figure 13-1.

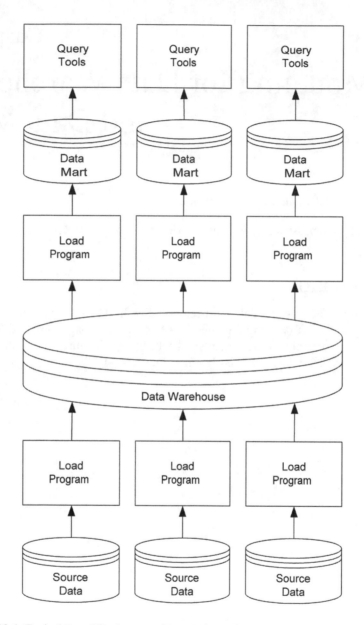

Figure 13-1. Typical Data Warehouse and Data Mart Architecture

The terminology in the diagram is typical, but the term "data warehouse" is sometimes used loosely to include data marts as well. And while we're clarifying terms, in this chapter, I use the term "operational" to distinguish databases and systems intended to support transaction processing rather than management queries.

The diagram shows that data is extracted periodically from the source systems, consolidated in the data warehouse, and then extracted to data marts which serve particular users or subject areas. In some cases, the data marts may be fed directly, without an intermediate data warehouse, but the number of extraction programs needed multiplies quickly as the number of source systems and marts increases. Another option is for the data marts to be logical "views" of the warehouse; in this scenario, there is no physical data mart, but rather a window into the data warehouse, with data being selected and combined for each query.

Data warehouses are now widely used, and often need to be developed in-house, primarily because the mix of source systems varies so much from organization to organization. Reporting requirements, of course, may also vary. This is good news for data modelers, because data warehouses and data marts are databases, which of course must be specified by data models. There may also be some reverse engineering work to be done in order to understand the organization and meaning of the data in the source systems.

Data modeling for data warehouses and marts, however, presents a range of new challenges, and has been the subject of much debate amongst data modelers and database designers. An early quote indicates how the battle lines were drawn:

> *"Forget everything you know about entity relationship data modeling … using that model with a real-world decision support system almost guarantees failure[46]."*

On the other side of the debate were those who argued that "a database is a database" and nothing needed to change.

---

[46] Kimball, R. & Strehlo, K., "Why Decision Support Fails and How to Fix It", *Datamation* (June 1, 1994).

Much has been written, and will continue to be written, on the subject, some of it built on sound foundations – some not. Some techniques are more appropriate for particular products or architectures, and that picture will continue to change as the products develop. No list of techniques can cover every situation, and in a single chapter we cannot do more than provide an overview of what has become a specialist discipline in its own right.

We therefore focus on the key requirements and principles, to provide you with a basis for evaluating techniques and making sound design decisions. We first look at how the requirements for data marts and data warehouses differ from those for operational databases. We then reexamine the rules of data modeling, and find that although the basic objectives (evaluation criteria/quality measures) remain the same, their relative importance changes. As a result, we need to modify some of the rules and add some general guidelines for data warehouse and data mart modeling. Finally, we look specifically at the issues of organizing data to suit the multidimensional database products that underpin many data marts.

Characteristics of Data Warehouses and Data Marts

The literature on data warehouses identifies a number of characteristics that differentiate warehouses and marts from conventional operational databases. Virtually all of these have some impact on data modeling.

Data Integration – Working with Existing Databases

A data warehouse is not simply a collection of copies of records from source systems. It is a database which "makes sense" in its own right. We would expect to specify one Product table even if the warehouse drew on data from many overlapping product tables or files with inconsistent definitions and coding schemes. The data modeler can do little about these historical design decisions, but needs to define target tables into which all of the old data will fit – after some translation and/or reformatting. These tables will in turn need to be further combined, reformatted and summarized as required to serve the data marts, which may also have been developed prior to the warehouse. (Many organizations originally developed individual data marts, fed directly from source systems – and often called "data warehouses" - until the proliferation of load programs forced the development of an intermediate warehouse). Working within such constraints adds an extra challenge to the data modeling task and means that we will often end up with less than ideal structures.

Loads Rather than Updates

Data marts are intended to support queries and are typically updated through periodic batch loading of data from the warehouse. Similarly, the data warehouse is likely to be loaded from the source systems through batch programs, which are not expected to run concurrently with other access. This strategy may be adopted not only to improve efficiency and manage contention for data resources, but also to ensure that the data warehouse and data marts are not "moving targets" for queries that need to produce consistent results.

Recall our discussion of normalization. One of the strongest reasons for normalizing beyond first normal form was to prevent "update anomalies" where one occurrence of an item is updated but others are left unchanged. In the data warehouse environment, we can alternatively achieve that sort of consistency by careful design of the load programs – knowing that no other update transactions will run against the database.

Of course, there is not point in abandoning or compromising normalization just because we can tackle the problem in another (less elegant) way. There needs to be some payoff – and this may come through improved performance or simplified queries. And if we chose to "trickle feed" the warehouse using conventional transactions, update anomalies would become an issue again.

Less Predictable Database "Hits"

In designing an operational database, we usually have a good idea of the type and volumes of transactions that will run against it. We can optimize the database design to process those transactions simply and efficiently, sometimes at the expense of support for lower-volume or unpredicted transactions.

Queries against a data mart are less predictable – and indeed, the ability to support ad hoc queries is one of the major selling points of data marts. A design decision (such as use of repeating group, as described in chapter 2) that favors one type of query at the expense of others will need to be very carefully thought through.

Complex Queries – Simple Interface

One of the challenges of designing data marts and associated query tools is the need to support complex queries and analyses in a relatively simple way. It is not usually reasonable to expect users of the facility to navigate complex data structures in the manner of experienced programmers – yet typical queries against a fully normalized database may require data from a large number of tables. (I say "not *usually* reasonable" because some users of data marts, such as specialist operational managers, researchers and data miners may be willing and able to learn to navigate sophisticated structures if the payoff is sufficient).

Perhaps the central challenge for the data mart modeler comes from the approach that tool vendors have settled on to address the problem. Data mart query tools are generally intended for use with a *multidimensional* database based on a central "fact" table and associated look-up tables – called *dimension tables* or just *dimensions* (Figure 13-2 in chapter 13 shows an example). The data modeler is required to fit the data into this shape. We can see this as an interesting variation of the "elegance" objective discussed in chapter 1. From a user perspective, the solution is elegant, in that it is easy to understand and use – and consistent from one mart to the next. From the data modeler's perspective, some very inelegant decisions may need to be taken to meet the constraint.

Summarization

The data warehouse seldom contains complete copies of all data held in operational databases. Some is excluded, and some may be held only in summary form. Whenever we summarize, we lose information; and the data modeler needs to be fully aware of the impact of summarization on all potential users.

History

The holding of historical information is one of the most important characteristics of a data warehouse. Managers are frequently interested in trends, whereas operational users of data may only require the current position. Such information may be built up in the data warehouse over a period of time, and retained long after it is not longer required in the source systems. The challenge of modeling time-dependent data may be greater for the data warehouse designer than for the operational database designer.

Quality Criteria for Warehouse and Mart Models

It's interesting to take another look at the evaluation or quality criteria for data models that we identified in chapter 1, but this time in the context of the special requirements of data warehouses and marts. All remain relevant, but their relative importance changes – so our trade-offs are likely to be different.

Completeness

In designing a data warehouse, we are limited by the data available in the source systems – although there is sometimes scope to capture some data directly to supplement it. We have to ask not only "What do we want?" but also "What have we got?" Practically, this means acquainting ourselves with the source system data either at the outset or as we proceed. For example:

The *user* says "I want to know what percentage of customers spend more than a specified amount on CDs when they shop here."

Modeler: "We only record sales – not customers, so what we can tell you is what percentage of sales exceed a certain value."

User: "Same thing, isn't it?"

Modeler: "Not really – what if the customer buys a few CDs in the classical section then stops by the rock section and buys some more."

User: "That'd actually be interesting to know – can you tell us how often that happens?" And what about if they see another CD as they're walking out and come back and buy it – they see the display by the door …"

Modeler: "We can get information on that for those customers who use their store discount card, because we can identify them …"

… and so on.

The users of data warehouses, interested in aggregated information, *may* not make the same demands for absolute accuracy as the user of an operational system. Accordingly it may be possible to compromise completeness to achieve simplicity (as discussed below under Business Rules). Of course, this needs to be verified at the outset: there are examples of warehouses that have lost credibility because the outputs did not balance to the last cent. What we can't afford to compromise is good documentation, which should provide the user with information on the currency, completeness, and quality of the data, as well as the basic definitions.

Finally, we may lose data by summarizing it to save space and processing. The summarization may take place either when data is loaded from source systems to the warehouse (a key design decision) or when it is loaded from the warehouse to the marts (a decision more easily reversed).

Nonredundancy

We can be a great deal less concerned about redundancy in data warehouses and data marts than we would be with operational databases. As discussed earlier, since data is loaded through special load programs or utilities, and not updated in the usual sense, we do not face the risk that fields may be updated inconsistently. Redundancy does of course still cost us in storage space and data warehouses can be very large indeed.

Particularly in data marts, denormalization is regularly practiced to simplify structures, and we may also carry derived data, such as commonly used totals.

Enforcement of Business Rules

We tend not to think of a data warehouse or mart as *enforcing* business rules in the usual sense, because of the absence of traditional update transactions.

Nevertheless, the data structures will determine what sort of data can be loaded – and if the data warehouse or mart implements a rule that is not supported by a source system, we will have a challenge to address! Sometimes, the need to simplify data leads us to (for example) implement a one-to-many relationship even though a few real world cases are many-to-many. Perhaps an insurance policy can occasionally be sold by more than one salesperson – but we decide to build our data mart around a Policy table with a Salesperson dimension. We've specified a tighter rule – and we are going to end up trading some "completeness" for the gain in simplicity.

Data Reusability

Reusability is the *raison d'être* of most data warehouses and marts. More so than in operational databases, we have to expect the unexpected as far as queries concerned. Data marts may be constructed to support a constrained set range of queries (we can build another mart if necessary to support an new requirement), but the data warehouse itself needs to be able to feed virtually any conceivable mart that uses the data which it holds. Here is an argument *for* full normalization, and against any measures that irrecoverably lose data – such as summarization with removal of the source data.

Stability and Flexibility

One of the challenges of data warehouse design is to accommodate changes in the source data, which may reflect real changes in the business, or simply changes (including complete replacement) to the source systems.

Much of the value of a data warehouse may come from the build-up of historical data over a long period. We need to build structures that not only accommodate the new data, but also allow us to retain the old

It is a maxim of data warehouse designers that "data warehouse design is never finished." If users gain value from the initial implementation it is almost inevitable that they will require that the warehouse and marts be extended – often very substantially. Many a warehouse project has delivered a warehouse that cannot be easily extended, requiring new warehouses to be constructed as the requirements grow. The picture in Figure 13-1 becomes much less elegant when we add multiple warehouses in the middle, possibly sharing common source systems and data marts.

Simplicity and Elegance

As discussed earlier, data marts are often restricted to relatively simple structures that suit a range of query tools and are relatively easy for end-users to understand.

Communication Effectiveness

It is challenging enough to communicate "difficult" data structures to professional programmers, let alone end-users who may have only an occasional need to use the data marts. Data marts that use highly generalized structures and unfamiliar terminology, or that are based on a sophisticated original view of the business are going to cause problems.

Performance

Query volumes against data marts are usually very small compared with transaction volumes for operational databases. Response times can usually be much greater than would be acceptable in an operational system, but the time required to process large tables in their entirety – as is required for many analyses unless data has been summarized in advance – may still be unacceptable.

The data warehouse needs to be able to accept the uploading of large volumes of data, usually within a limited "batch window" when operational databases are not required for real time processing. It also needs to support reasonably rapid extraction of data for the data marts. Data loading may use purpose-designed utilities, which will dictate how data should be organized to achieve best performance.

The Basic Design Principle

The architecture shown in Figure 13-1 has evolved from earlier approaches in which the data warehouse and data marts were combined into a single database.

The separation is intended to allow the data warehouse to act as a bridge or clearinghouse between different representations of the data, while the data marts are designed to present simpler views to the end users.

The basic rule for the data modeler is to respect this separation.

Accordingly, we design the data warehouse much as we would an operational database, but with a recognition that the relative importance of goals (as discussed in the previous section) may be different. So, for example, we may be more prepared to accept a denormalized structure, or some data redundancy – provided of course there is a corresponding payoff. Flexibility is paramount – we can expect to have to accommodate growth in scope, new and changed source systems, and new data marts.

The data mart is a different matter. Here we need to fit data into a quite restrictive structure, and the modeling challenge is to achieve this without losing the ability to support a reasonably wide range of queries. We will usually end up making some serious compromises that may be acceptable for the data mart but would not be so for an operational database or data warehouse.

Modeling for the Data Warehouse

Many successful data warehouses have been designed by data modelers who tackled the modeling assignment as if they were designing an operational database. I have even seen examples of data warehouses that had to be completely redesigned according to this traditional approach, after ill-advised attempts to apply modeling approaches borrowed from the data mart theory.

You are unlikely to go too far wrong if you follow the principle stated in the previous section, and model normally, but with a clear understanding of the special purpose of the data warehouse and the restrictions of the source systems. That's why I devoted so much space at the beginning of this chapter to differences and goals: it is a proper appreciation of these rather than a brute application of some special technique that leads to good warehouse design.

There are, however, a few general tasks and issues worth looking at which are specific to data warehouse design.

An Initial Model

Data warehouse designers usually find it useful to start with an E-R model of the total business, or at least of the part of the business that the data warehouse may ultimately cover. The starting point may be an existing corporate data model (see chapter 14) or a generalization of the data structures in the most important source databases. If the former, the data modeler will need to check that it aligns reasonably closely with existing structures rather than representing a radical "future vision." Data warehouse designers are not granted the latitude of data modelers starting with a blank slate!

Understanding Existing Data

In theory, we could construct a data warehouse without ever talking to the business users, simply by consolidating data from the source systems. Such a warehouse would (again in theory) allow any query possible within the limitations of the source data.

In practice, we need user input to help select what data will be relevant to the data mart users (the extreme alternative would be to load every data item from every source system), to contribute to the inevitable decisions on compromises, and, of course, to "buy in" and support the project.

Nevertheless, a good part of data warehouse design involves gaining an understanding of data from the source systems and defining structures to hold and consolidate it. Usually the most effective approach is to use the initial model as a starting point, and map the existing structures against it. Initially we do this at an entity level, but as modeling proceeds in collaboration with the users, we add attributes and possibly subtypes.

Determining Requirements

Requirements are likely to be expressed in a different way to those for an operational database. The emphasis is on identifying business measures (such as monthly turnover) and the base data needed to derive them – and much of this discussion will naturally be at the attribute level. Prototype data marts can be invaluable in helping potential users to articulate their requirements. The data modeler also needs to have one eye on the source data structures and the business rules which they implement, in order to provide the user with feedback as to what is likely to be possible, and what alternatives may be available.

Determining Sources and Dealing with Differences

One of the great challenges of data warehouse design is in making the most of source data in legacy systems. If we are lucky, some of the source data structures may be well designed, but we are likely to have to contend with overloaded attributes, poor documentation of definitions and coding schemes, and (almost certainly) inconsistency across databases.

Our choice of source for a data item – and hence its definition in the data warehouse will depend on a number of factors.

- The objective of minimizing the number of source systems feeding the data warehouse, in the interests of simplicity, reduced need for data integration, and reduced development, maintenance, and running costs.

- The "quality" of the data item – a complex issue involving primarily the accuracy of the item instances (i.e., whether they reflect the real world), but also timeliness (when were they last updated?) and compatibility with other items (update cycles again). Timing differences can be a major headache. The update cycles of data vary in many organizations from real-time to annually. Because of this, the "same" data item may hold different values in different source databases.

- Whether multiple sources can be reconciled to produce a better overall quality. We may even choose to hold two or more versions of the "same" attribute in the warehouse, to enable a choice of the most appropriate version as required.

- The compatibility of the coding scheme with other data. Incompatible coding schemes and data formats are relatively straightforward to handle – *as long as the mapping between them is simple*. If the underlying definitions are different, it may be impossible to translate to a common scheme without losing too much meaning. It's easy to translate country codes – as long as you can agree what a country is! One police force recognizes three eye colors, another four.

- Whether overloaded attributes can be or need to be unpacked. For example, one database may hold name and address as a single field, while another may break each down into smaller fields – initial, family name, street number, etc. Programmers often take serious liberties with data definitions – many a field has been redefined well beyond its original intent. Usually, the job of unpacking it into primitive attributes is reasonably straightforward once the rules are identified.

In doing the above, the data warehouse designer may need to perform work more properly the responsibility of a data management or data administration team. Indeed the problems of building data warehouses in the absence of good data management groundwork have often led to such teams being established or revived.

Shaping Data for Data Marts

How much should the data warehouse design anticipate the way that data will be held in the data marts? On the one hand, the data warehouse should be as flexible as possible – which means not organizing data in a way that will favor one user over another. Remember that the data warehouse may be required not only to feed conventional data marts, but may also be the common source of data for other analysis and decision support systems. And some data marts offer broader options for organizing data.

On the other hand, if we can be reasonably sure that all users of the data will first perform some common transformations such as summarization or denormalization, there is an argument for doing them once – as data is loaded into the warehouse – rather than each time it is extracted. And denormalized data can usually be renormalized without too much trouble (summarization is a different matter – base data cannot be recovered from summarized data). The data warehouse can act as a stepping-stone to greater levels of denormalization and summarization in the marts. When data volumes are very high, there is frequently a compelling argument for summarization to save space and processing.

Another advantage of shaping data at the warehouse stage is that it achieves a level of commonality across data marts. For example, we might decide that we would not hold details of all telephone calls but rather only those occurring during a set of representative periods each week. If the decision was made at the warehouse stage, we could decide once and for all what the most appropriate periods were. All marts would then work with the same sampling periods, and results from different marts could be more readily compared.

Sometimes the choice of approach will be straightforward. In particular, if the data marts are implemented as views of the warehouse, we will need to implement structures that can be directly translated into the required shape for the marts. Where you are in doubt, however, my advice is to lean towards the first option. One of the great lessons of data modeling is that new and unexpected uses will be found for data, once it is available, and this is particularly true in the context of data warehouses. Maximum flexibility and minimum anticipation are good starting points!

We will not cover the specific opportunities for data tailoring in this section, as they are essentially about moving the model closer to that which we would use to support a mart. We look at what this means in the next section.

Modeling for the Data Mart

The Basic Challenge

In organizing data in a data mart, the basic challenge is to present it in a form that can be understood by general business people. A typical operational database design is simply too complex to meet this requirement. Even our best efforts with views cannot always transform the data into something that makes immediate sense to non-specialists. Further, the query tools themselves need to make some assumptions about how data is stored if they are going to be easy to implement and use, and to produce reports in predictable formats.

Data mart users also need to be able to move from one mart to another without too much effort.

Multidimensional Databases, Stars and Snowflakes

Vendors of data marts have settled on a basic solution to the problem of providing a simple data structure. While some products offer variants and extensions (as is the case with relational databases and most competing software products!), most are built around the idea of a *star schema* or (equivalently for our purposes) a *multidimensional database.*

Figure 13-2 shows a star schema. The structure is very simple: a *fact table* surrounded by a number of dimension tables.

Figure 13-2. A Star Schema: the Fact Table is Sale

The format is not difficult to understand. The fact tables hold (typically) transaction data, either in its raw, atomic form or summarized. The dimensions effectively classify the data in the fact table into categories, and make it easy to formulate queries based on categories which aggregate data from the fact table: "what percentage of sales were in region 13?" "What was the total value of sales in region 13 to customers in category B?"

With our user hats on, this looks fine. Putting our data modeling hats on, we can see some major limitations – at least compared with the data structures for operational databases that we've been working with to date.

Before we start looking at these "limitations" it's interesting to observe that multidimensional databases have been around long enough now that there are professional designers who have modeled only in that environment. They seem to accept the star schema structure as a "given" and do not think of it as a limiting environment to work in. It's worth taking a leaf from their book if you're a "conventional" modeler moving to data mart design. Remember that relational databases themselves are far from comprehensive in the structures that they support – subtypes for example – yet we manage to get the job done!

One Fact Table per Star

While there is usually no problem implementing multiple stars, each with its own fact table (within the same[47] or separate data marts), we can have only one fact table in each star. Figure 13-3 illustrates the key problem that this causes.

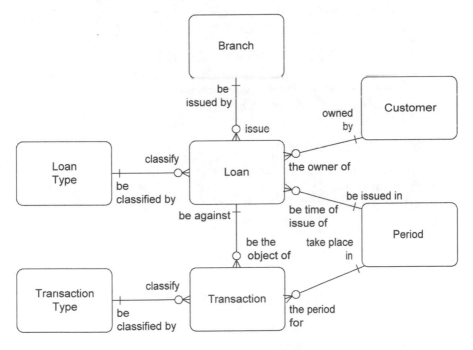

Figure 13-3. Which is the Fact Table – Loan or Transaction?

---

[47] Multiple stars in the same data mart can usually share dimension tables.

It's likely that we will hold numeric data and want to formulate queries at both the loan and transaction level. Some of the options we might consider are:

1. Move the data in the Loan table into the transaction table, which would then become the fact table. This would mean including all of the data about the relevant loan in each row of the transaction table. If there is a lot of data for each loan, and many transactions per loan, we could end up using a lot of space. Such denormalization would also have the effect of making it difficult to hold loans that did not have any transactions against them. Our solution might require that we add "dummy" rows in the transaction table, containing only loan data. Queries about loans and transactions would be more complicated than would be the case with a simple loan or transaction fact table.

2. Nominate the Loan table as the fact table, and hold transaction information in a summarized form in the Loan table. This would mean holding totals rather than individual items. If there were a relatively small maximum number of transactions per loan (perhaps more realistically we might be dealing with the number of assets securing the loan) we could hold a repeating group of transaction data in the Loan table – as always with some loss of simplicity in query formulation.

3. Implement separate star schemas, one with Loan as a fact table, the other with Transaction as a fact table. We would probably turn Loan into a dimension for the transaction schema, and might hold summarized transaction data in the loan table.

One Level of Dimension

A true star schema supports only one level of dimension. Some data marts do support multiple levels (usually simple hierarchies). These variants are generally known as *snowflake* schemas (Figure 13-4).

Figure 13-4. A Snowflake Schema. Sale is the Fact Table

To compress what may be a multi-level hierarchy down to one level, we have to denormalize (specifically from fully normalized back to first normal form). Figure 13-5 provides an example.

Figure 13-5. Denormalizing to Collapse a Hierarchy of Dimension Tables

While we may not need to be concerned about update anomalies from denormalizing, we do need to recognize that space requirements can sometimes become surprisingly large if the tables near the top of the hierarchy contain a lot of data. We may need to be quite brutal in stripping these down to codes and (perhaps) names, so that they function only as categories. (In practice, space requirements of dimensions are seldom as much of a problem as those of fact tables).

Another option is to summarize data from lower level tables into higher-level tables, or completely ignore one or more levels in the hierarchy (Figure 13-6). This option will only be workable if the users are not interested in some of the (usually low level) classifications.

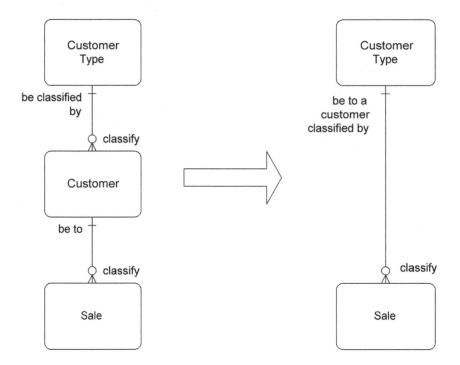

Figure 13-6a. Ignoring One or More Levels in the Hierarchy.

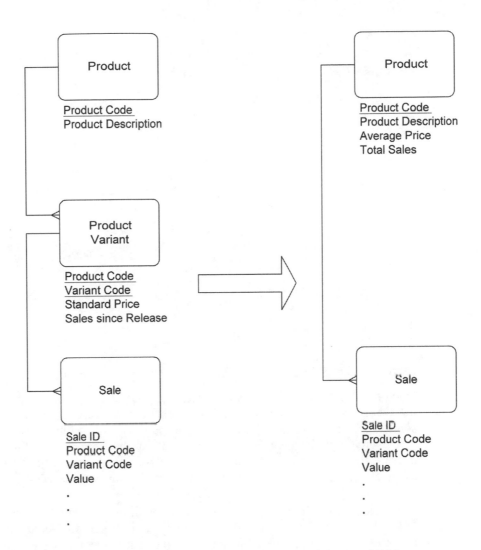

Figure 13-6b. Summarizing Data from Lower Level Tables into Higher Level Tables.

One-to-Many Relationships

The fact table in a star schema is in a many-to-one relationship with the dimensions. In the discussion above on collapsing hierarchies, we also assumed that there were no many-to-many relationships amongst the dimensions, in which case simple denormalization would not work.

What do we do if the real world relationship is many-to-many, as in Figure 13-7? Here, we have a situation in which, most of the time, sales are made by only one salesperson, but on occasions, more than one salesperson shares the sale.

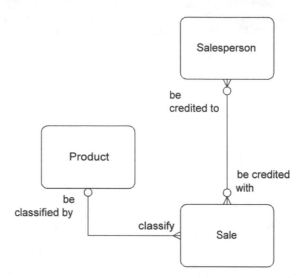

Figure 13-7. Many-to-Many Relationship between Dimension and Fact Tables.

One option is to ignore the less common case, and tie the relationship only to the "most important" or "first" salesperson. Perhaps we can compensate to some degree by carrying the number of salespersons involved in the Sale table, and even (say) the percentage involvement of the key person. For some queries, this compromise may be quite acceptable – but it would be less than satisfactory if a key area of interest was sales involving multiple salespersons.

We could modify the Salesperson table, to allow it to accommodate more than one Salesperson, through use of a repeating group. It's an inelegant solution, and breaks down once we want to include (as in the previous section) details from higher-level look up tables. Which region's data do we include – that of the first, the second or the third salesperson?

Another option is to in effect resolve the many-to-many relationship, and treat the sale-by-salesperson table as the fact table (Figure 13-8). We'll probably need to include the rest of the sale data in the table.

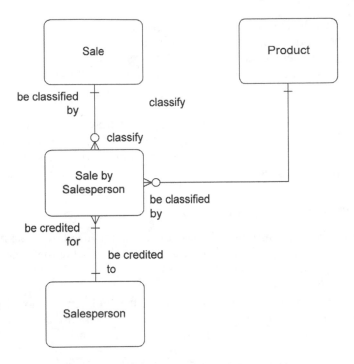

Figure 13-8. Treating the Sale-by-Salesperson Table as the Fact Table.

Once again, we have a situation in which there is no single, mechanical solution. We need to talk to the users about how they want to "slice and dice" the data, and work through with them the pros and cons of the different options.

Modeling Time-Dependent Data

The basic issues related to the modeling of time, in particular the choice of "snapshots" or history are covered in chapter 11, and apply equally to data warehouses, data marts and operational databases. This section covers a few key aspects of particular relevance to data mart design.

Time Dimension Tables

Most data marts include one or more dimension tables holding time periods, to enable that dimension to be used in analysis (e.g., "what percentage or sales were made by sales people in Region X *in the last quarter*?") The key design decisions are the level of granularity (hours, days, months, years?) and how to deal with overlapping time periods (financial years may overlap with calendar

years, months may overlap with billing periods, etc). The finer the granularity
(i.e., the shorter the periods), the fewer problems we have with overlap and the
more precise our queries can be. However, query formulation may be more
difficult or time-consuming in terms of specifying the particular periods to be
covered.

Sometimes, we will need to specify a hierarchy of time periods (as a
snowflake, or collapsed into a single-level denormalized star). Alternatively, or
in addition, we may specify multiple time dimension tables, possibly covering
overlapping periods.

Slowly-Changing Dimensions

One of the key concerns of the data mart designer is how quickly the data in
the dimension tables will change, and how quickly fact data may move from
one dimension to another.

Figure 13-9 shows a simple example of the problem in snowflake form for
clarity. This might be part of a data mart to support analysis of customer
purchasing patterns over a long period.

Figure 13-9. Slowly Changing Dimensions

It should be clear that if customers can change from one customer group to another over time, and our mart only records the current group, we will not be able to ask questions such as "what sort of vehicles did people buy whilst they were in group 'A'?" (We *could* ask "what sort of vehicles did people *currently* in group 'A' buy over time" – but this may well be less useful).

In the operational database such data will generally be supported by many-to-many relationships and/or matching of timestamps and time periods as described in chapter 11. There are many ways of reworking the structure to fit the star schema requirement. For example:

1. Probably the neatest solution to the problem as described is to carry *two* foreign keys to Customer Group in the Purchase table. One key points to the customer group which the customer belonged to at the time of the purchase; the other to the customer group which the customer currently belongs to. In fact, the information supported by the latter foreign key may not be required by the users, in which we can delete it, giving us a very simple solution.

2. Of course, setting up the mart in this form will require some translation of data held in more conventional structures in the operational databases and (probably) the data warehouse.

3. If the dimension changes sufficiently slowly in the timeframes in which we are interested, then the amount of error or uncertainty which it causes may be acceptable. We may be able to influence the speed of change by deliberately selecting or creating dimensions (perhaps at the data warehouse stage), which change relatively slowly. For example, we may be able to classify customers into broad occupational groups ("professional, manual worker, technician") rather than more specific occupations, or even develop lifestyle profiles that have been found to be relatively stable over long periods.

4. We can hold a history of (say) the last three values of Customer Group in the Customer table. This approach will also give us some information on how quickly the dimension changes

Summary

Logical data warehouse and data mart design are important subdisciplines of data modeling, with their own issues and techniques.

Data warehouse design is particularly influenced by their role as a staging point between operational databases and data marts. Existing data structures in operational databases or (possibly) existing data marts will limit the freedom of the designer, who will also need to support high volumes of data and load transactions. Within these constraints, data warehouse design has much in common with the design of operational databases.

The rules of data mart design are largely a result of the star schema structure – a limited subset of the full E-R structures used for operational database design – and lead to a number of design challenges, approaches and patterns peculiar to data marts. The data mart designer also has to contend with the limitations of the data available from the warehouse.

Chapter 14

Corporate Data Modeling

"Always design a thing by considering it in its next larger context – a chair in a room, a room in a house, a house in an environment, an environment in a city plan."

– Eliel Saarinen

Introduction

So far, we have discussed data modeling in the context of database design: We have assumed that our data models will ultimately be implemented more or less directly using some database management system. Our focus has been on the data requirements of individual application systems.

But data models also have a role to play in data planning and management for an enterprise as a whole. A **corporate data model** (sometimes called an **enterprise-wide data model**) is a model that covers the whole of, or a very significant part of, an organization. We can use such a model to:

- classify or index existing data

- provide a target for database and systems planners

- provide a context for specifying new databases

- support the evaluation and integration of application packages

- guide data modelers in the development or implementation of individual databases

- provide input to business planning

- specify an organization-wide database-in particular a data warehouse.

These activities are part of the wider discipline of data management – the management of data as a corporate resource – that warrants a book in itself. In this chapter, we look briefly at data management in general, then discuss the uses of corporate data models. Finally, we examine how development of a corporate data model differs from development of a conventional project-level data model.

But first, a word of warning. Far too many corporate data models have ended up "on the shelf" after considerable expenditure on their development. The most common reason, in my experience, is a lack of a clear idea of how the model is to be used. It is vital that any corporate data model be developed in the context of a data management or information systems strategy, within which its role is clearly understood, rather than as an end in itself.

Data Management

Problems of Data Mismanagement

The rationale for data management is that data is a valuable corporate resource, and therefore needs to be properly managed. Parallels are often drawn with physical assets, people, and money, all of which need to be managed explicitly if the enterprise is to derive the best value from them. But as with management of other assets, we can best understand the need for data management by looking at the results of not doing it.

Databases have traditionally been implemented on an application-by-application basis – one database per application system. Indeed, databases are often seen as being "owned" by their parent applications. The problem is that some data may be required by more than one application. For example, a bank may implement separate applications to handle personal loans and savings accounts, but both will need to hold data about customers. Without some form of planning and control, we will end up holding the same data in both databases. This is where the element of choice in data modeling works against us – we have no guarantee that the modelers working on the two systems will have represented the common data in the same way, particularly if they are software package developers working for different vendors, rather than in-house staff. Not only will the data be duplicated, it will be very difficult to document, reconcile, and control the duplication.

The effects of duplication and inconsistency across multiple systems are similar to those that arise from poor data modeling at the individual system level.

There are the costs of keeping multiple copies of data in step (and repercussions from data users, including customers, managers, and regulators, if we don't). Most of us have had the experience of notifying an organization of a change of address, and later discovering that only some of their records have been updated.

Pulling data together to meet management information needs is far more difficult if definitions, coding, and formats vary. An airline wants to know the total cost of running each of its terminals, but the terminals are identified in different ways in different systems – sometimes only by a series of account numbers. An insurance company wants a breakdown of profitability by product, but different divisions have defined "product" in different ways. Problems of this kind constitute *the* major challenge in data warehouse development (chapter 13).

Finally, poor overall data organization can make it difficult to use the data in new ways as business functions change in response to market and regulatory pressures and internal initiatives. Often, it seems easier to implement yet another single-purpose database than to attempt to use inconsistent existing databases. A lack of central documentation also makes reuse of data difficult – we may not even know that the data we require is held in an existing database. The net result, of course, is still more databases, and an exacerbation of the basic problem. Alternatively, we may decide that the new initiative is "too hard" or economically untenable. Advocates of Business Process Reengineering point out that good data management is a prerequisite for organizations that want to be responsive and "nimble" in changing their processes.

I have seen banks with fifty or more "Branch" files, retailers with more than thirty "Stock Item" files, and organizations that are supposedly customer-focused with dozens of "Customer" files. Often, just finding out the scope of the problem has been a major exercise. Not surprisingly, it is the data that is most central to an organization (and hence used by the greatest number of applications) that is most frequently mismanaged.

Managing Data as a Shared Resource

Data management aims to address these issues by taking an organization-wide view of data. Instead of regarding databases as the sole property of their parent applications, we treat them as a shared resource. This may entail documenting existing databases; encouraging development of new, sharable databases in critical areas; establishing standards for data representation; and setting an overall target for data organization. These tasks are usually assigned to a data management (or "data administration") team, which may also serve as a center of expertise in data modeling.

The (theoretical) ideal solution to data management problems would be to build a single shared database covering all of the enterprise's data requirements. Unfortunately, the approach seldom makes sense logistically or economically, as some organizations found to their cost in the 1970s. (Some who failed to learn from others' experiences discovered the same thing for themselves in the 1980s and 1990s!)

More recently, data managers saw themselves as akin to town planners. They could not tear down existing databases and start again, but attempted to coordinate an orderly migration to a better overall position. Data managers seldom initiated projects, but were responsible for ensuring that individual initiatives contributed to a harmonious whole. And like town planners, they encountered considerable resistance along the way, as builders asserted their preference for operating without outside interference!

This approach, too, was only rarely successful. A number of factors worked against it, including the widespread use of packaged software in preference to in-house development, and greater pressure to deliver results in the short-to-medium term. Today, we are increasingly seeing data managers taking a more proactive role, initiating projects to improve data management in specific areas, rather than attempting to solve all of an organization's data management problems.

A corporate data model has been central to all of these approaches to data management. In the following sections, we examine the most important roles that it can play.

Classification of Existing Data

Most organizations have a major investment in existing databases and files. Often, the documentation of these is of variable quality and held locally with the parent applications.

The lack of a central, properly indexed register of data is one of the greatest impediments to data sharing. If we don't know what data we have (and where it is), how can we hope to identify opportunities for its reuse? The problem is particularly apparent to builders of data warehouses (chapter 13) and executive information systems. Much of the data needed to provide summarized information for management must be drawn from existing operational systems. Sourcing this is often a major challenge. Correctly interpreting it in the absence of adequate documentation has proved an even greater one, and serious business mistakes have been made as a result of incorrect assumptions.

Commercial data dictionaries and "repositories" have been around for many years to hold the necessary **metadata** i.e., data about data. Some organizations have built their own, with mixed success. But data inventories are of limited value without an index of some kind: We need to be able to ask, "What files or databases hold data about flight schedules?" or "Where is 'Country Code' held?," remembering that 'Country Code' may be called 'CTRY-ID' in one system, and 'F12345' in another. Or an attribute named 'Country Code' may mean something entirely different to what we expect. I recall encountering a 'Vehicle ID,' which in fact identified salespersons; the salesperson was the "vehicle" by which the sale was made.

A standard set of "keywords" that are then associated with each existing data item provides a partial solution to the indexing problem. But by the time we provide a tight definition for each keyword, and handle the problems of completeness and overlap, we have performed a task not too dissimilar to defining entities and attributes for a corporate data model. Given the value of a corporate data model for other purposes, it makes sense to use it, rather than keywords, as our indexing technique.

In developing a corporate data model specifically to index existing data, remember that the mapping between entities and existing files will be simpler if the two are based on similar concepts. Avoid radically new, innovative corporate data models unless there is an adequate payoff! Of course, if the business has changed substantially since the databases were built, the corporate data model may well, by necessity, differ significantly from what is currently in place. It then becomes an important tool for assessing the completeness and quality of information systems support for the business.

One of the most effective approaches to building an indexed inventory of data is to develop a fairly generalized corporate data model, and to devote the major effort to improving documentation of individual databases. The corporate model is mapped against existing data at the entity level, and serves as a coarse index to identify databases in which any required data may be held; the final assessment is made by close examination of the local documentation.

A Target for Planning

Just as a town plan describes where we aim to be at some future date, a corporate data model can describe how we intend to organize our total set of computerized data at some point in the future.

It is here that corporate data modelers have frequently encountered trouble. It is one thing to start with a blank sheet of paper and develop an ideal model that may be conceptually quite different from the models on which existing systems are based. It is quite another to migrate from existing databases and files to new ones based on the model, or to find package vendors who share the same view of data organization.

There is a natural (and often economically sound) reluctance to replace current databases that are doing an adequate job. We may need to accept, therefore, that large parts of a corporate model will remain unimplemented, at least in the medium term.

This leads to a second problem: Should implementers of new systems aim to share data from existing databases, or duplicate the data, following the specification of the corporate data model? The former approach perpetuates the older structures; the latter increases the problems of data duplication. I have even seen developers refusing to use databases that were designed in accordance with a corporate data model because the corporate model had since changed.

Third, in many business areas, the most cost-effective approach is to purchase a packaged application. In these cases, we have little choice about the underlying data models (except insofar as we may be able to choose among packages that are better or worse matches with the corporate data model). With one purchase decision, we may render a large part of the corporate data model irrelevant.

Corporate data modelers frequently find themselves fighting both systems developers and users, who want economical solutions to their local problems, and who feel constrained by the requirement to fit in with a larger plan. There are arguments for both sides. Without an overall target, it will certainly be difficult to achieve better sharing of data. But too often data modelers forget the basic tenet of creative data modeling: There may be more than one good answer. I have seen data modelers arguing against purchase of a package because it does not fit "their" corporate model, when in fact the underlying database is built on a sound model and could readily be incorporated into the existing set of databases.

The "town planning" paradigm mentioned earlier, if pragmatically applied, can help us develop a target which balances the ideal vision with the practicalities of what is in place or available. The target needs to be a combination of existing databases that are to be retained, databases to be implemented as components of packages, and databases to be developed in-house. It is, in fact, a corporate data model produced within the constraints of other commitments, the most important being the existing systems and the applications development strategy. Some of it will be less than ideal: the structures that fit in best will often differ from those we would use if we had started with a "clean slate."

In developing this sort of model, you should set a specific date – typically, three to five years hence, and aim to model how the organization's data will look at that time. Some areas of the model can be very precise indeed, as they merely document current databases; others may be very broad because we intend to purchase a package whose data structure is as yet unknown.

Such a model represents a realistic target that can be discussed in concrete terms with systems planners, developers, and users, and used as a basis for assessing individual proposals.

A Context for Specifying New Databases

Determining Scope and Interfaces

In specifying a new database, three of the most fundamental questions we need to ask are:

What is included?

What is excluded?

What do we have to fit in with?

These questions need to be answered early in a systems development or acquisition project, as an important part of agreeing expectations and budgets, and of managing overlaps and interfaces among databases. Once a project team has planned and budgeted to design their own database in isolation (and all the associated processing to maintain it), it can be virtually impossible to persuade them to use existing files and databases. Similarly, once it has been decided (even if only implicitly) not to include certain data, it is very difficult to change the decision.

A "big picture" of an organization's overall data requirements – a corporate data model – is an invaluable aid to answering questions of scope and overlap, and highlighting data issues before it is too late to address them.

Incorporating the Corporate Data Model in the Development Lifecycle

Here is how a typical large organization ensures that databases are specified in the context of an overall data plan.

The organization requires that every information systems project beyond a certain size receive funding approval from a committee of senior managers, which looks at proposals in terms of overall costs and benefits to the business. The committee's brief is far broader than data management; its prime concern is that the organization's total investment in information systems is well directed, and that local needs do not override the best interests of the organization as a whole. (For example, they may enforce a preferred supplier policy for hardware).

The committee requires that each proposal include a one-page "data management" statement, prepared in consultation with the data management group. This involves project and data management representatives looking at the corporate data model and identifying the entities that will be required by the proposed system. The resulting "first-cut" data model for the system is a subset of the corporate data model produced by "slicing" in two dimensions: horizontally, to select which entities are to be included and vertically to select which subtypes of those entities are applicable to the project. For example, the project might decide that it requires the entity "Physical Asset" (horizontal selection), but only in order to keep data about vehicles (vertical selection). This exercise may lead to reconsideration of system scope, often to include other subtypes that are handled similarly. For example, it might turn out that with some minor enhancements the vehicle management system could handle all movable assets.

The data management group then advises on whether and in what form the required data is currently held, by reference to the data inventory. This in turn provides a basis for deciding where data will be sourced, and what new data structures the project will build. Where data is to be duplicated, and the need for common representation and/or interfaces can be established. The results of the discussions form the data management statement.

From time to time, disagreements as to data sourcing arise, typically because the project prefers to "roll its own" and the data management group favors data reuse. Ultimately, the committee decides, but most situations are resolved when the implications of each option are laid out and discussed.

In practice, this is a very simple process, with the data management statement typically taking less than a day to prepare. But it can make a real difference to the scope and cost of projects, and to the integration of systems. It does, however, depend upon having a corporate data model, and someone in authority that is interested in *overall* costs and benefits to the organization rather than the cost justification of each project in isolation.

The first-cut project data model can also be a valuable tool for estimating and budgeting. It is possible to make an estimate of system size in terms of function points using only a data model and some rules of thumb, such as average number of functions per entity. The accuracy of the estimate depends very much on how well data boundaries are defined; the corporate model approach does much to assist this.

Another benefit of an early look at project data requirements in the context of a corporate data model is that the terminology, definitions, and data structures of the corporate data model are communicated to the project team before they embark on a different course. The value of this in improving the quality and compatibility of databases is discussed in the next section.

Guidance for Database Design

A corporate data model can provide an excellent starting point for the development of project-level data models (and hence database designs).

It contains information about business data requirements that might not otherwise be available to data modelers working on a specific project. A corporate data model takes a broad view of the business, and is likely to incorporate contributions from senior management and strategic planners. In particular, it may highlight areas in which change can be expected, vital input to decisions as to the most appropriate level of generalization.

Because a corporate data model is usually developed by very experienced data modelers, it should specify technically sound data structures, and may include good and perhaps innovative ideas.

The corporate data model can also provide standard names and definitions for common entities (and attributes as well, though corporate modeling to this level of detail is less common). Pulling together data from multiple databases, or transferring data from one to another, is much easier if definitions, formats, and coding are the same. More and more, we need to be able to exchange data with external bodies, as well as among our own databases. The corporate data model can be the central point for specifying the necessary standard definitions and formats.

Achieving genuine consistency demands a high level of rigor in data definition. I recall an organization that needed to store details of languages spoken. One database treated Afghani as a single language, while another treated it as two – Pushtu and Pashto. What might seem to be an academic difference caused real problems when transferring data from one system to another, or attempting to answer simple questions requiring data from both databases. In cases of code sets like this, reference to an external standard can sometimes assist in resolving the problem. Often decisions at this level of detail are not taken in the initial corporate modeling exercise, but are "fed back" to the model by project teams tackling the issue, for the benefit of future project data modelers.

Input to Business Planning

A corporate data model provides a view of an important business resource (data) from what is usually a novel perspective for business specialists. As such, it may stimulate original thinking about the objectives and organization of the business.

In business, new ideas frequently arise through generalization: a classic example is redefining a business as "transportation" rather than "trucking." We as modelers make heavy use of generalization, and are able to support it in a formal way through the use of supertypes.

So we find that even if the more specialized entities in a corporate data model represent familiar business concepts, their supertypes may not. Or, commonly, the supertypes represent critical high-level concepts that cut across organizational boundaries, and are not managed well as a whole. In a bank, we may have "Loan" (whereas individual organization units manage only certain types of loan), in a telecommunications company "Customer Equipment Item" (whereas different organization units manage different products).

I have seen some real breakthroughs in thinking stimulated by well-explained corporate data models. Some of these have been attributable to a multi disciplinary, highly skilled corporate modeling team looking closely at a business's aims and objectives as input to the modeling exercise. Others have appeared as a result of the actual modeling.

Nevertheless, I would not encourage corporate data modeling for this reason alone. Better results can usually be achieved by the use of specific business planning and modeling techniques. We need to remember that data modeling was developed as a stage in database design, and its conventions and principles reflect this. Normalization is unlikely to help you set your business direction!

Unfortunately, there is a tendency among data modelers to see a business only from the perspective of data, and to promote the data model as representing a kind of "business truth." Given the element of choice in modeling, the argument is hard to sustain. In fact, corporate data models usually encourage a view of the business based on *processes*, as distinct from products, customers, or projects. For example, the high-level supertype "Policy" in an insurance model might suggest common handling of all policies, rather than distinct handling according to product or customer type. Sometimes the new view leads to useful improvements; sometimes it is counterproductive. The business strategy that allows for the most elegant handling of data certainly has advantages, but these may be outweighed by other considerations, such as business unit autonomy.

Specification of a Corporate Database

The last use of a corporate data model was historically the first. The dream in the early days of database management systems was to develop a database embracing all of an organization's computer data, fully normalized, nonredundant, and serving the needs of all areas of the organization.

A number of organizations actually attempted this, almost invariably without success. The logistics of developing a database of the necessary size and complexity and providing the associated processing were well beyond the project management capabilities (and budgets) of most organizations. Eventually, more urgent business priorities overrode these grand plans.

A variant is the "subject database" approach, in which the corporate data model is carved up into smaller, more manageable components, which are to be built one at a time. The difficulty lies in deciding how to partition the data. If we partition the data on an application-by-application basis we end up with duplication, resulting from data being required by more than one application (the same as if we had developed application databases without any plan!)

An alternative approach is to divide the data by supertypes: thus a bank might plan subject databases for Loans, Customers, Transactions, Branches, and so on. The problem here is that most practical systems require data from many of these subject databases. To implement a new loan product, the bank would probably require all of the databases mentioned above. The subject database approach is viable, but requires very careful management of the migration from existing databases. The subject databases are developed tactically, to complement application-specific databases. Organizations that have attempted to use subject databases to meet all of their data requirements have run into conflict between this long-term ideal and immediate business needs.

The choice of subject databases is important. Successful strategies have focused on widely used but centrally updated data, typically of low to medium volume. These databases are usually implementations of entities near the top of the one-to-many relationship hierarchy. Examples include data about products, organizational structure, regulations, and staff, as well as common codes and their meanings. Customer data does not quite fit the criteria, but is of sufficient importance to most organizations that support can frequently be gained for a customer database project.

Finally, it is almost always a mistake to develop databases in isolation. Successful projects deliver a *system*, even if this only provides for update and basic inquiries on the data. For example, rather than deliver a product database, we should aim to deliver a product management system for the marketing division. By doing this, we bring the subject database initiative into the mainstream of systems development and can manage it using well-understood procedures and roles. Most importantly, organizations have proved more reluctant to abandon the development of a conventional system with specific user sponsorship than an infrastructure project whose benefits may be less obvious and less clearly "owned."

Characteristics of Corporate Data Models

Although corporate data models use the same building blocks – entities, relationships, and attributes – as individual database models, they differ in several ways. Most of the differences arise from the need to cover a wide area, but without the detail needed to specify a database.

Ultimately, the level of detail in a corporate data model depends upon its role in the data management strategy – in other words, what it is going to be used for. An extreme example is the organization that produced, after considerable effort and investment, a corporate data model with only six entities. But suppose the organization was a bank, and the entities were Customer, Product, Service, Contract, Account, and Branch. If the model was successfully used to win agreement throughout the organization on the meaning of these six terms, drove the construction of six shared databases, and encouraged a review of the way each was managed, then the six-entity model would have justified its cost many times over.

More typical corporate data models contain between 50 and 200 entities. This relatively low number (in comparison with the model that would result from consolidating all possible project-level models) is achieved by employing a high level of generalization – often higher than we would select for implementation. Corporate models, as initially developed, seldom specify the full set of attributes for each entity. In some cases no attributes at all are recorded; in others, sample and key attributes may be included to clarify entity definitions.

Corporate models may also omit some of the "less important" entities, or incorporate them into other entities through denormalization. For example, a model might include the entity Contract, but exclude Contract Change, Contract Type, and Client Involvement in Contract. The last is a resolution entity that could be implied through a many-to-many relationship (Client may be involved in Contract) rather than shown explicitly.

Even after this amount of trimming, a corporate data model may still be too complicated to be readily understood. Many business specialists have been permanently discouraged from further participation in the modeling process by a forbiddingly complex "circuit diagram" of boxes and lines. In these cases, it is worth producing a very high-level diagram showing less than ten very generalized entities. Ruthless elimination of entities that are not critical to communicating the key concepts is essential. Such a diagram is intended solely as a starting point for understanding, and you should therefore make decisions as to what to generalize or eliminate on this basis alone. Appendix B describes a more formal approach to presenting large data models.

Developing a Corporate Data Model

In developing a corporate data model, we use the same basic techniques and principles as for a project-level model. The advice in chapter 5 about using patterns and exploring alternatives remains valid, but there are some important differences in emphasis and skills.

The Development Cycle

Project-level models are developed reasonably quickly to the level of detail necessary for implementation. Later changes tend to be relatively minor (because of the impact on system structure), and driven by changes to business requirements.

In contrast, corporate models are often developed progressively over a long period. The initial modeling exercise may produce a highly generalized model with few attributes. But project teams using the corporate model as a starting point will need to "flesh it out" by adding subtypes, attributes, and new entities resulting from detailed analysis and normalization. To do so, they will spend more time analyzing the relevant business area, and will be able to cross check their results against detailed function models. They may also receive better quality input from users, who have a more personal stake in specifying a system than in contributing to the planning exercise that produced the corporate data model.

The results of project-level modeling can affect the corporate model in two ways. First, more detailed analysis provides a check on the concepts and rules included in the corporate model. Perhaps a one-to-many relationship is really many-to-many, or an important subtype of an entity has been overlooked. The corporate model will need to be corrected to reflect the new information.

Second, the additional subtypes, entities, and attributes that do not conflict with the corporate model, but add further detail, may be incorporated into the corporate model. Whether this is done or not depends on the data management strategy, and often on the resources and tools available to maintain a more complex model. Many organizations choose to record only data of "corporate significance" in the corporate data model, leaving "local" data in project models.

In planning a corporate modeling exercise, then, you need to recognize that development will extend beyond the initial study, and put in place procedures to ensure that later "field work" by project teams is appropriately incorporated.

Partitioning the Task

Project-level data models are usually small enough that one person or team can undertake all of the modeling. While a model may be notionally divided into sections that are examined one at a time, this is usually done by the team as a whole rather than by allocating each section to a different modeler.

With corporate models, this is not always possible. For many reasons, including time constraints, skill sets, and organizational politics, we may need to divide up the task, and have separate teams develop parts of the model in parallel.

If doing this, consider partitioning the task by supertype, rather than by functional area, as data is often used by more than one functional area. For example, assign a team to examine Physical Assets (supertype) rather than Purchasing (functional area). Although this approach may be less convenient from an organizational perspective, it means that different teams will not be modeling the same data. The element of choice in modeling inevitably leads to different models of the same data and long arguments in their reconciliation. I have seen teams spend far longer on reconciliation than on modeling, and corporate modeling projects abandoned for this reason.

If you choose to partition by functional area, ensure that you have an agreed framework of supertypes in place before starting, and meet very regularly to fit results into the framework and identify any problems.

The initial high-level model is essential whichever approach is taken. Its development provides a great opportunity for creative exploration of options – so great that corporate data modeling projects frequently spend months arguing or become seriously stuck at this point looking for the "perfect" solution. Beware of this. Document the major options and move quickly to collect more detailed information to allow them to be better evaluated.

Inputs to the Task

Few things are more helpful to corporate data modelers than a clearly documented business strategy that is well supported by management. In developing a corporate model, overall business objectives need to take the place of system requirements in guiding and verifying the model. The best answer to "why did you choose this particular organization of data?" is "because it supports the following business objectives in the following way."

Business objectives prompt at least three important questions for the data modeler:

1. What data do we need to *support* the achievement of each objective? A welfare organization might need a consolidated register of welfare recipients to achieve the objective "reduce the incidence of persons illegally claiming more than one benefit."

2. What data do we need to *measure* the achievement of each objective? A police force may have the objective of responding to urgent calls as quickly as possible, and could specify the key performance indicator (KPI) "Mean time to respond to calls classified as urgent." Base data needed to derive the KPI would include time taken to respond to each call, and classification of call.

3. How will pursuit of the objectives change our data requirements over time? An investment bank may have the objective of providing a full range of investment products for retail and commercial clients. Meeting the objective could involve introduction of new products and supporting data.

Ideally, the corporate data model will be developed within the context of a full information systems planning project, following establishment of a comprehensive business plan. In many cases, however, data modeling studies are undertaken in relative isolation, and we need to make the best of what we have, or attempt to put together a working set of business objectives as part of the project. Interviews with senior staff can help, but it is unrealistic to expect a corporate modeling project to produce a business strategy as an interim deliverable!

The best approach in these cases is to make maximum use of whatever is available: company mission statement, job descriptions, business unit objectives, annual plans. Interviews and workshops can then be used to verify and supplement these.

One of the most difficult decisions facing the corporate modeling team is what use to make of existing project-level models, whether implemented or not, and any earlier attempts at corporate or business unit models. I find the best approach is to commit only to taking them into account, without undertaking to include any structures uncritically. These existing models are then used as an important source of requirements, and for verification, but are not allowed to stand in the way of taking a fresh look at the business.

The situation is different if our aim is to produce a realistic target for planning that incorporates databases to which we are committed. In this case, we will obviously need to copy structures from those databases directly into the corporate model.

Expertise Requirements

Data modelers working at the project level can reasonably be forgiven any initial lack of familiarity with the area being modeled. The amount of knowledge required is limited by the scope of the project, and expertise can be gained as the model is developed, typically over several weeks or months.

In the case of a corporate data model, the situation is quite different. Wide ranges of business areas need to be modeled, with limited time available for each. And we are dealing with senior members of the organization whose time is too precious to waste on explaining basic business concepts.

Conducting an interview with the finance manager without any prior knowledge of finance will achieve two things: a slightly improved knowledge of finance on the part of the interviewer, and a realization on the part of the finance manager that he/she has contributed little of value to the model. On the other hand, going into the interview with a good working knowledge of finance in general, and of the company's approach in particular, will enable the interview to focus on rules specific to the business, and will help build credibility for the model and data management.

In corporate data modeling, then, modeling skills need to be complemented by business knowledge. The modeling team will usually include at least one person with a good overall knowledge of the business. In complex businesses, it can be worthwhile seconding business specialists to the team on a temporary basis to assist in examining their area of expertise. I find that there is also great value in having someone whose knowledge of the business area was acquired outside the organization: experienced recruits, consultants, and MBAs are often better placed to take an alternative or more general view of the organization and its data.

External Standards

External data standards are an important, but often overlooked input to a corporate data model. There is little point in inventing a coding scheme if a perfectly good (and hopefully well-thought-out) one is accepted as an industry, national, or international standard, nor in rewriting definitions and inventing data names for entities and attributes.

A major payoff in using external standards is in facilitating electronic commerce. Indeed, the corporate model can be the means by which the necessary standards are made available to development teams.

Choice, Creativity, and Corporate Data Models

Corporate data models can be a powerful means of promulgating innovative concepts and data structures. Equally, they can inhibit original thought by presenting each new project with a *fait accompli* as far as the overall structure of its model is concerned. In my experience, both situations are common, and frequently occur together in the one organization.

With their access to the "big picture" and strong data modeling skills, a corporate data modeling team is in a good position to propose and evaluate creative approaches. They are more likely than a conventional application project team to have the necessary access to senior management to win support for new ideas. Through the data management process, they have the means to at least encourage development teams to adopt them. Some of the most significant examples of business benefits arising from creative modeling have been achieved in this way.

On the other hand, a corporate data model may enshrine poor or outdated design, and inhibit innovation at the project level. There needs to be a means by which the corporate model can be improved by ideas generated by systems developers, and at least some scope for breaking out of the corporate data modeling framework at the project level. Too often, a lack of provision for changing the corporate data model in response to ideas from project teams has led to the demise of data management as the model ages.

It is vital that both systems developers and corporate modelers clearly understand the choice factor in modeling and recognize that:

- if the project model meets the user requirements but differs from the corporate model, the corporate model is not necessarily wrong; and

- if the corporate model meets business requirements but the project model differs, it too is not necessarily wrong.

Indeed, both models may be "right," but in the interests of data management we may need to agree on a common model, ideally one that incorporates the best of both.

A genuine understanding of these very basic ideas will overcome many of the problems that occur between corporate modelers and project teams, and provide a basis for workable data management standards and procedures.

Summary

Corporate data models cover the data requirements of complete enterprises or major business units. They are generally used for data planning and coordination rather than as specifications for database design.

A corporate data model should be developed within the context of a data management strategy. Data management is the management of data as a corporate resource, typically involving central control over its organization and documentation, and encouragement of data sharing across applications.

A corporate data model can be mapped against existing data, and thereafter used as an index to access it. It may also serve as a starting point for detailed project-level data modeling, incorporating ideas from senior business people and experienced data modelers.

Development of a corporate data model requires good business skills as well as modeling expertise. If the task is partitioned, it should be divided by data supertype rather than functional area.

While corporate data models can be powerful vehicles for promulgating new ideas, they may also stifle original thinking by requiring conformity.

Appendices

Check List for Data Model Review

I use the following checklist as a framework for reviewing data models developed by others. It is equally relevant to checking your own work.

The Context of the Model

Is there a formal data model? (chapter 1)

Some projects still do not include a formal data modeling phase at all, leaving all data organization decisions to the technical database designer.

Is there a commitment to using the model as a specification for database design? (chapter 1)

Modern methodologies generally require delivery of a data model. Sometimes, there is no real commitment to actually using it as a specification for the database. Always review the final logical database design as well as the model.

Who has been involved in developing the model? (chapters 1 and 6)

Look for evidence that users and business specialists participated in developing and reviewing the model.

Have other candidate models been proposed and considered? (Chapter 5)

Look for evidence that the modeler has not merely adopted the first workable solution.

How will performance problems be managed? (Chapter 1)

There should be a formal procedure in place for dealing with performance problems. Resolution should involve data modelers and users as well as physical database designers.

Is there a data management strategy in place?
Does the model conform to this? (Chapter 14)

Check with the Data Administrator as well as the project data modeler.

Are there any constraints imposed by existing systems and data?
Does the model take these into account? (Chapter 14)

Frequently, the data requirements of an application can be met at least partially from existing databases, either through direct data sharing or data transfer. The data model should identify any areas that are constrained to match existing structures.

Does the model conform to corporate standards for presentation, naming, and supporting documentation? (Chapters 5 and 10)

Check with the Data Administrator and standards group.

The Model as a Whole

How well presented and understandable is the model? (Chapter 4, Appendix B)

Consider the intended audience(s). There may be a need to present the model at different levels, or to provide "subject area" models for particular audiences. Ask other stakeholders whether they understand the model.

Does the model cover the full scope required?

Check with the initial project proposal; verify against a high-level function model.

Have history requirements been taken into account? (Chapter 11)

Identify any situations in which no mechanism exists for recording changes or past positions. Ensure that the user is willing to lose such data.

Has the data model been checked against a detailed function model? (Chapter 5)

Look for documented interaction analysis.

Is there any redundancy? (Chapter 4)

Look particularly for entities that overlap. The most common situations involve external people and organizations.

Have subtypes and supertypes been removed? (Chapter 4)

The final model for implementation should be supported by a fully subtyped model, and documentation justifying the chosen level of subtyping in each case.

Entities

Do all of the entities have meaningful, reasonably unambiguous names? (Chapter 3)

Some ambiguity is unavoidable, but watch out for genuinely misleading names and names that have multiple distinct meanings in the business. Names should be in the singular.

Are all the entity names supported by good definitions? (Chapter 3)

The definition should clearly state what is included and what is excluded and give examples of both. Poor entity definitions are one of the most common faults in data models.

Is the level of generalization appropriate? (Chapters 4 and 12)

Check that the rules implied by entities are expected to be stable for the life of the system. Ensure that higher levels of generalization are not an excuse for incomplete analysis (look for subtypes as evidence of more detailed investigation).

Relationships

Are relationships correctly documented? (Chapter 3)

Relationships should be named, preferably in both directions. Cardinality, optionality, and ideally transferability should be shown.

Have all many-to-many relationships been resolved? (Chapter 3)

Resolution is not totally mechanical – ensure that the key of the resolution entity is defined.

Is the level of generalization appropriate? (Chapter 7)

Look particularly at self-referencing many-to-many relationships – check that they do not hide simple hierarchies.

Are any relationships derivable? (Chapter 7)

Look particularly for "relationships" derivable from inequalities.

Attributes

Is there a full attribute list for each entity? (Chapters 2, 7 and 10)

The documentation should include a full list of attributes for each entity including foreign keys.

Do the attribute names conform to (internal) standards?
(Chapter 10)

If no naming standard is in place, look for inconsistencies, synonyms, and homonyms.

Do all attributes have definitions? (Chapters 2 and 10)

Look also for definitions of derivable attributes that do not appear in the entity lists.

Have all attributes been classified according to an appropriate taxonomy with respect to the way they will be used? (Chapter 10)

Distinguish between Identifiers, Categories, Quantities and Texts and between the various types of Quantity.

Keys and Normalization

Are primary keys defined for all entities? (Chapter 2)

It is not sufficient to identify all candidate keys – one key must be nominated as primary.

Do all primary keys meet the basic criteria of applicability, uniqueness, minimality, and stability? (Chapter 9)

Give special attention to stability, particularly for meaningful keys.

Have surrogate keys been used indiscriminately? (Chapter 9)

If all entities use surrogate keys, check that this is not expected to cause performance problems.

Are all candidate keys identified? (Chapters 8 and 9)

Multiple candidate keys may be associated with BCNF problems or indicate that an entity should be disaggregated into two or more entities linked by one-to-one relationships.

Are all foreign keys identified? (Chapter 7)

Ensure that the notation allows the related entity to be identified in each case. Check for overlapping and split foreign keys.

Are all tables fully normalized? (Chapters 2 and 8)

Check particularly for 4NF and 5NF problems with all-key tables.

Business Rules

Have all data validation rules been specified? (Chapter 12)

These are particularly important, and should include which attributes are mandatory, which attributes or sets of attributes (other than the primary key) are unique, and any other constraints on the values that each attribute may hold.

An Approach to Presenting Large Data Models

The material in this appendix was developed by my colleague Daniel L. Moody and described in a more formal paper[48]. The approach described has been proved to be a workable solution to the problem of presenting large data models, in particular corporate data models.

Step 1: Partition Data Model into Subject Areas

The first step is to divide the model into parts of manageable size (subject areas). The rules for doing this are:

1. Each entity must be assigned to one and only one subject area (i.e. no overlap between subject areas).

2. Each subject area should consist of a maximum of nine entities excluding subtypes (following the "seven plus or minus two" principle).

3. Each subject area should be named after one of the entities on the subject area (called the central entity).

To work out the number of subject areas required, divide the number of entities in the model (excluding subtypes) by seven. In the example data model, there are 23 entities, which means 3 subject areas are required.

---

[48] Moody, D. L., "A Leveled Architecture for Representing Enterprise Data Models", *Proceedings of the International Conference on Enterprise Modelling (IEMC'99)*, Verdal, Norway, June 14-16, 1999.

The diagram overleaf shows a data model partitioned into subject areas. Central entities are shaded, and boundary relationships (relationships between entities on different subject areas) are highlighted in the diagram.

Example Data Model Partitioned into Subject Areas

Step 2: Produce Context Data Model

The **Context Data Model** provides a summary of the model, showing all subject areas and how they fit together. Each subject area should be shown as a circle, with relationships between them shown using arrows, labeled by the meaning of the relationship. A relationship may be shown between subject areas when there is a boundary relationship between them. However there is no need to show all boundary relationships – *only the most important ones should be shown to avoid cluttering the diagram.*

The diagram below shows the Context Data Model for our example:

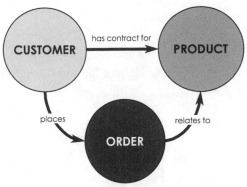

Context Data Model

Step 3: Produce Subject Area Data Models

Each subject area should be shown as a separate diagram. **Subject Area Data Models** include all entities assigned to that subject area plus cross-references to other subject areas (foreign entities). Subject area data models are shown as standard Entity-Relationship models with the following modifications:

- The central entity is shown at the center of the diagram and larger than all other entities.

- Relationships to entities on other subject areas are shown using foreign entities. Foreign entities are shown as dotted boxes, with their primary subject area in parentheses.

In our example, there is a boundary relationship between the Order Item entity (Order Subject Area) and the Product entity (Product Subject Area). In the Order Subject Area diagram, this would be shown as follows:

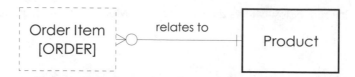

In the Product Subject Area diagram, the same relationship would be shown as:

Thus boundary relationships are duplicated in both subject areas involved. Foreign entities should be shown on the outside of subject area diagrams, since they act as entry points and exit points to subject areas.

Customer Subject Area Data Model

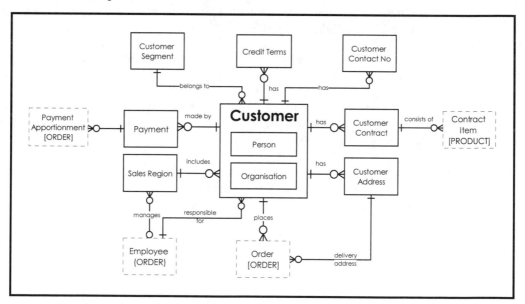

Order Subject Area Data Model

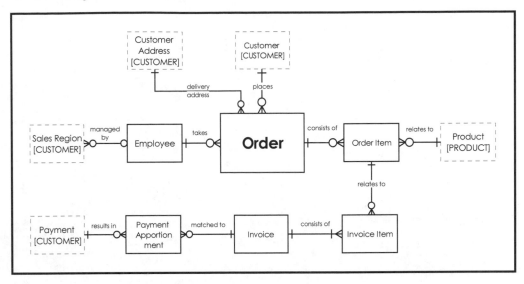

Product Subject Area Data Model

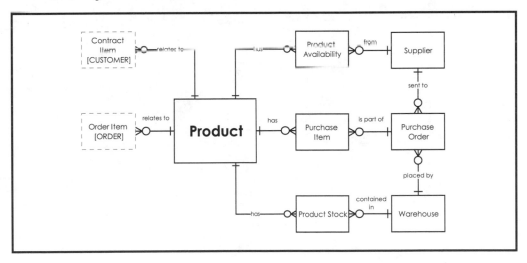

Index

Related Coriolis Technology Press Titles

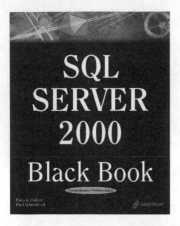

SQL SERVER™ 2000 BLACK BOOK

By Patrick Dalton and Paul Whitehead
ISBN: 1-57610-770-1 • Media: CD-ROM • Price: $59.99 U.S. • $89.99 CAN

This comprehensive SQL Server 2000 book addresses four main topics: architecture, administration, development, and performance and troubleshooting. It covers hardware and disk configuration, which is an extremely important but often overlooked area in other books. Provides solutions and examples for the new XML capabilities of the database, scripting, and other areas of application development. The included CD-ROMs contain many useful tools and an evaluation copy of Microsoft® SQL Server™ 2000.

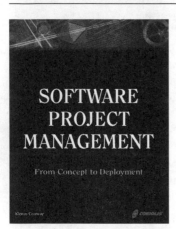

SOFTWARE PROJECT MANAGEMENT: From Concept to Deployment

By Kieron Conway
ISBN: 1-57610-807-4 • Media: CD-ROM • Price: $49.99 U.S. • $74.99 CAN

Written specifically for programmers and developers, this book follows a real-world small-scale project from beginning to end. Covers both object-oriented and non-object-oriented technologies, multimedia, and image handling, and ultimately provides a basic set of development skills to help developers complete projects on time and under budget. Introduces the reader to planning and costing software developments and demonstrates how to formalize and analyze requirements. Explores modular design and development and tackles issues of setting up software support. Presents the need for progress monitoring and the vital importance of change handling. This book helps bridge the gap between traditional development and genuine object-oriented development.

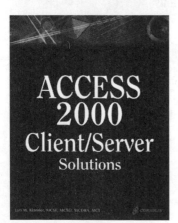

ACCESS 2000 CLIENT/SERVER SOLUTIONS

By Lars Klander
ISBN: 1-57610-417-6 • Media: CD-ROM • Price: $49.99 U.S. • $74.99 CAN

Designed for the intermediate to advanced Access developer, author Lars Klander shows you how to expand your existing Access skill set to enter the powerful world of true client/server development. This book is divided into logical segments designed to simplify your transition to client/server and n-tier development. You will learn to create client/server applications using multiple development tools including SQL Server and Oracle8. This book will help you master DAPs, ADOs, and ADPs; use Visual InterDev to develop Internet-based client/server applications; and much more

The Coriolis Group, LLC   Telephone: 480.483.0192 • Toll-free: 800.410.0192 • In Canada: 905.477.0722 • www.coriolis.com
Coriolis books are also available at bookstores and computer stores worldwide.

MANNING EBOOK PROGRAM

All ebooks are 50% off the price of the print edition!

In the spring of 2000 Manning became the first publisher to offer ebook versions of all our new titles as a way to get customers the information they need quickly and easily. We continue to publish ebook versions of all our new releases, and every ebook is priced at 50% off the print version!

Go to www.manning.com/payette to download the ebook version of this book and have the information at your fingertips wherever you might be.

MANNING EARLY ACCESS PROGRAM

Get Early Chapters Now!

In 2003 we launched MEAP, our groundbreaking Early Access Program, to give customers who can't wait the opportunity to read chapters as they are written and receive the book when it is released. Because these are "early" chapters, your feedback will also help shape the final manuscript.

Our entire MEAP title list is always changing and you can find the current titles at www.manning.com